TRADE ASSOCIATIONS MONOGRAPHS

THE COMMERCIAL BANKING INDUSTRY
The American Bankers Association

THE CONSUMER FINANCE INDUSTRY
National Consumer Finance Association

LIFE INSURANCE COMPANIES AS
FINANCIAL INSTITUTIONS
Life Insurance Association of America

MANAGEMENT INVESTMENT COMPANIES
Investment Company Institute

MORTGAGE COMPANIES: THEIR PLACE
IN THE FINANCIAL STRUCTURE
Miles L. Colean, for the
Mortgage Bankers Association of America

MUTUAL SAVINGS BANKING: BASIC CHARACTERISTICS
AND ROLE IN THE NATIONAL ECONOMY
National Association of Mutual Savings Banks

PROPERTY AND CASUALTY INSURANCE COMPANIES:
THEIR ROLE AS FINANCIAL INTERMEDIARIES
American Mutual Insurance Alliance
Association of Casualty and Surety Companies
National Board of Fire Underwriters

THE SAVINGS AND LOAN BUSINESS: ITS PURPOSES,
FUNCTIONS, AND ECONOMIC JUSTIFICATION
Leon T. Kendall, for the
United States Savings and Loan League

In addition to the Trade Associations Monographs, the Committee for Economic Development is publishing for the Commission on Money and Credit

THE FEDERAL RESERVE AND THE TREASURY: ANSWERS TO QUESTIONS FROM THE COMMISSION ON MONEY AND CREDIT

and fifty-nine individual essays organized into nine separate volumes, each centered around a particular aspect of monetary and fiscal policy. Their titles and the contributing authors are as follows:

IMPACTS OF MONETARY POLICY

Daniel B. Suits; Robert Eisner and Robert H. Strotz, with a bibliography by G. R. Post; Edwin Kuh and John R. Meyer; Leo Grebler and Sherman J. Maisel; Charlotte DeMonte Phelps; Irwin Friend

STABILIZATION POLICIES

E. Cary Brown, Robert M. Solow, Albert Ando, and John Kareken; Milton Friedman and David Meiselman; Lawrence E. Thompson; Arthur M. Okun; Merton H. Miller; Allan H. Meltzer; Oswald Brownlee and Alfred Conrad

MONETARY MANAGEMENT

Frank M. Tamagna; Warren L. Smith; Clark Warburton; Michael D. Reagan; C. P. Kindleberger; Robert Z. Aliber

FISCAL AND DEBT MANAGEMENT POLICIES

William Fellner; Richard A. Musgrave; James Tobin; James R. Schlesinger; Paul H. Cootner; Irving Auerbach; Ralph K. Huitt; John Lindeman

FEDERAL CREDIT AGENCIES

George F. Break; Jack Guttentag; Ernest Bloch; D. Gale Johnson; Dale E. Hathaway; George S. Tolley; John McCroskey

FEDERAL CREDIT PROGRAMS

Stewart Johnson; Warren A. Law; James W. McKie; D. Gale Johnson; James Gillies; Robert C. Turner and Ross M. Robertson; J. Fred Weston

PRIVATE CAPITAL MARKETS

Irwin Friend; Hyman P. Minsky; Raymond W. Goldsmith

PRIVATE FINANCIAL INSTITUTIONS

Paul M. Horvitz; Deane Carson and Paul Cootner; Victor L. Andrews; Thomas G. Gies, Thomas Mayer, and Edward C. Ettin; Lawrence L. Werboff and Marvin E. Rozen; Fred H. Klopstock; E. Gordon Keith

INFLATION, GROWTH, AND EMPLOYMENT

Joseph E. Conard; Jesse W. Markham; Franklyn D. Holzman; John W. Kendrick; Daniel Creamer; Stanley Lebergott; Lawrence R. Klein and Ronald G. Bodkin; Tibor and Anne Scitovsky

LIFE INSURANCE COMPANIES
AS FINANCIAL INSTITUTIONS

PRENTICE-HALL INTERNATIONAL, INC.

London · *Tokyo* · *Sydney* · *Paris*

PRENTICE-HALL OF CANADA, LTD.

PRENTICE-HALL DE MEXICO, S.A.

Life Insurance Association of America

LIFE INSURANCE COMPANIES AS
FINANCIAL INSTITUTIONS

A MONOGRAPH
PREPARED FOR THE

Commission on Money and Credit

Prentice-Hall, Inc.
Englewood Cliffs, N.J. | *1962*

The Commission on Money and Credit was established in 1957 as an independent organization by the unanimous vote of the Board of Trustees of the Committee for Economic Development. The bylaws governing the Commission on Money and Credit state that "It shall be the responsibility of the Commission to initiate studies into the United States monetary and financial system."

This volume was especially prepared for the Commission on Money and Credit as part of its research program leading to the publication in June 1961 of its final report: *Money and Credit: Their Influence on Jobs, Prices, and Growth.* It is published by direction of the Commission according to its bylaws, as a contribution to the understanding of the monetary and financial system of the United States. It is one of more than 100 research studies prepared for the Commission by trade organizations, individual scholars, the Federal Reserve System, and the Treasury of the United States.

A selected group of such papers will be published for the Commission by the Information Division of the Committee for Economic Development in accordance with commitments to The Ford Foundation and the Merrill Foundation which provided main financial support for the Commission.

Publication of this volume does not necessarily constitute endorsement of such study by the Commission, its Advisory Board, its Research Staff, or any member of any board or committee, or any officer of the Committee for Economic Development, The Ford Foundation, the Merrill Foundation, or any other organization participating in the work of the Commission.

FOREWORD

One facet of the Commission on Money and Credit's investigation was an inquiry into the functioning of our financial system in order to arrive at a judgment of the adequacy of that system and its regulation to serve the needs of a growing economy.

In addition to examining other sources of information and having special studies prepared, the Commission also sought the advice, experience, and opinion of practitioners in the financial area. In this latter connection the Life Insurance Association of America was invited to prepare a monograph on the life insurance industry.

In soliciting the monograph, the Commission indicated the desirability of having it provide information on the following six topics:

1. The nature of government regulation of life insurance companies, including tax treatment, and its impact upon the functioning of the industry.
2. The operations and practices of the industry, in terms of flow of funds, portfolio practices, liquidity requirements, and so forth.
3. The role of life insurance companies in the economy, in terms of their influence upon economic growth, their contribution to economic stability, and their impact upon the allocation of resources.
4. The effects of monetary-debt management policy upon the industry and the role of life insurance companies in transmitting these policies throughout the economy.
5. The structure and competitive position of life insurance companies both within the industry and vis-à-vis other financial intermediaries.
6. The view of the life insurance industry regarding possible changes in regulatory or tax provisions.

The Life Insurance Association of America responded willingly to the invitation of the Commission and was most cooperative in working out with the staff of the Commission the scope and detailed outline of the planned monograph. The preparation of the monograph itself was a large task, and the finished product was a valuable contribution to the Commission.

In making its request to the LIAA for a monograph on the life insurance industry, the Commission indicated its desire and expectation to publish important background and research materials which it used in the course of its work. We are pleased that the Association consented to the inclusion of the monograph among the supporting documents of the Commission and agreed to revise for publication the original paper in order to make this further contribution to the general fund of knowledge on the nature of the life insurance industry and its role in the economy.

On behalf of the Commission and its staff we would like to express our thanks to the Life Insurance Association of America for the preparation of this study.

BERTRAND FOX
Research Director

ELI SHAPIRO
Deputy Research Director

December 1961

PREFACE

The monograph *Life Insurance Companies as Financial Institutions* was prepared at the request of the Commission on Money and Credit by the Economic Research Staff of the Life Insurance Association of America. It has been reviewed by the Joint Committee on Monetary and Fiscal Policy of the LIAA and the American Life Convention and has benefited a great deal from their criticisms and suggestions. Responsibility for the monograph rests, however, with the Economic Research Staff of the LIAA.

Much has been written about the functioning of commercial banks, mutual savings banks, and other types of financial institutions. Although considerable information has been published about life insurance companies as financial institutions, there has not been any comprehensive treatment; it is hoped that this monograph will help to meet this need. It is based on much of the research which has been conducted by the LIAA's Economic Research Department in the past several years.

I would like to acknowledge the work done by several members of my staff in the preparation of the monograph. Elizabeth Holt Bancala and Elizabeth Shaull participated in writing some of the individual chapters and contributed much of the supporting material for others, and in addition did considerable editing of the text. Kenneth Wright, now Senior Economist of the First National City Bank, contributed invaluably to the preparation of a number of chapters. In addition, Charles A. Van Orden, Jr., attorney of the LIAA staff, prepared the tables included in the appendix to Chapter 5. These tables, outlining the laws governing life insurance company investments in nineteen important states for life insurance, represent a most valuable piece of work. Josephine Skinner, Senior Research Assistant of the Statistical Department of the LIAA, prepared the material and wrote the portion of Chapter 11 dealing with the geographical distribution of life company investments over a period of time. In addition to these specific acknowledgments, we have also received valuable general aid from the Statistical Department of the LIAA and from the Institute of Life Insurance.

I am grateful, also, for the criticisms and suggestions received from Bruce E. Shepherd, Executive Vice President of the LIAA, and Eugene M. Thoré, Vice President and General Counsel of the LIAA.

Finally our secretarial staff did yeoman work in preparing the manuscript and I would like to express my gratitude to Irene Herriet, Judith Ash, and Harriet Englisher for their important aid. In addition, George H. Larsen and his assistants were most helpful in the task of mimeographing the monograph.

JAMES J. O'LEARY
Vice President and
Director of Economic Research
Life Insurance Association of America

July 1961

CONTENTS

List of Charts

List of Tables

LIFE INSURANCE COMPANIES AS FINANCIAL INSTITUTIONS

Chapter 1

SUMMARY AND
CONCLUSIONS

The life insurance companies of the United States have a dual function. They afford the means whereby millions of American families, through their own initiative, obtain security against unpredictable contingencies and provide for their old age. They also are a highly important channel through which the American people save. Life insurance has produced the largest accumulation of personal saving in this country and has thus provided the greatest reservoir of capital funds to aid in financing the growth of the American economy.

The function which life insurance plays in meeting the security needs of our people is comparatively well known. Its role as a source of capital funds is much less understood. The objective of this monograph, therefore, is to consider life insurance companies as financial institutions. It explores such questions as the following. What is the nature of personal saving through life insurance? How large have these savings been, and what have been the ways in which the funds have been invested? What factors have governed the investments by life insurance companies? In what ways, if any, have federal actions influenced the savings and investment patterns of life companies? What procedures are followed by the life companies in their investment activities? Have the savings through life insurance been invested in accord with the capital needs of the country? And, to what extent has the investment of life insurance savings contributed to the growth of the American economy?

The discussion of life insurance companies as financial intermediaries in this monograph may be summarized as follows:

1) *Policyholders' Saving Through Life Insurance.* The regular and systematic purchase of life insurance by our people leads to an accumulation of reserves because of the level-premium plan used for many types of policies. Under the level-premium plan, the amount of the annual premium remains unchanged during the premium-paying periods although the likelihood of death of the insured person increases with the

1

passage of time. In the early years of a level-premium policy the occurrence of death is relatively low, and the premium paid for the policy is in excess of death claims (considering a group of insureds). In the later years of the policy the premium paid is less than the amount necessary to meet death claims that come with advancing years and rising mortality. The law requires that when a level-premium plan is issued a fund or reserve must be accumulated in the early years to meet the rising level of claims expected during the later years of such policies. These reserves form the basis of personal saving through life insurance.

Life insurance saving differs fundamentally from saving through deposit-type institutions such as mutual savings banks and savings and loan associations in at least three important respects: (1) it is long-term and contractual in nature and is therefore more stable; (2) it is motivated primarily by the desire for family financial protection in the event of untimely death; and (3) it is ordinarily expected to be left intact until the death of the insured rather than withdrawn for some consumer expenditure.

The record of growth of life insurance saving since the turn of the century has been outstanding. At the end of 1896 policyholders' accumulated savings in life insurance amounted to about $1.2 billion; at the end of 1959 accumulated savings totaled $108 billion. In the first decade of this century accumulated savings more than doubled with a rise from $1.5 billion to $3.2 billion over these years. A somewhat slower growth was experienced during the ten years ended in 1919 when accumulated savings grew by less than 90 percent in that decade. The fastest rate of growth took place during the 1920's when accumulated savings advanced from $6.2 billion to $15.3 billion for an increase in that decade of almost 150 percent. Adverse economic conditions during the great depression cut this growth rate in half with a net increase for the 1929-39 period of only 79 percent. Some revival took place during the decade of the 1940's when accumulated savings in life insurance more than doubled with a rise from $27.3 billion to $57.8 billion. During the most recent decade accumulated savings rose to $108 billion in 1959, less than 90 percent above 1949, reflecting a declining rate of growth during the 1950's. The somewhat slower growth rate was especially apparent in 1956-59.

The principal factors at work which have caused a leveling off in life insurance savings in the period 1949-59 appear to be the following: (1) an increase over time in the importance of term insurance; (2) a rise in surrender benefits; (3) a tendency for policyholders to be less willing to leave policy proceeds with the company under those supplementary contracts which are based solely in interest return; and (4) an increased drawing upon equity in life insurance through the use of policy loans.

Although the past few years have witnessed a somewhat reduced role of life insurance in the total savings picture, it is quite possible that this phase will prove to be temporary. There are a number of factors at work currently which give some promise of restoring a more vigorous growth of life insurance savings. One is the increasing concern among life companies that permanent cash-value life insurance has not been receiving the sales emphasis that it merits as a means of providing both financial protection and saving for the policyholder. It appears certain that renewed efforts will be made to build the volume of types of policies having a savings element. Another factor which would encourage saving through life insurance would be the building of greater public confidence that the value of the dollar would be stabilized. In 1960 and through the first half of 1961 the fear of inflation has receded. Finally, the general advance of incomes and living standards that is expected during the coming decade may strengthen the growth of life insurance saving as more and more families reach the stage at which greater saving in this form becomes an attainable goal of family budgeting.

2) *Trends in the Investment of Life Insurance Company Funds, 1899-1959.* Life insurance funds have been invested largely in fixed-income loans to individuals and business concerns in the private sectors of the economy, principally mortgages and corporate bonds. These two investment outlets have accounted for approximately three-fifths to three-fourths of total assets over most of the century. As a result of the depression of the Thirties, followed closely by World War II, however, there was an extended period of fourteen years, 1934-47, in which corporate bonds and mortgages fell below half of total assets, reaching a low of 37 percent at the end of 1945. During these years the demands of federal government financing dominated the capital markets and life insurance assets were increasingly channeled into U.S. Government securities; these holdings reached a peak of 46 percent of total assets by the last year of World War II.

In the case of mortgages, farm loans were of considerable importance during the earlier years of the century, but with the depression and federal lending programs for aid to the farming community, activity by the life insurance companies in farm loans declined. Farm mortgages have been less than 3 percent of life insurance assets for the past twenty years, as compared with nearly 20 percent during the early Twenties. In contrast, the unprecedentedly large demands for residential and other non-farm mortgage financing in the postwar period have resulted in these loans currently accounting for nearly one-third of life companies' assets.

The emphasis among corporate bond holdings of life insurance companies was on railroad bonds during the early years of the century but, as the public utility industry developed, investments of life companies flowed more into these securities. Utility bonds continue to be an important investment outlet for the companies, but the postwar period has been marked by particularly heavy investments in industrial and miscellaneous bonds. These now account for over one-half of all corporate bond holdings of life companies and alone account for 22 percent of assets.

In addition to U.S. Government securities and corporate bonds, life insurance companies have also invested in the bonds of state and local governments and of foreign central and local governments (mainly Canadian). These investments have generally not exceeded one-tenth of assets and have usually been much less, reaching their higher proportions during the Thirties. In the postwar period state and local government bonds have become a growing area of investment, particularly special revenue issues on which the yields are more competitive with other available investments. Additionally, in the past few years with the sizable increase in the federal income tax levied on life insurance companies, there has been an incentive for some companies to invest somewhat more in tax-exempt securities than formerly. The total investment in governmental bonds (other than U.S. Governments) was, however, only about 4 percent of assets at the end of 1959. The recent increases in the proportion represented by state and local government issues have been offset by decreases in the proportionate share accounted for by foreign central government bonds.

Holdings of stocks by life insurance companies have been comparatively small and indeed were of greater importance in the first years of the century than at any time since. During most of the period for which information is available preferred stocks were favored over common, but in the last several years common stocks have become of greater importance. This is in part due to the increased market valuations on such holdings (common stocks are valued at year-end market). In the area of stock investments, in particular, the policies of individual companies have varied widely with respect to the proportion of assets so invested, but the combined industry average has for most of the century (1911-49) been less than 3 percent of assets and during the last ten years has not exceeded 4 percent of the total.

Real estate holdings have for most of the period been a minor asset of life insurance companies. At the beginning of the century they accounted for about 10 percent of assets but since then the proportion has followed a declining trend, except in the Thirties when mortgage foreclosures were heavy. Investments made in income real estate—residential properties in the early years after World War II but especially commercial and industrial rental properties in more recent years—have contributed to a rise in the share of assets represented by real estate, although they are currently only about 3 percent of the total.

Changes in the composition of life insurance assets, with the share of some investment classifications increasing while others were decreasing, reflect to a high degree changes in the economy. Despite decreases in the proportionate share of some asset classifications, the absolute amount of each major class of investment was nevertheless larger in 1959 than in 1899 because of the large gain in total assets—from $1.6 billion to $113.6 billion.

3) *The Basic Factors Governing the Investment Policies of Life Insurance Companies.* There are three types of factors governing the investment policies of life companies, as follows: (1) financial, economic, and public interest; (2) statutory; and (3) the regulations governing valuation of securities held by life companies.

With regard, first, to the financial, economic, and public interest factors, it is pertinent that life insurance and annuity contracts are long-term in nature and are typically written on the basis of an assumed rate of interest at which earnings on policy reserves will be compounded over the course of time. This factor inclines investment policy toward the placement of reserves in long-term investments bearing a fixed rate of return, with regular payments of interest over the life of the loan, and with scheduled repayment in a fixed number of dollars. Thus, investment in long-term obligations provides a characteristic of stability over time which parallels the contractual obligations assumed by the life insurance company with the policyholder.

In order to carry out their role as managers and trustees of policyholders' funds, life insurance companies place these funds in outlets in which the risk of loss through default is kept to a minimum, and the margin of safety is often greater than required under the limits of the investment laws governing their operations. At the same time, however, it is a mistake to assume that life companies are unwilling to assume reasonable risks in their lending. On the contrary, reasonable risks are assumed after careful evaluation, with the investment yield adjusted in accordance with the risk.

In placing policy reserves into various investment outlets within the limits of the safety of the principal, the objective of life insurance investment officers is to obtain the maximum rate of return available for these funds. The incentive to maximize yield on the investment portfolio is directly related to the net cost of insurance to the policyholder, since earnings above and beyond the assumed interest rates of policy contracts are a direct factor in the size of policyholders' dividends. To the extent that a particular life insurance company is able to produce a higher yield on its portfolio than the rate assumed in policy contracts, it is in a position to reduce the net cost of insurance below that of its competitors.

In addition to the factors which lead life insurance companies to place their funds in longer-term obligations at the maximum investment yields consistent with safety of principal, there are also certain liquidity requirements governing life company investments. There are three basic reasons why life insurance companies, like any other business concerns, would wish to have available at any given time a fund of liquid assets or a source of liquidity upon which to draw. The first and most obvious is the need to maintain working balances of cash and bank deposits in order to carry on the normal transactions of receiving payments and making disbursements. The second need for liquidity stems from the possibility of unforeseen contingencies. Among these are the possibilities of war, epidemics, economic crises or other catastrophies which would sharply increase death benefits and other claims or lead to widespread withdrawals of cash values in life insurance through policy surrenders or policy loans. A third reason for maintaining some liquidity is to remain sufficiently flexible to take advantage of worth-while investment opportunities which may arise.

In addition to these and other less important economic and financial factors, the life insurance companies have been motivated by direct public interest considerations in their investments. This has been especially true of their emphasis upon residential mortgage lending, their direct investment in housing projects, and their lending to small business concerns.

Along with the economic, financial, and public interest factors, the investments of life insurance companies in the United States are also governed by the investment laws of the fifty states and the District of Columbia. The purpose of these investment laws is to specify appropriate areas and to establish standards for the investment of life insurance company funds, with a view to ensuring the financial soundness of the company and protecting the interest of the policyholder by preventing improper practices or speculative excesses. Accordingly, life insurance investment laws take the form either of prohibiting certain investments or of prescribing the permissible categories of investments which may be made subject to certain limitations. For the major classes of investments the state laws typically stipulate the quality standards which must be met, together with the maximum percentage of assets which may be placed in a particular class of investment either in the aggregate or as issued by one issuer.

The investment laws are administered in each state by the state insurance department (headed by a commissioner or superintendent of insurance), or by the state department of banking and insurance. These departments are responsible for the licensing of companies to sell insurance in their respective states. They require life companies to submit annual financial statements which include the details of their investment operations during the course of the year. For example, this annual statement includes a listing of every security acquired, held, and disposed of during the year together with the particulars of each transaction. A triennial examination of each company also is conducted by the state insurance departments.

Chapter 5 traces the history of statutory regulation of life insurance company investments and analyzes the specific standards set forth in state laws for the eligibility of corporate bonds, mortgages, preferred and common stock, and income real estate. It also describes the statutory limits established for holdings of the various classes of investments, as well as other provisions of the investment laws such as "leeway" or "basket" clauses, provisions regarding small business financing, investment in foreign securities, and geographic limits on investment. The tabular appendix to Chapter 5 provides a detailed state-by-state analysis, for the main insurance states, of the laws governing investments.

A third factor influencing the investment policies of life insurance companies is the regulations governing the valuation of securities for annual statement purposes, and the mandatory securities valuation reserves. These regulations are set by the state insurance departments and commissions to implement the state insurance laws. Under the guidance of the National Association of Insurance Commissioners they have become substantially uniform between the various states. The valuation standards are for a number of reasons a basic factor in the formulation of the investment policies of life insurance companies. The majority of large life insurance companies are mutual organizations. Mutuals, in fairness to all generations of policyholders, return most of their excess premium deposits and investment income to their policyholders each year. In fact, the New York law limits the accumulation of surplus by mutual companies to 10 percent of net policy reserves and policy liabilities. The laws of a number of other states impose similar limitations. Competition from the mutual companies precludes the stock companies from accumulating large surplus. With surplus thus limited, valuation of investments becomes a factor to be considered in everyday investment decisions. Securities which would be subject to large writedowns in value would pose particular difficulties for life companies.

Chapter 6 traces the history of valuation of investments held by life insurance companies. It outlines the nature of the existing system of valuation and the mandatory securities valuation reserves.

4) *The Investment Process in Life Insurance Companies.* Responsibility for the investment activities of a life insurance company rests ultimately with the finance committee of its board of directors. This body is composed typically of five or seven members, but there are sometimes as few as three or as many as ten members. As might be expected, a background in banking or finance predominates among its members because of the nature of the decisions which the finance committee is called

upon to make. In order that there may be a balanced representation, one or two members are likely to be executives of manufacturing or commercial concerns or public utilities, bringing a business viewpoint to the work of the committee. Lawyers or those with legal training are also to be found on the finance committees of life insurance companies, and a background in construction or in the real estate field is considered desirable in many appointments. Among medium-sized and smaller life companies, but less frequently in larger companies, the members of the finance committee will often include the president or the financial vice president of the insurance company.

The finance committee carries the ultimate responsibility for investment activities of the life insurance company and controls the broad direction of these operations. To facilitate the administration of this broad investment policy and to allow flexibility in timing, the committee quite often will delegate authority for loans of limited amounts; even these loans are subject to later review by the committee. In the main, the bulk of new investments are approved only after individual scrutiny by the committee, based on the detailed analysis and recommendations presented by the financial officers of the company. While the financial officers concern themselves with making investment selections, the finance committee is continually called upon to exercise its judgment in shaping the investment philosophy of the company and in making the final investment decisions.

The typical practice among life insurance companies is for a single investment officer, usually designated as the financial vice president, to have jurisdiction over all investment operations including both bonds and mortgages. This officer often is a member of the finance committee and serves as a direct liaison between that body and the investment staff. In a number of companies, however, there is no single investment manager with over-all responsibility; instead, separate vice presidents head the securities department and the mortgage department, respectively, and report directly to the finance committee and to the company president. In such cases, it is more likely that the allocation of funds between securities and mortgages is fixed by the finance committee. Where a financial vice president exists, that officer normally has the authority to determine the allocation of investment flows between the departments under his charge, sometimes subject to ratification by the finance committee.

Approximately $11 billion annually flows into the investment departments of the life insurance companies of this country for investment in long-term outlets such as bonds, stocks, and mortgage loans. The sources of this cash flow, analyzed in Chapter 7, may be classified into three groupings. The first of these is the "new money" arising from the net savings by policyholders in life insurance companies. This source provides over \$4.5 billion per year. The second source is the return flow from invested funds arising from amortization, maturities, and other repayments of bonds and mortgages, currently running at just under \$5 billion. Thirdly, funds for new investment may be obtained through the outright sale of long-term assets from the investment portfolio or the drawing down of cash and short-term securities holdings. The amounts from this source are more variable but have exceeded \$1 billion in recent years. Trends in component elements of the cash flow of life companies during 1957-59 are reviewed in Chapter 7.

The practice by life insurance companies of making forward investment commitments has its foundations in the relative stability of their cash flow available for investment, the objective of maintaining a fully invested position, and the need of borrowers to know that funds will be forthcoming when required. A forward investment commitment may be defined as a binding agreement on the part of the company to lend a specific amount of money at a given interest rate for a certain number of years, within an agreed upon time period. The process thus enables borrowers to plan their capital expenditures with assurance that external funds will be available and enables lenders to schedule disbursements to balance, as closely as possible, with their expected inflow of funds.

The time period covered by a forward commitment runs all the way from one month to two and one-half years, with the period varying by type of investment, size of borrower and lender, and also whether new or existing construction is involved.

The commitment process is very closely bound to the steady flow of cash available for investment and is in a sense a counterpart of cash flow. Chapter 7 analyzes the ratio of life insurance investment commitments to cash flow for the period from the fourth quarter of 1957 through the fourth quarter of 1960.

5) *The Influence of Federal Government Policy Measures on Life Insurance Company Investments.* It is sometimes asserted that the investment policies and activities of life insurance companies are largely unaffected by federal policy measures, and particularly unaffected by monetary policy. This view is not substantiated by the facts.

General credit controls by the Federal Reserve authorities exert prompt and important effects upon life insurance investment operations, as follows: (1) they influence the direction of flow of life company investments, encouraging (because of the rigidity of FHA and VA rates) an expanding flow of funds into VA-FHA mortgages during a period of credit ease, and an expanding flow of funds into corporate bonds and conventional mortgages (along with a contracting flow into VA-FHA mortgages) during a period of credit restraint; (2) by having an impact upon interest rates, general credit controls affect the value of assets held by life companies, and thus the ability of the companies to raise cash for new investment by sale of assets; (3) they influence the total cash flow for investment of life companies through the effects interest rate changes have on policy loans, mortgage repayments, and funds left on deposit with the companies under settlement options; and (4) they affect the forward commitment policy of the companies through the influence exerted on investor expectations about the movement of interest rates. That is, when general credit control policy contributes to the expectation of rising interest rates, life companies tend to be marginally less willing to expand their forward commitments, with the reverse being true when policy leads to the expectation of falling rates.

During the Korean emergency in 1950-52 the life insurance companies were subjected to two types of selective credit control, namely Regulation X and the Voluntary Credit Restraint Program. Because of the buildup of forward commitments on pre-Regulation X terms, along with the difficulty of drafting rules to cover the complicated functioning of the home mortgage market, it is generally recognized that the restrictive effects on home-building of Regulation X were considerably delayed. The Voluntary Credit Restraint Program demonstrated that in an emergency the life insurance companies and other lending institutions can be enlisted in an effective voluntary effort to avoid obviously inflationary uses of credit, but at the same time it demonstrated that there is no real substitute for general credit controls.

Just as Federal Reserve policy measures, by restricting or easing the availability of credit, affect the level of interest rates and investors' expectations, and hence life insurance company investments, so federal debt management operations can similarly influence life company investments in four main ways: (1) they cause shifts in the direction of flow of life company funds; (2) they affect the capital values of assets held by life companies, and thus the ability of companies to raise cash for investment; (3) they lead to changes in the total cash flow of the companies; and (4) they affect the forward commitment policies of the companies. Moreover, just as is true of monetary policy, the Treasury can have a powerful effect toward encouraging or discouraging inflation through its debt management policies, with the expectation of continuing inflation or control of inflation having an important bearing on life company investments.

Other federal policy measures have an impact upon life insurance investments. One of these is government insurance and guaranty of residential mortgages. Another is the regulation by the FHA of downpayment and amortization terms on insured mortgages. Still another is the regulation by the SEC and FPC of redemption features in bond issues of utilities coming under their jurisdiction. The insistence by these authorities that bonds be immediately callable at low call prices has severely restricted life company purchases of utility bonds.

The new federal tax levied on life insurance companies is based on so many variables that it is virtually impossible to reach any generalized conclusions as to its effect on life company investment policy. Under the new law some companies will find tax-exempt bonds more attractive than formerly, common and preferred stocks will be somewhat more attractive because of the restoration of the intercorporate dividend credit, the popularity of purchase and lease-back investments may suffer somewhat, and investment policy will henceforth be required to take account of capital gains and losses.

6) *The Gurley-Shaw Thesis and the Impact of Monetary Policy on the Life Insurance Companies.* In recent years Professors John Gurley and Edward Shaw have developed a widely discussed thesis, outlined in Chapter 9, to the effect that the monetary authorities have direct control over the ability of the commercial banks to create money (demand deposits), and they have some control over the volume of time deposits of commercial banks by reason of being able to control the interest rate paid on time deposits, but they have no direct control over the ability of nonmonetary financial intermediaries such as mutual savings banks, savings and loan associations, and life insurance companies to sell their liquid claims for money and thus to add to the supply of close money substitutes in the hands of the public. Likewise, it is argued, the monetary authorities have no control over the volume of loanable funds of these nonmonetary institutions. Concerning life insurance companies, the following conclusions may be reached.

(a) The Gurley-Shaw thesis has little applicability to life insurance companies for a number of important reasons. One is that life insurance policy reserves are not regarded as liquid assets by the great majority of policyholders and are not a close substitute for money. Secondly, the life companies are not "deposit rate" institutions, a key assumption made in the application of the thesis. An important argument by Gurley and Shaw is that the net rate of return earned by nonmonetary institutions, relative to the deposit rate they pay, determines their willingness to supply their own "indirect securities" to the public. In other words, in the case of a mutual savings bank, for example, the net rate of return earned by the bank on bonds and mortgages relative to the rate it must pay on deposits determines the willingness of the bank to expand its deposits. But, clearly, the rate of return earned on assets by the life insurance companies relative to any "deposit rate" is not the determining factor in the willingness of life companies to sell life insurance contracts. Thirdly, life insurance companies have characteristics which differentiate them importantly from the deposit institutions.

(b) As discussed earlier, life insurance companies are powerfully affected by policies of the monetary authorities, even though not directly.

(c) There is no convincing reason for instituting any direct control of life insurance companies by the monetary authorities. The indirect controls already available are powerful and fully adequate. The inevitable result of any direct control would be to injure the possibilities for further expanding the public's saving through life insurance, so greatly needed to facilitate a more rapid rate of national economic growth.

(d) What is needed most in connection with the Gurley-Shaw thesis is a careful examination into the indirect ways in which monetary controls affect nonmonetary intermediaries. It is logical to expect that powerful indirect effects of monetary policy, similar to those felt by life companies, are also experienced by other nonmonetary intermediaries. Moreover, it is significant that Gurley and Shaw do not even mention two of the fastest-growing intermediaries, namely, the corporate uninsured pension funds and the state and local funds. Together, their annual growth in assets today is about as large as that of the life insurance business. The nature of these funds indicates that the Gurley-Shaw thesis would have as little applicability to them as it has to life insurance companies. Finally, one may well raise the question of whether the Gurley-Shaw thesis gives enough recognition to the fact that monetary policy is directed to regulating the *effective* supply of money, that is, the quantity multiplied by the rate of turnover. There is little doubt that a rise in the velocity of money has at times made the task of the authorities more difficult, but far from unmanageable.

7) *Life Insurance Company Investments and National Economic Growth.* The heart of the economic growth process has been the willingness of the American people to save a significant proportion of their current income and to make these savings available for investment in capital goods. The principal channel of saving by the American people in the past sixty years has been life insurance. During that period, over $106 billion of savings have been accumulated in this form.

During the period 1948-59, inclusive, one of pronounced economic growth, American business and industrial corporations borrowed *net new money* amounting to about $53 billion in order to aid in financing new plant and equipment and for working capital. Of this total, nearly $29 billion was obtained from the life insurance companies of the country. In other words, about 54 percent of the net new money obtained in the capital markets by business and industrial corporations to finance their expansion, modernization, and working capital requirements in this period came from life insurance companies alone. About 66 percent of these funds went to business and industrial firms, with the remainder going to public utilities, and in small measure the railroads. During the same period the life insurance companies added to their holdings of mortgages on business and industrial properties, and apartment buildings, in an amount equal to $8.5 billion. Since the total mortgage debt of this type increased by $32 billion in this period, the life companies provided about 26 percent of the total of this financing. Thus, these are the funds which in the past twelve years have been employed to build office build-ings, warehouses, department stores, shopping centers, and many other commercial and industrial facilities which have meant so much to the growth of the country. It is largely through this channel that life com-panies have provided millions of dollars of financing to small business concerns.

Perhaps most interesting is the enormous contribution which life insur-ance savings have made to better housing of our people, which certainly improves national productive capacity as well as our living standards. During these past twelve years the life insurance companies have ex-panded their holdings of mortgages on one- to four-family houses in an amount equal to $20 billion. In other words, about 20 percent of the total increase of $103 billion in home mortgage debt in the country as a whole during this period has gone to life insurance companies. But this really underestimates the total impact of life insurance companies in home financing because it does not take account of amortization of mort-gages and other mortgage repayments. Reliable information reported to the Life Insurance Association of America shows that since 1946 the life insurance companies of the country have actually made about $45.5 billion of home mortgage loans, of which $13.3 billion have been FHA-insured loans, $10.6 billion have been VA-guaranteed loans, and ap-proximately $22 billion have been uninsured home loans. On the assump-tion that the average mortgage loan during this period was $10,000, the life insurance companies provided the financing making possible the purchase of homes by 4,550,000 American families.

These, then, are the principal ways in which the life insurance savings of our people have provided the financing of sound economic growth. They are not the only ways, however. There have been other types of life company investments of lesser magnitude such as the purchase of state and local government bonds which have provided the financing for toll highways and other public improvements. The same is true of direct investment in real estate and housing facilities, and many other invest-ments.

8) *Life Insurance Companies and the Allocation of Capital.* In judging the effectiveness of life insurance companies as financial inter-mediaries engaged in the channeling of savings into various investment outlets, the question arises as to how well they have performed their function as allocators of capital. Have the funds that pass through life companies been placed into those areas where they have been most productive in an over-all economic sense? Has the investment of these funds contributed in the most desirable way to the social, as well as the economic, make-up of the country?

Life insurance companies eminently qualify as efficient allocators of financial resources in a market economy for the following reasons. First, their investments are made in almost every sector of the capital market and they are constantly considering a wide array of potential investment outlets. Second, the investment decisions of life insurance companies are based on a philosophy of maximizing their rate of return, within the bounds of state investment laws and the principle of safeguarding the security of the funds invested. The incentive for life companies to maximize their rate of return on investments arises from the effect of this return upon policyholders' dividends and on the net cost of insurance. Thus the rate of investment return becomes an important factor in the competition among the companies in their sales of life insurance to the public. Under these conditions of a wide variety of investment outlets and a yield-maximizing philosophy of investments, life insurance companies allocate their funds to those investments on which the rate is highest, i.e., where economic priorities fixed by the market are the greatest. Life insurance companies therefore perform most efficiently in a market system to allocate available savings among the wide range of competing demands from various sectors of the economy.

In addition to economic priorities, there are a number of social priorities which have affected the allocation of life insurance funds. Immediately following the war, for example, the social priorities accorded to housing facilities in urban areas were recognized by the life companies through the erection or financing of large-scale housing projects to meet existing shortages. The more general social priorities accorded to home owner- ship have been given national recognition through the insurance and guaranty programs of the Federal Housing Administration and the Veterans Administration and life companies have been one of the largest suppliers of residential mortgage funds under these programs.

Life insurance company investments have been highly responsive to the changing geographical structure of the American economy. For example, during the past thirty-five years there has been a significant shift in investment emphasis from the older areas of the country to the rapidly developing areas such as the Pacific Coast and the West South Central States. Similarly, there have been important changes in the past thirty-five years in the types of investments life companies have made. Farm mortgages have declined in importance and city mortgages have increased sharply. Railroad securities, once the largest investment hold- ing, have dwindled in importance, whereas there has been a sharp increase in holdings of public utility and industrial bonds.

A remaining question relates to the ability of life companies to innovate in response to new demands in the economy. An impressive list of innova- tions may be cited to demonstrate the ability of life companies to meet the need for new forms of investment or new techniques of financing during the past several years. In some instances it has been necessary to amend state investment laws to allow such innovations to be introduced, but the passage in many states of leeway or basket clauses now provides flexibility, within prescribed limits, to depart from conventional practice in investment policy.

A few examples from recent years will illustrate the willingness of life companies to invest their funds in new ways or through new outlets. The erection and management of large-scale housing projects brought life companies into new fields during and immediately after World War II; these pioneering efforts in the use of their funds were designed to alleviate the critical shortage of urban housing. Another frontier of investing was crossed when life companies worked out the purchase-lease-back technique in which an office building or other real property of a business corporation is purchased by a life company and then leased to the selling corporation for occupancy; this technique allows a borrower to raise new money without adding to his long-term indebtedness. Oil and gas production loans, based on the expected revenue from proven oil reserves still underground, are another innovating form of investment. The financing of pipeline construction in the postwar period has been facilitated by life company loans based on delivery contracts and certificates of necessity issued by the Federal Power Commission. Many other investment innovations may be cited.

The record shows, therefore, that life insurance companies have proved to be a highly efficient means for channeling capital funds into those areas of the national economy, and into those uses, in which market demands have been strongest. They have responded quickly and imaginatively to the changing capital requirements of the American economy.

Chapter 2

POLICYHOLDERS' SAVING
THROUGH LIFE INSURANCE

The Mechanics of Saving Through Life Insurance

The Accumulation of Reserves. The regular and systematic purchase of life insurance by the public leads to an accumulation of reserves and a build-up of life insurance company assets because of the level-premium plan used for most types of policies. The extent to which the regular payment of premiums produces policyholders' saving and an accumulation of policy reserves depends upon the particular type of policy involved.

Under the level-premium plan the amount of the annual premium remains unchanged during the premium-paying period although the likelihood of death of the insured increases with the passage of time. In the early years of a level-premium policy the occurrence of death is relatively low, and the premium paid for the policy is in excess of death claims (considering a group of insureds). In the later years of the policy the premium paid is less than the amount necessary to meet death claims that come with advancing years and rising mortality. The law requires that when a level-premium plan is issued a fund or reserve must be accumulated in the early years in order to meet the rising level of claims expected during the later years of such policies.

An alternative to level-premium insurance would be yearly-renewable term insurance, for which an accumulation of reserves is not required since the premium is set to match the expectation of death claims over the next year. Under this approach premiums would be initially low but ultimately would rise steeply to almost prohibitive levels as the mortality expected for a given age increases. On the other hand, level-premium insurance plans present a more practical means for an individual to acquire permanent insurance extending to the later years of life. The accumulation of reserves in life insurance companies is a direct outgrowth of this latter approach.

Even under the level-premium plan, the degree to which reserves are

16

built up depends upon the type of policy written. For example, a five-year term policy would likely be written on a level-premium basis, but the short duration of the policy would not require a reserve accumulation during those five years of the size that would be necessary under a "straight-life" policy extending many years hence (on the average) to the death of the insured. Term life insurance is comparable in some respects to fire insurance since it covers the *possibility* of death during the period of coverage, while a straight life policy is based on the eventual *certainty* of death of the insured and the certainty that death benefits must be paid. Term insurance is designed to provide current temporary protection during the short period covered. It contains very little of the savings element through accumulation of a reserve. At the other extreme, the savings element and the accumulation of a reserve for an endowment policy is quite substantial since the payment of benefits is a *certainty*, either at the specified maturity date of the policy or at the death of the insured.

Reserves and Cash Values. Reserves are funds the law requires the company to set aside to assure the fulfillment of its level-premium plan contracts. In view of the fact that during the early years of level-premium policies the premiums paid are in excess of the death claims, the law requires that such policies provide cash surrender values. An equitable share of these accumulations in the hands of the company may be obtained by the policyholder through surrender of his policy. Moreover, life insurance policies also stipulate that the policyholder may borrow against the surrender value without forfeiting his policy. Thus these savings being accumulated in the life insurance company are available to the policyholders.

It is through these two features of the usual life insurance contract—cash surrender values and policy loan options—that savings in life insurance derive their "liquidity." The bulk of savings in life insurance thus is available, if the need arises, for a temporary or permanent recovery of the sums accumulated in earlier years. Accordingly, savings in life insurance is sometimes considered a "liquid asset" which can be rather quickly converted into cash. As noted in Chapter 8, however, it cannot be regarded as a "close substitute" for money.

The liquidity of any asset may best be measured by the ease or rapidity of its conversion into cash or demand deposits, which are the ultimate in liquidity since they are readily accepted as the means of payment. On the one hand, a tangible asset such as a house or automobile is considered illiquid because of the time required to find a buyer and convert it into money at a fair price. On the other hand, securities such as Government bonds or listed stocks are viewed as highly liquid since there are active organized markets for the ready sale of such assets.

Somewhere along this spectrum of liquidity of assets lie the cash values of life insurance policies convertible into money through policy surrenders or policy loans. Other forms of financial savings may also be withdrawn for conversion into money, which leads many observers to compare life insurance savings to savings through institutions such as the mutual savings banks, the savings and loan associations, and the time deposit departments of commercial banks. It must be recognized, however, that there are a number of fundamental differences between savings deposited with these latter institutions and life insurance policy savings.

Comparisons With Other Types of Institutional Savings. First of all, the inflow of savings through premiums to life insurance companies is contractual in nature and reflects long-term programs of insurance protection. To keep the insurance contract in force the policyholder pays his premiums on a regular and recurrent basis—annually, quarterly, monthly, or even weekly. In most cases, the conscious decision to embark on such a program had been made earlier, when the policy was first written. Some of the saving through life insurance companies is even done automatically through payroll deductions, as in the case of employee pension plans handled by life insurance companies. In contrast, regular and periodic saving in the form of time or savings deposits or savings and loan shares usually involves a series of decisions each requiring a visit to the deposit institution. Moreover, any departure from savings patterns in these forms does not involve a disruption of contractual relationships as in the case of life insurance. As a result, saving through life insurance historically has been extremely stable in comparison with the more volatile movements in savings trends at the deposit institutions.

Secondly, the basic motivation of saving through life insurance differs from the deposit type of institutional saving. The accumulation of savings through life insurance is secondary or incidental to the main purpose of providing financial protection for beneficiaries in the event of the death of the insured. As explained above, the convenience and practicality of a level-premium plan of insurance leads to a build-up of a reserve fund in the early years of the policy which will be sufficient to meet claims arising in the later years when the likelihood of death increases. It is probably safe to say that the typical policyholder is uncertain, and even unconcerned, as to the cash value of his policy as of any particular month or year, although he is aware that a fund is being built up which he can draw upon if the need arises. On the other hand, the typical depositor in a savings bank or a savings and loan association is more likely to know the exact dollar amount of his current account by reason of holding a passbook or deposit book. Moreover, the motivation of a depositor-saver is often to accumulate a certain sum for a planned expenditure such as a down payment on a home, a vacation trip, or some similar outlay.

Saving through deposit institutions with the expectation of subsequent withdrawal presents a third contrast with saving through life insurance.

For savings and loan associations, voluntary withdrawals in recent years have run about two-thirds of the gross amounts deposited,[1] while the withdrawal ratio for mutual savings bank regular deposits averages over 85 percent.[2] On the other hand, withdrawals from life insurance companies in the form of surrender benefits and policy loans have been about 20 percent or less of the gross inflow of life insurance premiums and considerations for annuities and supplementary contracts. In the case of life insurance companies, the withdrawal of accumulated savings takes place principally at the death of the insured in the form of payments to the beneficiaries of the face amount of the policy.

In summary, life insurance saving differs fundamentally from saving through deposit-type institutions in at least three important respects: life insurance saving is long-term and contractual in nature and is therefore more stable; it is motivated primarily by the desire for family financial protection in the event of untimely death; and it is ordinarily expected to be left intact until the death of the insured rather than withdrawn for some consumer expenditure.

The Growth of Life Insurance Savings, 1896-1959

Over-all Trends Since 1896. Owing to the contractual and long-term nature of the life insurance contract, saving through life insurance has exhibited relative stability during the past half century. Although the rate of growth of life insurance savings has shown some variation in response to changing economic conditions during these years, there has never been a year in which saving through life insurance failed to be on the positive side. Thus, the amounts of accumulated savings through life insurance have exhibited a continuous upward trend.

At the end of 1896, policyholders' accumulated savings in life insurance amounted to about $1.2 billion; at the end of 1959, accumulated savings totaled $108 billion (see Table 2-1). In the first decade of this century accumulated savings more than doubled with a rise from $1.5 billion to $3.2 billion over these years. A somewhat slower growth was experienced during the ten years ended in 1919 when accumulated savings grew by less than 90 percent in that decade. The fastest rate of growth took place during the 1920's when accumulated savings advanced from $6.2 billion to $15.3 billion for an increase in that decade of almost 150 percent. Adverse economic conditions during the great depression cut this growth rate in half with a net increase for the 1929-39 period of only 79 percent. Some revival took place during the decade of the 1940's when

---

[1] United States Savings and Loan League, *Savings and Loan Fact Book* (1959), p. 17.

[2] National Association of Mutual Savings Banks, *Savings Bank Journal* (January 1960), p. 92.

TABLE 2-1
The Growth of Savings Through Life Insurance, 1896-1959

Year	Accumulated Savings At Year-End (1) ($ millions)	Net Savings During Year (2) ($ millions)	Percentage Gain In Accumulated Savings During Year (3) (Percent)
1896	1,244	n.a.	n.a.
1897	1,327	83	6.67
1898	1,429	102	7.69
1899	1,538	109	7.63
1900	1,659	121	7.87
1901	1,800	141	8.50
1902	1,959	159	8.83
1903	2,127	168	8.58
1904	2,307	180	8.46
1905	2,502	195	8.45
1906	2,708	206	8.23
1907	2,868	160	5.91
1908	3,040	172	6.00
1909	3,248	208	6.84
1910	3,453	205	6.31
1911	3,691	238	6.89
1912	3,915	224	6.07
1913	4,140	225	5.75
1914	4,342	202	4.88
1915	4,595	253	5.83
1916	4,930	335	7.29
1917	5,303	373	7.57
1918	5,822	519	9.79
1919	6,150	328	5.63
1920	6,643	493	8.02
1921	7,136	493	7.42
1922	7,745	609	8.53
1923	8,504	759	9.80
1924	9,286	782	9.20
1925	10,295	1,009	10.87
1926	11,530	1,235	12.00
1927	12,765	1,235	10.71
1928	14,101	1,336	10.47
1929	15,251	1,150	8.16
1930	16,299	1,048	6.87
1931	17,083	784	4.81
1932	17,357	274	1.60
1933	17,887	530	3.05
1934	19,122	1,235	6.90
1935	20,667	1,545	8.08
1936	22,389	1,722	8.33
1937	24,023	1,634	7.30
1938	25,614	1,591	6.62
1939	27,329	1,715	6.70
1940	29,152	1,823	6.67
1941	31,314	2,162	7.42
1942	33,775	2,461	7.86
1943	36,643	2,868	8.49

(Continued)

Table 2-1 (Continued)

Year	Accumulated Savings At Year-End (1) ($ millions)	Net Savings During Year (2) ($ millions)	Percentage Gain In Accumulated Savings During Year (3) (Percent)
1944	39,829	3,186	8.69
1945	43,277	3,448	8.66
1946	46,679	3,402	7.86
1947	50,287	3,608	7.73
1948	53,910	3,623	7.20
1949	57,828	3,918	7.27
1950	61,818	3,990	6.90
1951	65,964	4,146	6.71
1952	70,761	4,797	7.27
1953	75,761	5,000	7.07
1954	80,979	5,218	6.89
1955	86,490	5,511	6.81
1956	92,059	5,569	6.44
1957	97,260	5,201	5.65
1958	102,599	5,339	5.49
1959	108,038	5,439	5.30

Life insurance savings in column 2 are defined as the net increase in total admitted assets of all U.S. life insurance companies, less the increase in policy loans and after adjusting for net capital gains and losses. Column 1 is the accumulated total of such savings beginning with 1896.

Source: Data for 1896-1947 are derived from R. W. Goldsmith, *A Study of Saving in the United States*, Vol. I, p. 450; subsequent years have been calculated by the LIAA using consistent definitions.

accumulated savings in life insurance more than doubled with a rise from $27.3 billion to $57.8 billion. During the most recent decade accumulated savings rose to $108 billion in 1959, less than 90 percent above 1949, reflecting a declining rate of growth during the 1950's.

Table 2-1 also shows for each year since 1896 the dollar amount of net savings in life insurance, as well as the percentage increase in accumulated savings for the year. The dollar amount of net savings in each year has shown an upward trend as population, incomes, and life insurance coverage have expanded. From annual net savings of about $100 million at the turn of the century, life insurance savings currently amount to about $5.5 billion each year. However, it is the annual percentage gains which facilitate comparison of the growth rate in life insurance savings over this span of years.

During the first few years of this century, life insurance savings grew at a steady 8.5 percent per annum (see Table 2-1). A sudden drop to 5.9 percent took place in 1907, probably associated with the country-wide financial panic which occurred that year. After some recovery in this rate just before World War I, the percentage increase dropped below 5 percent in 1914 followed by a strong recovery to almost 10 percent during the last year of World War I. A break in this upward trend took place in 1919 when the growth rate plummeted to 5.6 percent.

As noted earlier, the 1920's witnessed the most rapid accumulation of savings through life insurance during this century. In four years of this decade the growth rate exceeded 10 percent and in 1926 reached an all-time peak of 12 percent. The depression years brought a marked slow-down in saving through life insurance, as it did for saving in almost every other form. From a level of over 10 percent in the 1920's, the growth rate sagged to 6.9 percent in 1930, 4.8 percent in 1931, and 1.6 percent in 1932. Not only did the public reduce its purchases of new insurance, they also drew upon savings previously accumulated in life insurance by surrendering their policies or taking out policy loans. Nevertheless, there continued to be positive net savings through life insurance in those dark years. The later stages of the depression were accompanied by a revival in life insurance saving with the growth rate rising to 8.3 percent in 1936 followed by a temporary setback to lower levels until the outbreak of World War II. The war years of the early 1940's brought a revival in life insurance saving as incomes increased and employment grew. In 1944, the growth rate reached 8.7 percent which carried through the following year.

From the recent high of 8.7 percent in 1944 and 1945, the growth rate of life insurance savings has exhibited a broad downward trend during the postwar years. During each of the three postwar recessions there has been a decline in the rate which may be associated with the adverse economic conditions of those periods. However, recovery from these recessions has not always brought a recovery in the growth rate of life insurance savings. It was not until 1952 that the downward trend beginning in 1948 was reversed, and in 1955-56 and 1959 there was no noticeable recovery in the growth rate at all. Apparently a more pervasive influence has been at work during the postwar years, exerting a depressing influence powerful enough to override the upward trend which might be expected to develop during years of economic expansion and rising levels of income. As may be seen in Table 2-1, the growth rate dropped to 5.5 percent in 1958 and continued to decline in 1959.

Factors Affecting Life Insurance Savings Since 1951. The recent growth rate in life insurance savings has been the lowest of the past twenty-five years. To look deeper into this downward trend for the basic factors at work, this section will examine in detail the gross inflows and outflows of funds through life insurance companies such as premiums, investment income, benefits, and expenses.

To summarize the conclusions at the outset, the principal findings of this examination of the gross flows are as follows. First, a strong shift has taken place in the "product mix" of life insurance toward term insurance and away from plans with a substantial savings element, apparently stemming from increased sales emphasis upon individual term and group business, and possibly to some limited extent from public fears of inflation and a consequent reluctance to save through long-term fixed-dollar contracts. Second, in addition to whatever effect rising unemployment in recession years may have on new purchases of life insurance, an adverse effect on life insurance savings appears to have resulted from the impact of recession on policy loans and surrender benefits. This is noticeable for both the 1953-54 and the 1957-58 recessions. Third, rising interest rates in other parts of the economy have had an adverse effect on life insurance savings through the impact on policy loans and on supplementary contracts.

The major items of gross inflow and gross outflow which produced the net accumulation of individuals' savings in life insurance for the years 1952 through 1959 are set forth in Table 2-2. This period has been chosen because data on a fairly complete and consistent basis are available for these years. These statistics are drawn from the combined annual statements of all legal reserve life insurance companies in the United States, as tabulated by the Institute of Life Insurance. A brief description of each category may be helpful in understanding the nature of the flows specified.

Premiums on life insurance and annuity policies constitute by far the largest single source of life company income. The data of Table 2-2 relate to all forms of such policies, reflecting premiums on outstanding policies as well as new business. Life companies also are important in the accident and health insurance field and the premiums from this type of business have grown rapidly in recent years. The category shown as "consideration for supplementary contracts" represents the funds received through settlement options on life and annuity policies. The simplest example of such contracts would be one in which a widow took her life insurance benefits in the form of monthly income for a fixed period of years or for the remainder of her life, rather than as a lump-sum payment equal to the face amount of the policy. Dividends left on deposit arise from policyholder decisions to leave dividends to accumulate at interest with the company.

Investment income constitutes a major form of inflow for life companies, second in amount only to life and annuity premiums. The investment income data in Table 2-2 are on a net basis, i.e., after deducting investment expenses, depreciation on real estate and federal income taxes associated with investment income. Consistent data for the 1952-59 period are available only for net investment income, but more complete

TABLE 2-2
Gross Flow of Savings Through U.S. Life Insurance Companies

Accrual Basis

(In millions of dollars)

	1952	1953	1954	1955	1956	1957	1958	1959
Premiums—life and annuity	8,322	8,968	9,448	10,191	10,885	11,649	12,177	12,981
Premiums—accident and health	1,561	1,879	2,115	2,356	2,699	3,126	3,294	3,641
Consideration for suppl. contracts	707	737	777	794	778	774	818	784
Dividends left on deposit	226	250	280	312	354	386	424	453
Net investment income	2,160	2,353	2,590	2,801	3,063	3,331	3,492	3,879
Policy loan repayments	383	378	448	506	515	566	689	726
Miscellaneous income	63	84	69	91	86	67	43	52
Gross inflow*	13,422	14,649	15,727	17,051	18,380	19,899	20,937	22,516
Life and annuity benefits	3,448	3,742	4,060	4,398	4,796	5,467	5,900	6,072
Accident and health benefits	1,055	1,248	1,393	1,598	1,902	2,282	2,425	2,652
Payments on suppl. contracts	621	666	693	738	808	902	881	990
Disbursement of dividends left on deposit	111	126	153	169	192	235	274	307
Insurance commissions, expenses, taxes	2,265	2,498	2,697	2,932	3,240	3,631	3,864	4,191
Dividends on life policies	832	941	1,062	1,203	1,304	1,427	1,517	1,617
Dividends on accident and health policies	36	44	55	68	54	47	49	48
Dividends to stockholders	59	92	91	105	135	137	153	180
Interest on policy or contract funds	10	11	13	15	18	22	25	27
Policy loan extensions	506	579	661	669	744	916	1,008	1,156
Less: due and unpaid items	318	298	369	355	382	368	498	163
Gross outflow*	8,625	9,649	10,509	11,540	12,811	14,698	15,598	17,077
Net savings	4,797	5,000	5,218	5,511	5,569	5,201	5,339	5,439
Plus: net increase in policy loans	123	201	213	163	229	350	319	430
Plus: net capital gains	177	-	522	272	-	-	613	201
Minus: net capital losses	-	43	-	-	219	253	-	-
Net increase in total assets	5,097	5,158	5,953	5,946	5,579	5,298	6,271	6,070

*It should be noted that some of the items of "inflow" and "outflow" are not flows in a real sense but only in an accounting sense.

data on gross investment income for the past three years indicate that the net figures understate the gross amounts by approximately one-sixth.

Policy loan repayments represent the funds repaid to life companies by those policyholders who previously have borrowed against the cash value of their insurance.[3] Miscellaneous income is a fairly minor item in the gross inflow statement and consists of receipts from various operations which do not fall under the classifications listed above.

Turning next to the gross outflow side of Table 2-2, life and annuity benefits constitute the largest single type of disbursement. Not all of these benefits are paid in cash to policyholders; as noted above, some benefits are converted to settlement options for supplementary contracts and appear on the inflow side (in an accounting sense) of the statement. Actual payments on such supplementary contracts are shown on the outflow side of the statement in Table 2-2. Accident and health benefits constitute the offset to the inflow of accident and health premiums, with the difference between premiums and benefits largely accounted for by expenses of handling such business. These operations may be ignored, since the accident and health side of the life insurance business does not give rise to net savings by individuals or to any significant build-up in the assets of life insurance companies.[4] The remaining items shown on the outflow side are largely self-explanatory, except to note that dividends on life policies may be left with the company to accumulate at interest, or credited toward policies, or taken in cash by the policyholder. The final item shown on the gross outflow side is a negative adjustment taking account of a number of deferrals and accruals such as due and unpaid dividends, commissions, expenses, and taxes, as well as advance premiums and other items. On balance, they result in a build-up of liabilities and must be offset against the outflows listed above to arrive at the gross outflow shown in Table 2-2.

The net inflow of funds resulting from these gross inflows and outflows is used in this study as the measure of policyholders' saving through life insurance. Conceptually, the same measure of saving may be arrived at by starting with the net increase in total admitted assets, subtracting the capital gains (or adding losses), and subtracting the net increase in policy loans. This method corresponds closely to those used by Friend and Natrella and by Raymond Goldsmith as the measure of saving through life insurance.[5]

---

[3] Policy loan repayments and extensions are not shown as income and disbursements in life company annual statements, but the amount outstanding is reported as an asset of the company. In this report they are treated as gross flows between the policyholder and the company, since the net extension of policy loans is a factor necessary in computing policyholders' saving through life insurance.

[4] Over the period 1952-59 inclusive, aggregate reserves against accident and health policies rose only $460 million, largely reflecting the increased gross volume of business.

[5] The definition by Friend and Natrella in their monograph *Individuals' Savings: Volume and Composition* (New York: John Wiley & Sons, 1954) also takes account of nonadmitted assets and makes an adjustment for the assets and policy loans attributed to foreign policyholders. The inability to make the latter adjustment on

With few exceptions, the gross flow categories presented in Table 2-2 show a steady upward trend in dollar terms over the 1952-59 period. In this form, however, it is difficult to discern which of the flows have accelerated relatively and which have remained steady or have slowed down. In order to give the dollar statistics a common denominator, the data of Table 2-2 have been recast in Table 2-3 as percentages of the

TABLE 2-3
Gross Flow of Savings Through U.S. Life Insurance Companies

Accrual Basis

(As percent of gross inflow)

	1952	1953	1954	1955	1956	1957	1958	1959
Premiums—life and annuity	62.0	61.2	60.1	59.8	59.2	58.5	58.2	57.7
Premiums—accident and health	11.6	12.8	13.4	13.8	14.7	15.7	15.7	16.2
Consideration for suppl. contracts	5.3	5.0	4.9	4.7	4.2	3.9	3.9	3.5
Dividends left on deposit	1.7	1.7	1.8	1.8	1.9	1.9	2.0	2.0
Net investment income	16.1	16.1	16.5	16.4	16.7	16.7	16.7	17.2
Policy loan repayments	2.9	2.6	2.8	3.0	2.8	2.8	3.3	3.2
Miscellaneous income	.5	.6	.4	.5	.5	.3	.2	.2
Gross inflow	100.0	100.0	100.0	100.0	100.0	100.0	100.0	100.0
Life and annuity benefits	25.7	25.5	25.8	25.8	26.1	27.5	28.2	27.0
Accident and health benefits	7.9	8.5	8.9	9.4	10.3	11.5	11.6	11.8
Payments on suppl. contracts	4.6	4.5	4.4	4.3	4.4	4.5	4.2	4.4
Disbursement of dividends left on deposit	.8	.9	1.0	1.0	1.0	1.2	1.3	1.4
Insurance commissions, expenses, taxes	16.9	17.1	17.1	17.2	17.6	18.2	18.5	18.6
Dividends on life policies	6.2	6.4	6.8	7.1	7.1	7.2	7.2	7.2
Dividends on accident and health policies	.3	.3	.3	.4	.3	.2	.2	.2
Dividends to stockholders	.4	.6	.6	.6	.7	.7	.7	.8
Interest on policy or contract funds	.1	.1	.1	.1	.1	.1	.1	.1
Policy loan extensions	3.8	4.0	4.2	3.9	4.0	4.6	4.8	5.1
Less: due and unpaid items	2.4	2.0	2.3	2.1	2.1	1.8	2.4	.7
Gross outflow	64.3	65.9	66.8	67.7	69.7	73.9	74.5	75.8
Net savings	35.7	34.1	33.2	32.3	30.3	26.1	25.5	24.2

Because of rounding, details may not add to totals shown.

total gross inflow for each year. Viewed in this way, it is apparent that the net inflow remaining as savings with life companies declined from

---

individual flow categories has made it necessary to ignore these factors in this study; however, the differences involved are quite small. The definition of policyholders' saving used by Raymond Goldsmith, *A Study of Saving in the United States,* Vol. II, makes still further adjustments for the increase in capital stock, liabilities to other than policyholders, and deferred and uncollected premiums.

about one-third of the gross inflow in 1952 to only one-quarter of gross inflow in 1959.

Premiums on life and annuity policies have declined steadily since 1952 as a percentage of gross inflow, falling from 62 percent to 58 percent between 1952 and 1959. Another way to approach the trend in premium income is in relation to the *net* inflow of savings. For every $100 of net saving in 1952, $173 was paid in as life and annuity premiums; in 1959, $239 of premium income was paid in against every $100 of net savings. Although it is not possible to make a close reckoning of the composition of premiums as between those with a strong savings element and

TABLE 2-4
Trends in Life and Annuity Premiums of All U.S. Life Insurance Companies

	1952	1953	1954	1955	1956	1957	1958	1959
				(In millions of dollars)				
Industrial	1,404	1,467	1,508	1,548	1,571	1,531	1,511	1,566
Ordinary-life	4,948	5,306	5,614	6,034	6,504	7,013	7,410	7,935
-disability	86	94	103	106	119	135	138	145
-accidental death	81	88	93	99	108	118	127	138
-individual annuities	247	259	235	238	230	223	230	236
Group -life	709	823	921	1,116	1,290	1,444	1,567	1,704
-annuities	847	931	974	1,050	1,063	1,185	1,194	1,257
Total life and annuities premiums	8,322	8,968	9,448	10,191	10,885	11,649	12,177	12,981
				(As percent of total premiums)				
Industrial	16.9	16.4	16.0	15.2	14.4	13.1	12.4	12.1
Ordinary-life	59.5	59.2	59.4	59.2	59.8	60.2	60.9	61.1
-disability	1.0	1.0	1.1	1.0	1.1	1.2	1.1	1.1
-accidental death	1.0	1.0	1.0	1.0	1.0	1.0	1.0	1.1
-individual annuities	3.0	2.9	2.5	2.3	2.1	1.9	1.9	1.8
Group -life	8.5	9.2	9.7	11.0	11.9	12.4	12.9	13.1
-annuities	10.2	10.4	10.3	10.3	9.8	10.2	9.8	9.7
Total life and annuities premiums	100.0	100.0	100.0	100.0	100.0	100.0	100.0	100.0
				(As percent of gross inflow)				
Industrial	10.5	10.0	9.6	9.1	8.5	7.7	7.2	7.0
Ordinary-life	36.9	36.2	35.7	35.4	35.4	35.2	35.4	35.2
-disability	.6	.6	.7	.6	.6	.7	.7	.6
-accidental death	.6	.6	.6	.6	.6	.6	.6	.6
-individual annuities	1.8	1.8	1.5	1.4	1.3	1.1	1.1	1.0
Group -life	5.3	5.6	5.9	6.5	7.0	7.3	7.5	7.6
-annuities	6.3	6.4	6.2	6.2	5.8	6.0	5.7	5.6
Total life and annuities premiums	62.0	61.2	60.1	59.8	59.2	58.5	58.2	57.7

Because of rounding, details may not add to totals shown.

those furnishing only current protection, it is obvious that a sharp decline in the savings element has taken place.

Some indication of the trend toward term insurance may be seen in Table 2-4, which breaks down premium income by broad policy types. Plans with a large savings element—individual annuities and group annuities—have declined as a percent of total premiums while group life insurance, which is almost entirely term insurance, has shown rapid gains.

Another approach to this question is through the type of life insurance policies in force. Table 2-5 summarizes data collected by the Institute of Life Insurance on the composition of life insurance in force over the period 1920 through 1959. The face amount of life insurance in force with United States life companies more than doubled between 1951 and 1959, rising by $310 billion. Of that increase, three-fifths represented the growth in group life term insurance and ordinary term insurance. As a result, these major forms of term insurance rose from 31 percent of the total to 46 percent of total life insurance in force at the end of 1959. While life insurance in force rose by 118 percent over these years, life insurance premiums increased only 68 percent, indicating a shift to lower premium plans such as term insurance.

Still another way to assess the trend in premiums is in conjunction with benefit payments. While premiums have declined as a percent of gross inflow, life and annuity benefits have risen slightly. However, the bulk of this rise has taken place in surrender benefits rather than in death or disability benefits, maturing of endowments, or payment of annuities (see Table 2-6). Surrender benefits result from the surrender of a policy for the cash value accumulated in earlier years; the proceeds may be used to obtain paid-up or extended term insurance but more usually are taken as cash. As might be expected during periods of growing unemployment, the trend of surrenders in relation to total benefits registered a noticeable increase in 1954 and again in 1957-58. An additional factor which may have played some part in 1957 and 1958 was the introduction by many life companies of "family plan" policies which were purchased heavily in those years. In taking out family plan policies, many policyholders may have surrendered small existing policies on wives and children in the process of redesigning their insurance programs.

Supplementary contracts arising from settlement options fixed by the insured or the beneficiary have typically provided a net flow of savings to life insurance companies. In the years 1952 through 1955, consideration received exceeded payments on supplementary contracts. However, payments have outstripped consideration received during the period 1956 through 1959 with a resultant drain on policyholders' saving in this form. It is noteworthy that the net drain has resulted from an actual dollar decline in consideration received on contracts *without* life con-

TABLE 2-5
Composition of Life Insurance in Force by Type of Insurance
1920 - 1959

U.S. Life Insurance Companies

(In billions of dollars)

Year	Ordinary life and endowment (1)	Industrial	Ordinary term (2)	Group (3)	Total in force
1920	30.9	7.2	2.5	1.6	42.3
1921	33.7	8.0	2.7	1.6	46.0
1922	35.6	8.9	4.0	1.8	50.3
1923	39.7	10.1	4.5	2.5	56.8
1924	43.9	11.3	5.3	3.2	63.8
1925	49.2	12.8	5.3	4.3	71.7
1926	54.1	14.2	5.9	5.4	79.6
1927	58.8	15.5	6.2	6.4	87.0
1928	63.9	16.7	6.6	8.0	95.2
1929	69.0	17.9	7.2	9.1	103.1
1930	72.4	18.3	7.3	9.9	107.9
1931	73.4	18.3	7.2	10.0	108.9
1932	70.1	17.3	6.7	9.1	103.2
1933	65.8	17.2	6.1	8.9	98.0
1934	65.5	17.7	5.8	9.6	98.5
1935	66.5	18.3	5.4	10.5	100.7
1936	68.4	19.5	5.4	11.5	104.7
1937	70.7	20.6	5.4	12.9	109.6
1938	71.7	21.0	5.6	12.8	111.1
1939	73.2	21.1	5.6	14.0	114.0
1940	75.1	21.3	6.0	15.4	117.8
1941	78.3	22.3	6.0	18.0	124.7
1942	81.0	23.3	6.1	19.9	130.3
1943	85.5	25.6	6.2	23.0	140.3
1944	92.9	27.0	4.7	24.4	149.1
1945	99.3	28.5	5.1	22.8	155.7
1946	109.9	30.2	6.2	28.2	174.6
1947	116.2	31.5	10.0	33.6	191.3
1948	123.5	31.8	12.2	39.2	206.7
1949	129.8	33.0	14.7	43.1	220.5
1950	137.0	34.4	18.1	52.6	242.0
1951	144.9	35.9	21.1	60.3	262.3
1952	156.0	37.6	22.9	70.6	287.1
1953	165.3	38.9	28.6	83.9	316.7
1954	175.4	39.8	33.6	99.4	348.1
1955	189.7	40.8	38.8	119.8	389.1
1956	207.3	41.2	44.9	138.9	432.3
1957	229.3	41.2	52.0	159.9	482.4
1958	246.8	40.6	59.7	174.8	521.9
1959	267.2	40.7	68.1	194.7	570.8

(1) All ordinary life insurance except term.
(2) Includes individual credit life insurance.
(3) Includes group credit life insurance.
Because of rounding, details may not add to totals shown.

Source: Spectator Year Book and Institute of Life Insurance.

TABLE 2-6
Gross Outflow of Benefits from U.S. Life Insurance Companies

Accrual Basis

	1952	1953	1954	1955	1956	1957	1958	1959
	(In millions of dollars)							
Death benefits	1,881	2,024	2,112	2,290	2,495	2,786	2,972	3,171
Matured endowments	441	475	543	615	656	733	760	625
Annuity benefits	369	411	417	453	503	529	578	629
Disability benefits	113	118	119	118	118	128	133	127
Surrender benefits	644	714	869	922	1,024	1,291	1,457	1,520
Total life and annuity benefits	3,448	3,742	4,060	4,398	4,796	5,467	5,900	6,072
	(As percent of total benefits)							
Death benefits	54.5	54.1	52.0	52.1	52.0	51.0	50.4	52.2
Matured endowments	12.8	12.7	13.4	14.0	13.7	13.4	12.9	10.3
Annuity benefits	10.7	11.0	10.3	10.3	10.5	9.7	9.8	10.4
Disability benefits	3.3	3.1	2.9	2.7	2.5	2.3	2.2	2.1
Surrender benefits	18.7	19.1	21.4	20.9	21.3	23.6	24.7	25.0
Total life and annuity benefits	100.0	100.0	100.0	100.0	100.0	100.0	100.0	100.0
	(As percent of gross inflow)							
Death benefits	14.0	13.8	13.4	13.4	13.6	14.0	14.2	14.1
Matured endowments	3.3	3.2	3.4	3.6	3.6	3.7	3.6	2.8
Annuity benefits	2.7	2.8	2.7	2.7	2.7	2.7	2.8	2.8
Disability benefits	.8	.8	.8	.7	.6	.6	.6	.6
Surrender benefits	4.8	4.9	5.5	5.4	5.6	6.5	7.0	6.8
Total life and annuity benefits	25.7	25.5	25.8	25.8	26.1	27.5	28.2	27.0

Because of rounding, details may not add to totals shown.

tingencies, i.e., based on a fixed number of payments designed to spread the policy proceeds over a number of years (see Table 2-7). In such contracts, the interest rate used in determining the size of payments is paramount, while the life expectancy of the beneficiary is of no importance. The fact that policy proceeds could be taken in a lump sum and placed elsewhere in the capital market at extremely attractive interest rates during the 1956-57 period and again in 1959 may explain the decline in such funds left with life insurance companies. In 1958, the net drain on this account subsided somewhat, when interest rates had generally softened in the securities markets. In contrast to these developments, supplementary contracts with the size of payments related to life expectancy continued to provide a net savings inflow during 1956-59 although in smaller amounts than in earlier years. It appears that contracts based on insurance mortality calculations continued to be attrac-

TABLE 2-7
Gross Flows of Supplementary Contracts and Dividend Accumulation
in U.S. Life Insurance Companies

	1952	1953	1954	1955	1956	1957	1958	1959
			(In millions of dollars)					
Suppl. contracts with life contingencies:								
Consideration received	135	150	165	176	178	193	204	210
Payments incurred	99	108	118	129	142	160	174	196
Net	36	42	47	47	36	33	30	14
Suppl. contracts without life contingencies:								
Consideration received	572	587	612	618	600	581	614	574
Payments incurred	522	558	575	609	666	742	707	794
Net	50	29	37	9	-66	-161	-93	-220
Dividends left on deposit:								
Dividends left on deposit	226	250	280	312	354	386	424	453
Dividends and interest disbursed	111	126	153	169	192	235	274	307
Net	115	124	127	143	162	151	150	146

tive, while contracts based only on interest rates diminished in attraction relative to opportunities elsewhere in those years.

Dividends left on deposit to accumulate at interest might be expected to be sensitive to interest rate factors, but they have actually shown little noticeable change in recent years, on either a gross basis or net of disbursements. As a percentage of total gross inflow, both accumulations and disbursements have grown modestly during the period (see Table 2-3). In actual dollar terms there was a steady increase in net amounts left with the companies until 1957-59 when a slight decline occurred (see Table 2-7). This decline might be thought to stem from interest rate trends, but the fact that 1956 was unaffected (unlike the trend in supplementary contracts) casts some doubt on this hypothesis.

Policy loan repayments and extensions may best be examined in dollar amounts with reference to Table 2-2. The pattern of policy loan flows is an unstable one, and apparently is sensitive to short-term economic cycles. The net increase in outstanding policy loans showed a fairly sharp rise in 1953 which continued in 1954. Many observers attribute this trend to the recession of those years, with unemployed policyholders finding it necessary to meet current expenses by withdrawing in the form of policy loans part of their past savings in life insurance. With the economic recovery in 1955, the net rise in policy loans diminished as repayments rose and extensions were virtually unchanged. In late 1956 and through 1957, net policy loans again began to rise although unemployment was of modest proportions. This latter trend may be interpreted as a response to rising costs of consumer borrowing and the tightening of credit availability. With fixed interest rates on policy loans and rising rates and tightened credit standards elsewhere, it appears that many policyholders drew upon their equity in life insurance to obtain funds for such purposes as down payments on houses or working capital in their businesses. The easing of interest rates in 1958 may have reversed this trend while the rise in unemployment may have led to increased drawing upon policy loans to meet current expenses. The net increase in policy loans that year was less than in 1957 but remained high by historical standards. With rising interest rates in 1959, net policy loans turned up again and increased above the 1957 level. In any case, very little is actually known as to the purpose of policy loans and attempts to explain their movements over this period must be through inference rather than direct evidence.

Dividends on life policies have edged up slightly in relation to the gross inflow of funds, as may be seen in Table 2-3. Approximately four-fifths of such dividends were left with the companies either to accumulate at interest or to be applied either to pay premiums or to purchase additional insurance. The share of dividends taken in cash has been quite stable over these years with the exception of 1957 when a slightly higher proportion was paid in cash.

Insurance commissions, expenses, and taxes [6] have shown an increase relative to the gross inflow of funds to life insurance companies, rising from 16.9 percent in 1952 to 18.6 percent in 1959. As may be seen in Table 2-8, general insurance expenses accounted almost entirely for this rise while commissions and insurance taxes, licenses, and fees were fairly stable as a percent of gross inflow. Only in 1957 did commissions register a significant gain associated with the large volume of new business that year. The increase in general insurance expenses became most noticeable after 1955. It probably reflects the cost of putting an increased volume of new policies on the books as well as the general rise in the cost of wages, salaries, and materials.

The inflow from net investment income has shown a rising tendency from 1952 through 1959 in dollar terms, but a leveling off in 1956-58 with a sharp rise in 1959 when expressed as a percent of gross inflow (see Table 2-3). Part of the rise in net investment income in 1959 may be due to the allocation of a larger share of federal income taxes against insurance operations. Investment income reflects the interest and dividend receipts on assets currently in portfolio, many of which were acquired

---

[6] Before 1958, federal income taxes were largely allocated against investment income rather than insurance operations and have therefore been taken into account under "net investment income" on the inflow side. Revision of the federal income tax base for 1958 resulted in a larger part of the tax being shown against insurance operations.

TABLE 2-8
Gross Outflow of Insurance Commissions, Expenses, Taxes
of U.S. Life Insurance Companies

Accrual Basis

	1952	1953	1954	1955	1956	1957	1958	1959
				(In millions of dollars)				
Commissions	941	1,050	1,102	1,189	1,307	1,446	1,495	1,593
General insurance expenses	1,082	1,200	1,326	1,440	1,597	1,820	1,962	2,086
Insurance taxes, licenses, fees	242	248	269	303	336	365	407	512
Total	2,265	2,498	2,697	2,932	3,240	3,631	3,864	4,191
				(As percent of gross inflow)				
Commissions	7.0	7.2	7.0	7.0	7.1	7.3	7.1	7.1
General insurance expenses	8.1	8.2	8.4	8.4	8.7	9.1	9.4	9.3
Insurance taxes, licenses, fees	1.8	1.7	1.7	1.8	1.8	1.8	1.9	2.3
Total	16.9	17.1	17.1	17.2	17.6	18.2	18.5	18.6

during periods of relatively low interest rates. The effect of higher rates on new investments made during the more recent years is therefore damped down by the presence of earlier investments. Net investment income has become an increasingly important element in the accumulation of savings through life insurance. Expressed as a percent of the net inflow of savings to life insurance companies, net investment income has risen from 45 percent of net savings in 1952 to 71 percent in 1959. Had it not been for the gain in investment earnings resulting from the rise in interest rates, policyholders' savings would have declined even more than the record indicates.

Having examined the gross flows in some detail, we can now summarize these trends in terms of their impact on the net inflow of funds, i.e., policyholders' savings through life insurance. The principal factors at work which have caused a leveling off in 1956 and a decline to lower amounts of saving in 1957-59 appear to be the following:

(a) an increase in the importance of term insurance during the period under review;

(b) a rise in surrender benefits, i.e., cashing in of existing policies by the insured;

(c) a growing reluctance to leave policy proceeds with the company under those supplementary contracts which are based solely on interest rates;

(d) an increased drawing upon equity in life insurance through the use of policy loans; and

(e) a rise in general operating expenses of life insurance companies.

It is worth noting that the upward trend of interest rates since 1955 has had opposite effects on life insurance savings. While there has been an adverse effect of rising interest rates because of the impact on policy loans and supplementary contracts, the beneficial effect on net investment income has been an important factor in sustaining the amount of savings through life insurance.

The Relationship of Life Insurance to Other Forms of Saving

The trends in life insurance saving described above must be appraised against the background of the more general trend of saving in all forms by individuals in the United States. This section will therefore relate life insurance saving trends to the flows of saving into other types of thrift institutions during the postwar period, and also to the postwar trend of over-all personal saving out of disposable personal income.

Relationship to Other Types of Institutional Savings. Accumulated savings through life insurance companies have represented the largest single form of institutional savings throughout the postwar period. At the end of 1959, for example, the accumulated savings of policyholders in U.S. life insurance companies was in excess of $108 billion, compared with $61 billion accumulated in savings and loan associations and $39 billion in mutual savings banks. Uninsured corporate pension funds accounted for $25 billion at the end of 1959, while savings accumulated in state and local government retirement funds approximated $17 billion.[7]

Despite the apparent dominance of life insurance savings as reflected in these accumulated totals, the relative importance of the life insurance business in the savings process during the postwar period has been steadily declining. That is, life insurance savings have continued to grow, but the growth trend in other forms of institutional savings since the end of World War II has been more rapid. The result has been that life insurance companies account for a declining share of the total flow of institutional savings.

These trends are apparent from an examination of Table 2-9, showing the dollar amount going into various forms of institutional savings during the years 1947-59, and the percentage share that each institution represents in the total. Life insurance savings in 1947 amounted to $3.6 billion, rising steadily to $5.6 billion in 1956 and then declining somewhat thereafter. A far more rapid rate of growth has been shown by the savings and loan associations which rose from a $1.3 billion inflow of

---

[7] Time deposits at commercial banks are not included in this discussion of savings in institutional form, since the data available on time deposits include a large amount of foreign funds which cannot be segregated. Shifts in foreign funds produce wide swings in time deposits for reasons independent of domestic savings trends.

TABLE 2-9
Postwar Growth of Various Forms of Institutional Savings

	Life insurance companies	Mutual savings banks	Savings & loan ass'ns	Noninsured pension funds	State & local gov't retire- ment funds	Investment companies	Credit unions	Total
	(1)	(2)	(3)	(4)	(5)	(6)	(7)	
				(In millions of dollars)				
1947	3,608	1,010	1,345	600	200	148	96	7,007
1948	3,623	760	1,293	600	500	150	110	7,036
1949	3,918	1,019	1,685	600	848	260	126	8,456
1950	3,990	892	1,870	900	706	235	178	8,771
1951	4,146	1,054	2,335	1,376	822	360	193	10,286
1952	4,797	1,794	3,388	1,506	928	584	318	13,315
1953	5,000	1,897	3,990	1,840	1,152	431	379	14,689
1954	5,218	2,146	4,977	1,931	1,250	452	375	16,349
1955	5,511	1,998	5,427	2,077	1,298	776	473	17,560
1956	5,569	2,037	5,418	2,409	1,465	960	528	18,386
1957	5,201	1,857	5,231	2,680	1,650	1,005	539	18,163
1958	5,339	2,611	6,936	2,775	1,753	1,171	537	21,122
1959	5,439	1,484	7,448	3,213	1,968	1,525	682	21,759
				(As percent of total)				
1947	51.5	14.4	19.2	8.6	2.9	2.1	1.4	100.0
1948	51.5	10.8	18.4	8.5	7.1	2.1	1.6	100.0
1949	46.3	12.1	19.9	7.1	10.0	3.1	1.5	100.0
1950	45.5	10.2	21.3	10.3	8.0	2.7	2.0	100.0
1951	40.3	10.2	22.7	13.4	8.0	3.5	1.9	100.0
1952	36.0	13.5	25.4	11.3	7.0	4.4	2.4	100.0
1953	34.0	12.9	27.2	12.5	7.8	2.9	2.6	100.0
1954	31.9	13.1	30.4	11.8	7.6	2.8	2.3	100.0
1955	31.4	11.4	30.9	11.8	7.4	4.4	2.7	100.0
1956	30.3	11.1	29.5	13.1	8.0	5.2	2.9	100.0
1957	28.6	10.2	28.8	14.8	9.1	5.5	3.0	100.0
1958	25.3	12.4	32.8	13.1	8.3	5.5	2.5	100.0
1959	25.0	6.8	34.2	14.8	9.0	7.0	3.1	100.0

(1) Life insurance saving as defined in Table 2-1 above.

(2) Net increase in total assets of all mutual savings banks. Figures for 1959 are adjusted for the merger of a savings bank into the commercial bank system in January 1959.

(3) Net increase in total assets, less net increase or decrease in borrowings of savings and loan associations.

(4) Net increase in total assets (at book value) of noninsured corporate pension funds.

(5) Net increase in total assets of state and local government retirement systems.

(6) Sales less repurchases of shares of open-end investment companies, and net new capital of closed-end investment companies.

(7) Net increase in total assets of credit unions.

savings in 1947 to a savings inflow of more than $7 billion in 1959. A rise of almost the same proportion is shown by the uninsured pension funds which accounted for $3.2 billion in savings during 1959 as against $600 million in 1947. The importance of investment companies (largely mutual funds) has also gained sharply over this period, rising from $148 million to $1.5 billion in annual savings flow between 1947 and 1959.

Mutual savings banks have experienced a growth in their annual net inflow of savings over these years, but this trend has been more volatile than for most other types of thrift institutions. For example, the net inflow into savings banks remained close to $1 billion per year until 1952 when it jumped to $1.8 billion and later to $2.1 billion in 1954. After some moderation of this trend, assets of savings banks grew by a record amount of $2.6 billion in 1958, but in 1959 growth in assets dropped to $1.5 billion. The latter figure probably is explained by the issuance of the "magic fives" by the U.S. Treasury in 1959 which drained some funds from the savings banks. Credit unions, although still of minor importance in the institutional savings picture, have shown a fairly rapid growth rate in recent years with a net inflow in 1959 approximately seven times the amount saved in this form in 1947 (see Table 2-9).

A somewhat better perspective of these growth rates may be seen in the lower panel of Table 2-9 which sets forth the percentage share of each institution in the total institutional savings flow. The most striking trend is that for life insurance companies, showing a decline from more than one-half of all institutional savings in 1947 and 1948 to barely one-fourth of institutional savings in 1959. Savings and loan associations, on the other hand, advanced steadily from 19.2 percent of the total in 1947 to 34.2 percent in 1959, while noninsured pension funds moved up from 8.6 percent to 14.8 percent during these years. The share of the total accounted for by investment companies advanced from 2.1 percent to 7 percent while credit unions moved up from 1.4 percent to 3.1 percent.

If the exceptionally low percentage for 1947 is ignored, state and local government retirement funds have maintained a fairly stable share of total institutional savings during the postwar period with a tendency to rise in more recent years. Mutual savings banks have also maintained a fairly stable proportion of the total, running somewhat better than 10 percent in all of the postwar years except 1959, with fluctuations inversely related to the business cycle.

This examination of institutional savings trends produces the conclusion that life insurance saving has experienced a sharp decline relative to other forms of institutional savings during the postwar period. All other thrift institutions with the possible exception of mutual savings banks have exhibited a rising percentage share of the total or at least maintained their relative position.

The question remains as to whether personal saving in general has shifted away from institutional channels or whether it has shifted away from life insurance only. Analysis of this question requires an examination of this trend in relation to disposable personal income in the postwar period.

Relationship to Disposable Personal Income. Disposable personal income (hereinafter abbreviated as DPI) is a measure of the amounts available for either spending or saving. It is defined as the income to persons and unincorporated businesses from salaries and wages, proprietors' income, dividends, interest, rents and royalties, and transfer payments, *less* personal income taxes and contributions to social insurance.

Total personal saving, as defined in R. W. Goldsmith's *Study of Saving in the United States,* includes saving in all forms whether through purchase of homes, consumer durables, or business properties, institutional savings or direct investment in securities; it also makes allowance for increases in mortgage or personal debt. The trend in this form of personal saving is shown in Table 2-10. Taken as a percent of DPI, personal

TABLE 2-10
Relationship of Various Types of Saving
to Disposable Personal Income

	Percent of disposable personal income going into:		
Year	Personal saving	Institutional saving	Life insurance saving
	(1)	(2)	(3)
1947	11.9%	4.1%	2.1%
1948	14.1	3.7	1.9
1949	11.8	4.5	2.1
1950	14.4	4.2	1.9
1951	15.8	4.5	1.8
1952	15.7	5.6	2.0
1953	15.8	5.8	2.0
1954	15.2	6.4	2.0
1955	14.6	6.4	2.0
1956	15.4	6.3	1.9
1957	14.9	5.9	1.7
1958	14.2	6.6	1.7
1959	14.2	6.5	1.6

(1) Based upon Dr. Raymond W. Goldsmith's *Study of Saving*; his data through 1949 have been extended by the Metropolitan Life Insurance Company (Business Research Bureau).

(2) Institutional saving as defined in Table 2-9.

(3) Life insurance saving as defined in Table 2-1.

saving has run relatively stable during much of the 1950's—the proportion ranging narrowly between 14 and 16 percent.

The total of institutional savings (as defined in Table 2-9) is also shown as a percentage of DPI in Table 2-10. The data indicate a rise in the share of DPI that has been placed in institutional savings. From an average of around 4 percent in the early postwar period, institutional savings have risen to nearly 7 percent of DPI during more recent years.

Life insurance has not shared in this growing importance of institutional savings during the postwar period. Immediately after World War II, life insurance savings held close to 2 percent of total DPI, falling to 1.8 percent in 1951 (see Table 2-10). During the years 1952 through 1955 the percentage remained at 2 percent but began to drift downward in 1956, falling to only 1.6 percent of DPI in 1959. Thus, saving through life insurance has not only failed to keep pace during recent years with the over-all growth of institutional forms of saving, it has begun to fall behind the growth in disposable personal income.

The saving trend of the postwar period may be summarized as follows. The American public has been saving a fairly constant percent of its current disposable income in the postwar period. A growing share of these savings have been channeled into institutions such as savings and loan associations, noninsured pension funds, mutual funds, and credit unions. Life insurance has failed to hold its share of these institutional savings. In fact, life insurance savings have declined from more than one-half of the total in 1947 and 1948 to only one-quarter in 1959. Moreover, life insurance savings recently have represented a declining share of total disposable personal income, falling from 2 percent of DPI to only 1.6 percent in 1959.

The Prospects for Life Insurance Savings

What is likely to be the future trend of life insurance savings in the years immediately ahead? Although the past few years have witnessed a declining importance of life insurance in the total savings picture, it is quite possible that this phase will prove to be temporary. There are a number of factors at work currently which give some promise of a reversal of the recent downward trend.

For one thing, there has been a growing awareness among life insurance companies that permanent cash-value life insurance has not been receiving the emphasis that it deserves as a means of providing both financial protection and saving for the policyholder. The top management of many companies has spoken out increasingly on the need for more vigorous sales efforts in the case of the whole-life and endowment type of policy rather than group insurance and other forms of terms insurance which have no savings element. To the extent that this shift of emphasis can be carried out through the sales efforts of the life insurance business, it holds the promise of an augmented flow of savings into life insurance in the decade ahead.

Another factor which would encourage saving through life insurance would be the halting of price inflation and the disappearance of an inflationary psychology among the American public. As pointed out earlier, one of the factors that may underlie the rising importance of term insurance during the postwar period is a concern on the part of the public that the purchasing power of life insurance dollars may fall over time. Bringing inflation to a halt would put an end to such fears and encourage confidence in the long-run value of savings placed in life insurance and other forms of fixed-dollar saving. Although it is difficult to be confident that the battle against inflation has been won, there are some signs that the postwar inflation has run its course and that a prolonged rise in the general price level is not to be expected in the years ahead. A good share of the excessive liquidity in the economy has been wrung out since the end of World War II, thus allowing monetary policy to operate more effectively in combatting inflationary tendencies. If inflation can be eliminated as a major cause of concern over the economic future of this country and its currency, a return to more normal levels of saving in fixed-dollar forms such as life insurance can be expected.

Finally, the general advance of incomes and living standards that is expected during the coming decade may benefit the trend of life insurance savings as more and more families reach the stage at which saving in this form becomes an attainable goal of family budgeting. Rising productivity and advances in technology give promise of allowing a growing share of American families to satisfy their basic requirements and also meet their needs for permanent life insurance and for savings.

In conclusion, it well may develop that the declining trend in life insurance savings during the late 1950's represented a passing phase and the underlying conditions that produced this trend may be transitory. In any case it is not safe to assume that the recent downward trend will continue indefinitely into the future.

Chapter 3

TRENDS IN THE INVESTMENT OF
LIFE INSURANCE FUNDS, 1899-1959

This chapter provides statistical data on the distribution of assets held by life insurance companies during the period 1899-1959, with emphasis on 1939-59. During this sixty-year period total assets grew from $1.6 billion to $113.6 billion, with increases occurring in each year. The annual percentage gains ranged from 5 to 12 percent except in the severest depression years. As may be seen in Table 3-1, over the entire period corporate bonds and mortgage loans have been the principal investments of life insurance companies with the exception of a few years in the mid-Forties. In those years holdings of United States Government bonds were larger than those of corporate bonds and mortgages combined and reached a record high of 46 percent of assets at the end of 1945, as compared with 37 percent for the combined total of corporate bonds and mortgages.

United States Government Securities

At the turn of the century and until World War I, U.S. Government securities were of little importance in the total assets of life insurance companies, amounting to $10 million or less and constituting less than one percent of assets. During World War I, however, they increased rapidly in importance and by the end of 1919 reached a high point of 11.5 percent of assets. With the prosperous times of the Twenties and the consequent strong demands for capital funds from private sectors of the economy, U.S. Governments receded in relative importance to less than 2 percent of assets by the beginning of the Thirties. The depression years, with the accompanying expansion of borrowing on the part of the federal government and the decline in demands from private sectors of the capital market, found Governments again on the increase. By 1939 they had reached 18 percent of assets and during the ensuing war years continued to rise, amounting to 46 percent of the total by the end of 1945. In order

TABLE 3-1
Distribution of Assets of U.S. Life Insurance Companies, 1899-1959

(In millions of dollars)

End of year	U.S. Governments	Mortgages	Corporate bonds	Corporate stocks	Other assets	Total assets
1899	10	468	471	83	563	1,595
1909	2	1,084	1,373	146	1,039	3,644
1919	780	2,094	1,968	76	1,873	6,791
1929	339	7,316	4,579	416	4,832	17,482
1939	5,276	5,683	7,951	587	9,746	29,243
1940	5,767	5,972	8,645	605	9,813	30,802
1941	6,796	6,442	9,573	601	9,319	32,731
1942	9,295	6,726	9,707	608	8,595	34,931
1943	12,537	6,714	9,842	652	8,021	37,766
1944	16,531	6,686	9,959	756	7,122	41,054
1945	20,583	6,636	10,060	999	6,519	44,797
1946	21,629	7,155	11,775	1,249	6,383	48,191
1947	20,021	8,675	14,754	1,390	6,903	51,743
1948	16,746	10,833	18,894	1,428	7,611	55,512
1949	15,290	12,906	21,461	1,718	8,255	59,630
1950	13,459	16,102	23,300	2,103	9,056	64,020
1951	11,009	19,314	25,983	2,221	9,751	68,278
1952	10,252	21,251	29,200	2,446	10,226	73,375
1953	9,829	23,322	31,997	2,573	10,812	78,533
1954	9,070	25,976	34,194	3,268	11,978	84,486
1955	8,576	29,445	36,059	3,633	12,719	90,432
1956	7,555	32,989	38,184	3,503	13,780	96,011
1957	7,029	35,236	40,832	3,391	14,821	101,309
1958	7,183	37,062	43,220	4,109	16,006	107,580
1959	6,868	39,197	45,334	4,561	17,690	113,650

(In percent)

End of year	U.S. Governments	Mortgages	Corporate bonds	Corporate stocks	Other assets	Total assets
1899	.6	29.3	29.5	5.2	35.3	100.0
1909	.0	29.8	37.7	4.0	28.5	100.0
1919	11.5	30.8	29.0	1.1	27.6	100.0
1929	1.9	41.8	26.2	2.4	27.6	100.0
1939	18.1	19.4	27.2	2.0	33.3	100.0
1940	18.7	19.4	28.1	2.0	31.8	100.0
1941	20.8	19.7	29.2	1.8	28.5	100.0
1942	26.6	19.2	27.8	1.7	24.6	100.0
1943	33.2	17.8	26.1	1.7	21.2	100.0
1944	40.3	16.3	24.2	1.9	17.3	100.0
1945	45.9	14.8	22.5	2.2	14.6	100.0
1946	44.9	14.8	24.5	2.6	13.2	100.0
1947	38.7	16.8	28.5	2.7	13.3	100.0
1948	30.2	19.5	34.0	2.6	13.7	100.0
1949	25.6	21.6	36.1	2.9	13.8	100.0
1950	21.0	25.1	36.4	3.3	14.1	100.0
1951	16.1	28.3	38.1	3.3	14.3	100.0
1952	14.0	29.0	39.8	3.3	13.9	100.0
1953	12.5	29.7	40.7	3.3	13.8	100.0
1954	10.7	30.7	40.5	3.9	14.2	100.0
1955	9.5	32.6	39.9	4.0	14.1	100.0
1956	7.9	34.4	39.7	3.7	14.4	100.0
1957	6.9	34.8	40.4	3.3	14.6	100.0
1958	6.7	34.4	40.2	3.8	14.9	100.0
1959	6.0	34.5	39.9	4.0	15.6	100.0

to reach this proportion, the net investment in Governments exceeded the increase in assets during the four years of 1942-45. Although in aggregate dollar amount Governments reached their highest total in 1946, $21.6 billion, they have declined in relation to assets in each postwar year and had fallen to six percent of the total at the end of 1959.

Data on the maturity distribution of Government bond holdings of life insurance companies, available from the Treasury surveys of ownership, indicate that the increase in such holdings during World War II was largely concentrated in marketable issues having a first call date of over ten years. As may be seen in Table 3-2, issues classified by call class increased $14 billion from the end of 1941 to the end of 1945, with $13.9 billion of the increase accounted for by over ten-year issues.[1]

As the companies began to lighten their investment in Governments in 1947, they initially reduced their holdings of shorter-term issues (under ten years to call) relatively more than those of long issues. From 1946 through 1951 the decrease for all issues classified by call class came to $11.1 billion, of which $8.3 billion was accounted for by long-term Governments and the balance by shorter-term issues. In contrast, after 1951 as total classified issues declined $3.9 billion, over ten-year securities alone decreased $6.2 billion while those having call dates within ten years increased $2.2 billion. A large part of this change in the maturity distribution of the Government bond portfolios of life insurance companies is attributable to the passage of time, resulting in the shift of bonds from the over ten-year class to under ten years. Of the $6.2 billion net decline since 1951 in over ten-year holdings, $3 billion was accounted for by bonds, still in the portfolios, which had moved into the under ten-year class; another $4 billion had moved out of the portfolios, and this amount was but partially offset by net additions of $0.9 billion.

Mortgages

Over the sixty-year period of 1899-1959 the amount of mortgages (including all mortgages—residential, farm, commercial, and industrial) held by life companies increased from less than $500 million to $39.2 billion. Indeed, mortgage holdings increased in every year except for two periods: (a) the five years 1932-36, when the companies' combined mortgage portfolios declined $2.5 billion, and (b) the three years 1943-1945, when they decreased $90 million. These two periods were, of course, marked by depression and war in which residential and business construction requiring new mortgage financing was drastically curtailed. Although total mortgage debt outstanding in the United States declined in both of these periods, the reasons for the drop were quite different as between the

---

[1] It will be noted that these data are for surveyed companies only which, however, account for the bulk of life insurance companies' holdings.

TABLE 3-2

Trends in Holdings of U.S. Government Securities by Life Insurance Companies, 1899-1959

Distribution by Call Class (Dollar amounts in millions)

End of year	U.S. Government securities		Holdings due or callable within:[a]					Savings bonds & other[b]	Total holdings covered by Treasury survey	Holdings not covered by Treasury survey
	Amount	% of assets	1 year	1-5 years	5-10 years	Over 10 years	Total classified			
1899	$ 10	.6								
1909	2	.0								
1919	780	11.5								
1929	339	1.9								
1939	5,276	18.1								
1940	5,767	18.7								
1941	6,796	20.8	$321	$1,608	$1,681	$ 2,755	$ 6,365	$ 12	$ 6,377	$419
1942	9,295	26.6	204	1,336	2,248	5,056	8,844	12	8,856	439
1943	12,537	33.2	625	1,241	2,825	7,640	12,330	12	12,342	195
1944	16,531	40.3	181	1,328	2,978	11,836	16,324	97	16,421	110
1945	20,583	45.9	306	1,211	2,194	16,697	20,409	115	20,524	59
1946	21,629	44.9	755	1,425	2,233	16,981	21,394	131	21,525	104
1947	20,021	38.7	231	2,157	573	16,507	19,469	445	19,914	107
1948	16,746	30.2	250	1,459	519	13,884	16,112	541	16,653	93
1949	15,290	25.6	295	812	1,224	12,287	14,618	559	15,177	113
1950	13,459	21.0	655	398	906	10,779	12,737	613	13,350	109
1951	11,009	16.1	778	119	712	8,681	10,290	616	10,906	103
1952	10,252	14.0	577	120	1,127	7,689	9,513	622	10,135	117
1953	9,829	12.5	485	153	1,535	6,947	9,120	578	9,698	131
1954	9,070	10.7	546	483	2,158	5,183	8,371	557	8,928	142
1955	8,576	9.5	456	321	2,933	4,179	7,889	552	8,441	135
1956	7,555	7.9	333	328	3,211	3,016	6,888	517	7,405	150
1957	7,029	6.9	251	530	3,195	2,483	6,461	374	6,835	194
1958	7,183	6.7	612	537	2,761	2,680	6,591	344	6,935	248
1959	6,868	6.0	427	1,454	1,948	2,519	6,348	199	6,547	321

[a]Marketable public debt classified by call class and Investment Series B Bonds.
[b]Non-marketable public debt and small amounts of marketable debt (i.e., FHA debentures) not classified by call class.

43

two periods and the effects on life companies' assets also differed. On the one hand, the Thirties were years in which mortgagors were unable to keep up payments. Lenders, faced with serious delinquencies on loans in which the underlying security was depreciating rapidly, were forced to take title, either through foreclosure or voluntary conveyance, in order to protect the interests of policyholders, depositors, or shareholders. As a result, the decline in mortgage investments of life insurance companies was in part matched by a rise in real estate holdings. On the other hand, during the war years shortages of materials and manpower for non-defense construction sharply limited demands for mortgage financing. Repayments of outstanding mortgages exceeded extensions of new mortgages, reducing holdings of these investments and making funds available for other investments—primarily U.S. Governments.

In the early part of the century mortgage investments were generally around 30 percent of assets, reaching a high of almost 35 percent of the total in 1913 and 1914. Although continuing to increase in amount during the following years, they lost some ground in relation to other assets particularly in 1918 and 1919 (when Governments increased). By 1919 they had receded to 30.8 percent, a low proportion for the decade, but above the proportions for the first ten years of the century. From this level they mounted rapidly to reach 43.1 percent of total assets at the end of 1926 and 1927.[2] The proportion fell thereafter, at first slowly but then rapidly as the dollar amount of mortgages declined in the 1932-36 period. By the end of 1939 mortgages were only 19.4 percent of assets, an all-time low up to that time. During World War II, however, mortgages decreased even further in relative importance, reaching 14.8 percent of total assets by the end of 1945. Thus, although mortgages had increased from less than $500 million at the beginning of the century to $6.6 billion by the end of 1945, they had declined from almost 30 percent of assets to less than 15 percent.

After 1945, as the pent-up demands for housing and other construction began to be met, mortgages increased rapidly, reaching $39.2 billion at the end of 1959, or 34.5 percent of assets. This proportion was slightly below the postwar high of 34.8 percent at the end of 1957.

The breakdown of mortgages in Table 3-3 indicates that at the beginning of the century non-farm mortgages were of greater importance than farm loans but that by 1919 farm mortgages had come close to equaling the volume of non-farm loans.[3] By the end of the Twenties, however, total non-farm loans had increased to such an extent that they were

---

[2] During most of the 1920's the annual increase in mortgage holdings was in excess of $500 million, reaching a high of $770 million in 1926.

[3] If the mortgage portfolio is viewed as consisting of three major components, farm, residential, and commercial loans, it appears from the estimates in Table 3 that farm loans were the largest component during the early part of the century.

TABLE 3-3

Trends in Holdings of Mortgages by Life Insurance Companies, 1899-1959

(Dollar amounts in millions)

End of year	Residential			Commercial	Total non-farm		Total farm		Total mortgages	
	Government-insured and guaranteed	Conventional	Total		Amount	% of assets	Amount	% of assets	Amount	% of assets
1899	-	$ 172	$ 172	$ 163	$ 335	21.0	$ 133	8.3	$ 468	29.3
1909	-	358	358	339	697	19.1	387	10.6	1,084	29.8
1919	-	575	575	544	1,119	16.5	975	14.3	2,094	30.8
1929	-	2,704	2,704	2,511	5,215	29.8	2,101	12.0	7,316	41.8
1939	$ 385	2,181	2,566	2,228	4,794	16.4	889	3.0	5,683	19.4
1940	668	2,244	2,912	2,161	5,073	16.5	899	2.9	5,972	19.4
1941	815	2,420	3,235	2,294	5,529	16.9	913	2.8	6,442	19.7
1942	1,096	2,506	3,602	2,228	5,830	16.7	896	2.6	6,726	19.2
1943	1,286	2,520	3,806	2,067	5,873	15.6	841	2.2	6,714	17.8
1944	1,408	2,365	3,773	2,113	5,886	14.3	800	1.9	6,686	16.3
1945	1,394	2,312	3,706	2,154	5,860	13.1	776	1.7	6,636	14.8
1946	1,482	2,533	4,015	2,345	6,360	13.2	795	1.6	7,155	14.8
1947	2,241	2,829	5,070	2,710	7,780	15.0	895	1.7	8,675	16.8
1948	3,485	3,304	6,789	3,054	9,843	17.7	990	1.8	10,833	19.5
1949	4,677	3,712	8,389	3,379	11,768	19.7	1,138	1.9	12,906	21.6
1950	6,598	4,495	11,093	3,682	14,775	23.1	1,327	2.1	16,102	25.1
1951	8,387	5,254	13,641	4,146	17,787	26.1	1,527	2.2	19,314	28.3
1952	9,027	6,018	15,045	4,501	19,546	26.6	1,705	2.3	21,251	29.0
1953	9,572	6,986	16,558	4,878	21,436	27.3	1,886	2.4	23,322	29.7
1954	10,759	7,798	18,557	5,371	23,928	28.3	2,048	2.4	25,976	30.7
1955	12,469	8,744	21,213	5,959	27,172	30.0	2,273	2.5	29,445	32.6
1956	13,931	9,814	23,745	6,763	30,508	31.8	2,481	2.6	32,989	34.4
1957	14,472	10,520	24,992	7,660	32,652	32.2	2,584	2.6	35,236	34.8
1958	14,876	11,045	25,921	8,474	34,395	32.0	2,667	2.5	37,062	34.4
1959	15,359	11,880	27,239	9,114	36,353	32.0	2,844	2.5	39,197	34.5

45

almost 2½ times as large as farm mortgages. The latter had reached a peak of $2.2 billion in 1927. Over these years commercial mortgage loans were of about the same importance as residential loans among the non-farm mortgage investments of companies.

The economic hardships of the Thirties were particularly difficult for the farm community. Consequently, farm mortgage investments of life insurance companies showed no annual increase during any of the years of the Thirties. By 1939 farm loans had decreased $1.2 billion, or 58 percent, from their 1929 level. To a considerable extent the decline in farm mortgages was accounted for by foreclosures or voluntary conveyances of title, as data below on holdings of real estate indicate. Non-farm mortgages were some $400 million lower at the end of 1939 than at the end of 1929. These loans, however, had reached a high of $5.7 billion in 1931 and a low of $4.2 billion by the end of 1936, for a total net decline of $1.5 billion. Annual increases after 1936 brought the portfolio to $4.8 billion by the end of 1939. A large portion of the decline in non-farm mortgage holdings during the Thirties also resulted from foreclosures or voluntary conveyances.

In the post-World War II period both farm and non-farm mortgages increased annually. Non-farm loans gained $30.5 billion from 1945 through 1959 whereas farm mortgages increased $2.1 billion over the same period. The annual gains in non-farm mortgages were particularly large after 1947 but they were by no means equal in amount, ranging from $1.7 billion in 1958 to $3.3 billion in 1956. The variations in mortgage activity followed the pattern of housing starts, which during this period generally followed a countercyclical trend. In the first postwar recession of November 1948-October 1949, non-farm housing starts (privately financed) began a sharp rise early in the recession, peaking in mid-1950. In the July 1953-August 1954 recession, housing starts began to rise moderately at first but sharply toward the end of the period, peaking in 1955. In the August 1957-April 1958 recession, housing starts began to rise only in the last two months of the period, peaking at the end of 1958 and again in the early months of 1959. As a result, residential mortgages of life insurance companies, as shown in Table 3-4, increased substantially in both 1950 and 1951, reflecting the closing of loans on residences started in 1949 and 1950. They again represented a very large part of the increase in assets in 1955 and 1956, following the very high levels of housing starts in 1954 and 1955. The residential loan data in Table 3-4 reflect only partially the rise in housing starts in 1958 and 1959 since 1960 figures are not included.

Government-insured or guaranteed mortgages accounted for about 60 percent or more of the increase in non-farm mortgage holdings of life companies during the early postwar years of 1948-51 and again assumed importance during 1954-56. Conventional mortgages also in-

TABLE 3-4

Changes in Non-farm Mortgage Holdings of Life Insurance Companies
1947-1959

(In millions of dollars)

			Residential				Total
	FHA	VA	Total Govern-ment-backed	Conventional	Total	Commercial	non-farm
1947	170	589	759	296	1,055	365	1,420
1948	983	261	1,244	475	1,719	344	2,063
1949	1,073	119	1,192	408	1,600	325	1,925
1950	1,119	802	1,921	783	2,704	303	3,007
1951	684	1,105	1,789	759	2,548	464	3,012
1952	424	216	640	764	1,404	355	1,759
1953	331	214	545	968	1,513	377	1,890
1954	104	1,083	1,187	812	1,999	493	2,492
1955	279	1,431	1,710	946	2,656	588	3,244
1956	232	1,230	1,462	1,070	2,532	804	3,336
1957	124	417	541	706	1,247	897	2,144
1958	692	-288	404	525	929	814	1,743
1959	830	-347	483	835	1,318	640	1,958

creased substantially in the later period, particularly in 1956, so that Government-backed mortgages did not account for as large a proportion of the increase in non-farm mortgages as they had in the earlier postwar years. The largest annual increases for FHA loans held by life companies occurred in 1949 and 1950, when they gained $1.1 billion in each year. In 1951, VA mortgages took precedence over FHA loans, increasing $1.1 billion, while FHA loans increased about $700 million. During the mid-1950's FHA loans increased only moderately, but during the three years 1954-56, VA loans gained $1.1 billion, $1.4 billion, and $1.2 billion, respectively. In 1958 and 1959, FHA loans again were made in considerable volume and increased approximately $700 million and $800 million in the two years, while VA loans held by life companies showed net decreases. During the postwar period the net flows into conventional residential loans were considerably more steady than those into FHA or VA loans but nevertheless also showed years of large increases (e.g., 1956) and years of small gains (e.g., 1958). As discussed in Chapter 8, the variation in the net flows into various types of mortgages basically reflects differences in the relative attractiveness of investment yields at the time loans were authorized (as opposed to the year in which they are shown as having entered the assets of life insurance companies). Each broad category of mortgage loan—FHA, VA, conventional residential, or conventional business loan—has had to compete not only with other mortgages but also with other investment outlets such as corporate securities available to life insurance companies. Among the range of these outlets, corporate bonds have been particularly important.

Corporate Bonds

As seen in Table 3-5, over the entire period from 1899-1959 corporate bond holdings of life insurance companies have increased, almost without interruption, and have represented from about one-fourth to two-fifths of the assets of the companies. At the beginning of the century such bonds amounted to about $500 million, almost 30 percent of assets, and by the end of 1959 they totaled $45 billion, about 40 percent of assets.

TABLE 3-5
Trends in Holdings of Corporate Bonds by Life Insurance Companies, 1899-1959

(Dollar amounts in millions)

End of year	Railroad bonds Amount	% of assets	Public utility bonds Amount	% of assets	Industrial and miscellaneous bonds Amount	% of assets	Total corporate bonds Amount	% of assets
1899							$ 471	29.5
1909							1,373	37.7
1919	$1,798	26.5	$ 121	1.8	$ 49	.7	1,968	29.0
1929	2,853	16.3	1,432	8.2	294	1.7	4,579	26.2
1939	2,769	9.5	3,826	13.1	1,356	4.6	7,951	27.2
1940	2,830	9.2	4,273	13.9	1,542	5.0	8,645	28.1
1941	2,858	8.7	4,873	14.9	1,842	5.6	9,573	29.2
1942	2,712	7.8	5,165	14.8	1,830	5.2	9,707	27.8
1943	2,734	7.3	5,220	13.8	1,888	5.0	9,842	26.1
1944	2,777	6.7	5,299	12.9	1,883	4.6	9,959	24.2
1945	2,948	6.6	5,212	11.6	1,900	4.3	10,060	22.5
1946	2,872	6.0	5,587	11.6	3,316	6.9	11,775	24.5
1947	2,844	5.5	6,941	13.4	4,969	9.6	14,754	28.5
1948	3,002	5.4	8,741	15.7	7,151	12.9	18,894	34.0
1949	3,017	5.1	9,764	16.4	8,680	14.6	21,461	36.1
1950	3,187	5.0	10,587	16.5	9,526	14.9	23,300	36.4
1951	3,307	4.9	11,235	16.4	11,441	16.8	25,983	38.1
1952	3,545	4.8	11,953	16.3	13,702	18.7	29,200	39.8
1953	3,643	4.7	12,827	16.3	15,527	19.7	31,997	40.7
1954	3,757	4.5	13,511	16.0	16,926	20.0	34,194	40.5
1955	3,912	4.3	13,968	15.5	18,179	20.1	36,059	39.9
1956	3,877	4.0	14,520	15.1	19,787	20.6	38,184	39.7
1957	3,863	3.8	15,252	15.1	21,717	21.5	40,832	40.4
1958	3,843	3.6	15,938	14.8	23,439	21.8	43,220	40.2
1959	3,774	3.3	16,455	14.5	25,105	22.1	45,334	39.9

Annual totals of corporate bonds for all life insurance companies are not available for the years before 1920. It appears, however, that such bonds probably increased in almost every year, although there was no doubt a slowing down in their growth or perhaps some decline during and following World War I.

During the 1920's annual increases in corporate bonds ranged generally from $200 million to $450 million. These were years, however, when the net increases in mortgage holdings were consistently larger than those of corporate bonds. As a result, corporate bonds moved from 29 percent of assets at the end of 1919 to 26 percent by the end of 1929, having dipped below 25 percent in the early 1920's. In the first years of the 1930's corporate bonds gained little, actually declining $100 million in both 1932 and 1933. The period 1936-49 was one in which corporate bond holdings rose substantially each year, with the increase being considerably more than mortgage holdings. There were only moderate increases during the war years, but immediately after the war corporate bond holdings began to rise rapidly, reaching a peak annual increase of $4.1 billion in 1948, an amount larger than the net increase in total assets. Annual increases during the 1950's were substantial, ranging from $1.8 billion to $3.2 billion. In total, the net additions to the corporate bond portfolios of all companies amounted to more than $35 billion over the fourteen postwar years, compared with $32½ billion for mortgages.

In the first decades of the century corporate bond financing extended by life companies was very largely concentrated in securities of railroad companies, reflecting the dominance of the rail industry in the capital markets of those years. Railroad bonds generally comprised about 85-90 percent of the corporate bond holdings of the companies during the first twenty years of the century. In the early 1900's, indeed, railroad bonds accounted for an estimated one-third of total assets. However, as shown in Table 3-5, such holdings have gradually but consistently lost ground and by the end of 1959 represented but 3 percent of assets.

In contrast with the rails, the trend in holdings of public utility bonds and the bonds of business and industrial corporations has been one of increasing proportions in terms of total assets. Public utility bonds began their increase in relative importance during the Twenties when they went from 1.8 percent of assets at the beginning of 1920 to 8.2 percent at the end of 1929. They continued to gain as a proportion of assets each year (with the exceptions of 1932-33) through 1941, when they reached the pre-war peak of 14.9 percent of assets. During the war years, the proportion of assets represented by public utility bonds fell off each year although there generally were small increases in the dollar amount of such holdings. Almost immediately after the war public utility companies were in the forefront of those seeking external financing and life insurance companies responded to these demands, increasing holdings by almost $1.4 billion in 1947, $1.8 billion in 1948—an all-time record increase—and $1.0 billion in 1949. By the end of 1950, public utility bonds represented 16.5 percent of assets, the highest proportion on record. During the Fifties the annual increases in holdings of public utility bonds were all below the $1 billion level, ranging from about $450-$550 million in years such as 1955, 1956, and 1959, when mortgages registered large gains, to $700-$800 million in 1950 and 1957. By the end of 1959 public utility bonds amounted to $16.5 billion, or 14.5 percent of total assets.

The growth in holdings of industrial and miscellaneous bonds was quite gradual during the Twenties, going from $49 million, or 0.7 percent of assets, to $294 million, 1.7 percent of assets. During the late Thirties their growth accelerated and by the end of 1939 life companies' holdings of industrial and miscellaneous bonds approximated $1,350 million, or 4.6 percent of assets. They reached a pre-war high of $1.8 billion, or 5.6 percent of assets, by the end of 1941. Although there was a nominal increase in dollar holdings over the war years, by the end of 1945 these bonds had receded to 4.3 percent of assets. From this level they mounted rapidly, increasing by $23 billion in fourteen years. By the end of 1959 life companies' holdings of industrial and miscellaneous bonds totaled $25.1 billion, 22.1 percent of assets. This tremendous post-war growth reflected the response of life companies to the demands of all types of business and industrial concerns for external funds in order to finance plant and equipment modernization and expansion programs. Detailed industrial classification of the bond portfolio is not available in the annual statements of companies, but a special survey made by the Institute of Life Insurance as of 1957 indicated that about two-thirds of the industrial and miscellaneous bond portfolio was held in securities of manufacturing concerns and the remaining one-third in those of non-manufacturing concerns, such as finance, retail and wholesale trade, transportation and communications, and services.

In corporate bond financing, and particularly in industrial and miscellaneous bond financing, it is not unusual for borrowers to place their issues directly with investors, giving rise to offerings known as *direct placements*. The term may in its broadest sense also cover securities which, although not directly negotiated between borrower and lender, are placed with a limited number of investors and involve no general public distribution. The limited number of holders makes possible future changes in indenture terms or other modifications of the contract, thus giving these loans features characteristic of loans originally negotiated by borrower and lender. Based on studies made of companies accounting for 85 percent of the corporate bond holdings of the life insurance business, it is estimated that at the end of 1959 roughly two-thirds of the corporate bond holdings of all life insurance companies had been acquired through direct placement. The proportion varied considerably among the three major breakdowns with nearly one-fifth of rails, less than one-half of public utilities, and about 90 percent of industrial and miscellaneous bonds having been acquired via this investment route. These 1959 proportions resulted from gradual increases over time, but particularly during the postwar period. The development of direct placements has been an important feature in the investment process of life insurance companies and is discussed further in Chapter 7 in connection with the cash flow of companies and the forward commitment process.

Stocks

The value of stocks (preferred and common) held by life insurance companies increased from less than $100 million at the turn of the century to almost $4.6 billion at the end of 1959 (Table 3-6). As a proportion of assets, however, these holdings declined from 5.2 percent to 4.0 percent over the period, having reached a high of 7.3 percent in 1903 and a low of 0.6 percent during several years of the Twenties. During most of the period, from the end of 1911 through 1949, stock holdings were consistently less than 3 percent of assets.

There have been several factors influencing the amount of stocks held by the companies: (1) statutory requirements and limitations, (2) valuation regulations, and (3) investment policies. With respect to statutory provisions, which are discussed more fully in Chapter 5, the provisions of the New York State law in particular have had an important influence on the amount of stocks held by all life insurance companies since companies domiciled in the state have constituted a large, although varying, segment of the industry.[4] Under the New York law, investment in preferred stocks was not permitted from 1906 until 1928 and in common stocks from 1906 until 1951.[5] The laws of other states also have not permitted stock investment. When such investment has been permitted there have been limitations on the amount of such holdings. These limitations are often expressed as a percentage of assets or surplus and help to account for the relatively small investment in equities by life companies.

In addition, the method for valuing stocks required by the regulatory authorities has had some effect on the amount of such holdings by life insurance companies. Broadly speaking, over most of the sixty-year period under review stocks have been valued at year-end market prices, which, of course, may fluctuate widely. It is likely that market valuations may have been some deterrent to greater stock investment since these

---

[4] Table 5-2 of Chapter 5 provides statistical data on the proportion of total life insurance companies' assets accounted for by New York companies at various dates.

[5] During the years in which such investment was prohibited, stocks may have been held by the affected companies as a result, for example, of reorganization of a corporate borrower in which equities were accepted in exchange for debt instruments in order to protect the life company's interest.

fluctuations would have had a direct impact on surplus during most of the period.[6] Surplus is customarily small relative to policy reserves and liabilities, both because of legal limitations in some states and in general because of considerations of equity among various generations of policyholders. There is a natural reluctance on the part of companies to expose surplus to wide variations, possibly to a decrease, such as large stock investments might entail.

It should also be noted, in connection with the carrying values for stocks, that annual changes in holdings that might be computed from Table 3-6 cannot be used as a measure of net investment or disinvestment in equities on the part of life companies. A decline in market values

TABLE 3-6
Trends in Holdings of Stocks by Life Insurance Companies,
1899-1959

(Dollar amounts in millions)

End of year	Preferred	Common	Total stocks	% of assets
1899	$ n.a.	$ n.a.	$ 83	5.2
1909	n.a.	n.a.	146	4.0
1919	n.a.	n.a.	76	1.1
1929	n.a.	n.a.	416	2.4
1939	445	142	587	2.0
1940	455	150	605	2.0
1941	453	148	601	1.8
1942	460	148	608	1.7
1943	485	167	652	1.7
1944	550	206	756	1.9
1945	722	277	999	2.2
1946	908	341	1,249	2.6
1947	1,033	357	1,390	2.7
1948	1,055	373	1,428	2.6
1949	1,258	460	1,718	2.9
1950	1,454	649	2,103	3.3
1951	1,401	820	2,221	3.3
1952	1,483	963	2,446	3.3
1953	1,531	1,042	2,573	3.3
1954	1,732	1,536	3,268	3.9
1955	1,744	1,889	3,633	4.0
1956	1,551	1,952	3,503	3.7
1957	1,524	1,867	3,391	3.3
1958	1,561	2,548	4,109	3.8
1959	1,607	2,954	4,561	4.0

n.a. - Not available.

[6] Chapter 6 provides an historical summary of the valuation of securities and a description of the mandatory securities valuation reserve first provided for by the National Association of Insurance Commissioners in 1951.

from one year to another may obscure the net investment made in stocks, or an increase in values may exaggerate or even exceed the net investment actually made.

The investment policy of companies has varied widely with respect to common stocks, particularly as to the basic question of their appropriateness as investments for a life insurance company. Some companies hold that common stocks are not an appropriate investment outlet since the contractual liabilities of the companies are in terms of fixed dollar amounts and common stocks hold no promise to pay either the original investment or income. Other companies hold the view that all available avenues of investment should be utilized in order to obtain diversification not possible through loans and to realize the highest possible over-all rate of return. These companies believe that in view of the long-run nature of their contracts life companies are in a position to weather cyclical price changes. There are many other arguments advanced pro and con common stock investment, including social, economic, and public relations aspects of investment in equities on the part of life insurance companies. As a result of weighing the many considerations involved, the companies have reached diverse conclusions with the result that common stocks are not included among the assets of some companies while others hold upwards of 10 percent of their assets in such investments.

Classification of the industry's stock holdings as to preferred or common is available for only a relatively short period. It is probable that in the early part of the century common stocks predominated, but in most of the period for which the breakdown is available (i.e., from 1939, as shown in Table 3-6) preferred stocks were favored. The figures undoubtedly reflect the effect of the New York law of 1928 which permitted limited investment in preferred stocks while common stock investment continued to be prohibited. In the last few years common stocks have emerged as being of greater importance than preferreds, and this reflects not only the provisions of the New York law of 1951 and further liberalization in 1957 regarding common stock investment but also the high level of common stock prices during the Fifties.

Government Securities, Other Than U.S. Governments

The obligations of state and local governments and of foreign (mainly Canadian) governments, both central and local, have long been among life insurance companies' investments. The combined holdings of these bonds represented nearly 11 percent of assets at the beginning of the century but since then have generally been less than 10 percent of the total (Table 3-7). During the Thirties, holdings of state and local government issues (domestic) gained in importance with the result that all government bonds (other than U.S. Governments) increased from 6.2

TABLE 3-7
Trends in Holdings of Government Bonds, Other Than
U.S. Government Securities by Life Insurance Companies
1899-1959

(Dollar amounts in millions)

End of year	State and local			Foreign central governments	Total	% of assets
	U.S.	Foreign	Total			
1899	$ ...	$ ...	$ ...	$ ...	$ 173	10.8
1909	...	...	...	...	241	6.6
1919	...	...	320	173	493	7.3
1929	...	...	909	174	1,083	6.2
1939	1,940	318	2,258	249	2,507	8.6
1940	2,082	310	2,392	288	2,680	8.7
1941	1,995	291	2,286	396	2,682	8.2
1942	1,772	273	2,045	511	2,556	7.3
1943	1,488	285	1,773	684	2,457	6.5
1944	1,123	306	1,429	792	2,221	5.4
1945	722	325	1,047	915	1,962	4.4
1946	614	322	936	1,010	1,946	4.0
1947	609	336	945	1,037	1,982	3.8
1948	872	327	1,199	1,140	2,339	4.2
1949	1,052	341	1,393	1,130	2,523	4.2
1950	1,152	395	1,547	1,060	2,607	4.1
1951	1,170	566	1,736	922	2,658	3.9
1952	1,153	614	1,767	755	2,522	3.4
1953	1,298	692	1,990	586	2,576	3.3
1954	1,846	703	2,549	481	3,030	3.6
1955	2,038	658	2,696	410	3,106	3.4
1956	2,273	738	3,011	357	3,368	3.5
1957	2,376	787	3,163	332	3,495	3.4
1958	2,681	829	3,510	320	3,830	3.6
1959	3,200	935	4,135	349	4,484	3.9

percent of assets at the end of 1929 to 8.6 percent at the end of 1939. Despite sizable increases in holdings of foreign central government issues during World War II, these were more than offset by decreases in holdings of domestic state and local issues. By the end of 1945 the total of state and local and foreign governmental bonds had fallen below 5 percent of assets and during the postwar years has fluctuated around 3 or 4 percent of assets. Nevertheless, during the postwar period there has been substantial investment in the issues of state and local governments. These increased from $0.6 billion (1.2 percent of assets) at the end of 1947 to $3.2 billion (2.8 percent of assets) by the end of 1959. This investment was accompanied by increased investment also in the securities of foreign local governments but by a net decrease in holdings of foreign central government bonds, which returned to about their pre-war level (Table 3-7).

Although there are a number of factors influencing investment in these governmental bonds, it is probable that the most influential consideration has been the yield on these securities relative to other available investments. For example, during World War II when federal income tax rates were greatly increased and new issues of the U.S. Treasury were fully taxable, the issues of state and local governments became increasingly attractive to individuals and other investors and less attractive to life insurance companies for which the tax-exempt feature had little or no value. The very great demands for financing on the part of state and local governments during the postwar years have resulted in many issues being offered at yields attractive to life insurance companies. A large proportion of the companies' postwar investment in state and local issues represents special revenue bonds on which the yields are more competitive with other available outlets. The relatively large net additions to these holdings in 1958 and particularly in 1959 resulted in part from the substantial increase in the federal income tax levied on life insurance companies effective with their 1958 operations.

Real Estate

Real estate holdings of life insurance companies are of three broad classifications: properties owned for company occupancy, real estate acquired for investment (i.e., income-producing), and properties acquired in satisfaction of debt. At the turn of the century real estate holdings accounted for about 10 percent of total assets, as shown in Table 3-8, but this proportion gradually declined to 2-3 percent of assets in the Twenties, as holdings changed little and total assets steadily increased. Largely as a result of mortgage foreclosures in the Thirties, real estate holdings increased rapidly and accounted for nearly 9 percent of assets in the mid-Thirties. With more prosperous times these foreclosed properties were gradually disposed of and real estate again became negligible, amounting to only 1½ percent of assets by the end of 1946. Investments made in income real estate—residential properties in the early years after World War II but especially commercial and industrial rental properties in more recent years—have contributed to a rise in the share of assets represented by real estate. Nevertheless, total real estate holdings were only about 3 percent of assets at the end of 1959.

Policy Loans and Miscellaneous Assets

Policy loans (including premium notes) accounted for a larger share of assets during most of the sixty years under review than they did at either the beginning or end of the period. In 1899 loans to policyholders were just over 4 percent of assets (Table 3-9) but they mounted rapidly during the next ten years to reach 12 percent at the end of 1909. They

TABLE 3-8
Trends in Holdings of Real Estate by Life Insurance Companies, 1899-1959

(Dollar amounts in millions)

End of year	Company used	Investment Residential	Commercial	Other	Total	% of assets
1899	$ ...	$ ...	$ -	$ ...	$ 154	9.6
1909	...	...	-	...	167	4.6
1919	...	...	-	...	168	2.5
1929	191	10	-	263	464	2.7
1939	220	40	-	1,879	2,139	7.3
1940	220	75	-	1,770	2,065	6.7
1941	225	85	-	1,568	1,878	5.7
1942	225	105	-	1,333	1,663	4.8
1943	230	129	-	993	1,352	3.6
1944	230	135	-	698	1,063	2.6
1945	235	140	-	482	857	1.9
1946	235	150	89	261	735	1.5
1947	258	207	219	176	860	1.7
1948	299	240	384	132	1,055	1.9
1949	333	302	515	97	1,247	2.1
1950	353	349	657	86	1,445	2.2
1951	383	356	829	63	1,631	2.4
1952	418	461	985	39	1,903	2.6
1953	452	446	1,095	27	2,020	2.6
1954	519	456	1,297	26	2,298	2.7
1955	597	455	1,504	25	2,581	2.9
1956	680	437	1,679	21	2,817	2.9
1957	791	438	1,867	23	3,119	3.1
1958	853	425	2,063	23	3,364	3.1
1959	964	414	2,243	30	3,651	3.2

Detail for company used and investment real estate prior to 1947 are estimates from Raymond W. Goldsmith, *A Study of Saving in the United States*, Vol. I (Princeton University Press, 1955), p. 659.

then ranged around 12 to 15 percent of the total until the Thirties. Policy loans served as an important source of cash to policyholders during the worst years of the depression of the Thirties, particularly at the time of the banking crisis. At the end of 1932 they accounted for 18 percent of assets, having increased 60 percent above their 1929 level. They declined in amount and as a share of assets in each year 1933-46. During the years following World War II policy loans remained fairly constant at under 4 percent of assets until 1959 when their proportionate share again reached just over 4 percent.

Miscellaneous assets of life insurance companies include cash, due and deferred premiums, collateral loans, amounts receivable, and special in-

TABLE 3-9
Trends in Holdings of Policy Loans and Miscellaneous Assets
of Life Insurance Companies, 1899-1959

(Dollar amounts in millions)

End of year	Policy loans		Miscellaneous assets	
	Amount	% of assets	Amount	% of assets
1899	71	4.4	165	10.4
1909	446	12.3	185	5.1
1919	805	11.9	407	6.0
1929	2,379	13.6	906	5.2
1939	3,248	11.1	1,852	6.3
1940	3,091	10.0	1,977	6.3
1941	2,919	8.9	1,840	5.7
1942	2,683	7.7	1,693	4.9
1943	2,373	6.3	1,839	4.8
1944	2,134	5.2	1,704	4.1
1945	1,962	4.4	1,738	3.9
1946	1,894	3.9	1,808	3.8
1947	1,937	3.7	2,124	4.1
1948	2,057	3.7	2,160	3.9
1949	2,240	3.7	2,245	3.8
1950	2,413	3.8	2,591	4.1
1951	2,590	3.8	2,872	4.2
1952	2,713	3.7	3,088	4.2
1953	2,914	3.7	3,302	4.2
1954	3,127	3.7	3,523	4.2
1955	3,290	3.6	3,742	4.1
1956	3,519	3.7	4,076	4.2
1957	3,869	3.8	4,338	4.3
1958	4,188	3.9	4,624	4.3
1959	4,618	4.1	4,937	4.3

vestments such as transportation equipment—railroad cars and motor vehicles—owned for lease to other businesses. Detail of miscellaneous assets is not available except for recent years, but their total amount and proportion of assets are given in Table 3-9.

Chapter 4

SOME BASIC FACTORS GOVERNING
INVESTMENT POLICIES

Financial and Economic Factors

The purpose of this chapter is to outline the underlying economic and financial factors which are basic to the investment policies of life insurance companies. The following discussion develops the framework within which investment decisions are made, by setting forth the major economic and financial considerations which shape the over-all pattern of life insurance investing. Among these considerations are the nature of the obligation to life insurance policyholders, the principle of maximizing investment return consistent with safety of the principal, diversification of portfolio, and liquidity requirements. The following chapters will discuss the ways in which state laws and regulation of the valuation of life insurance company assets affect the investment policies of life companies.

Long-Term Nature of Life Insurance Contracts. As premium dollars flow into life insurance companies and additions are made to policyholders' reserves, as described in Chapter 2, there is an underlying presumption that, on the average, claims against these additions of reserves will not arise for many years hence, usually upon the death of the insured or at maturity of the endowment. Thus, the investment of these reserves is appropriately in obligations which also have their maturity many years hence. It is for this reason that the favored investments of life insurance companies have traditionally consisted of long-term obligations such as real estate mortgages and corporate, municipal, and U.S. Government bonds. This is not to say that the payment of policy claims necessarily must be made from the redemption of investment assets or that the maturity of specific investments is geared to the expected timing of benefit payments. Nevertheless, life insurance and annuity contracts involve a considerable time span which makes appropriate the investment of policyholders' reserves in longer-term investment outlets.

Life insurance and annuity contracts are typically written on the basis of an assumed rate of interest at which earnings on policy reserves will be compounded over the course of time. This factor inclines investment policy toward the placement of reserves in those investments bearing a fixed rate of return, regular payments of interest over the life of the loan, and scheduled repayment in a fixed number of dollars. Thus, investment in long-term obligations provides a characteristic of stability over time which parallels the contractual obligations made by the life insurance company to the policyholder.

In addition to this characteristic of stability, the emphasis on long-term investment has had additional advantages. During the greater part of the past thirty years, the rate of interest which could be derived from long-term investments has been substantially higher than that on shorter-term securities or loans. Moreover, the expense of frequent reinvestment of the return flow from maturities is avoided when funds are placed in obligations running fifteen, twenty, or thirty years in length. Finally, the policy of investing long-term provides a stability to the rate of return on the portfolio which could not be assured in any other way. If investments were concentrated in short-term outlets, thus requiring continual reinvestment at the prevailing rate, the volatility of short-term interest rates over the course of the business cycle would produce an instability in investment earnings which would be inconsistent with the long-term stability of assumed interest rates on policyholders' contracts.

The presence of an assumed interest rate on policy contracts, currently at 3 percent for many policies in force, provides a strong incentive to place investment funds in those forms which will provide a net yield of at least 3 percent. The assumed rate therefore has a strong influence upon investment policy, especially in periods of relatively low market interest rates. For example, the tremendous amounts of U.S. Government bonds acquired by life insurance companies during World War II provided a return of only 2½ percent. In order to obtain a yield which would cover the assumed rate, and also to take advantage of the attractive investment opportunities arising from the expansion of industry and home-ownership, life insurance companies after World War II liquidated a large portion of their low-yielding Governments in the process of investing elsewhere at more satisfactory rates of return.

Safety of Investments. The practice of investing policyholders' reserves in outlets that have a high degree of safety as to repayment of principal also stems from the nature of the life insurance contract and the liability to the policyholder. The basic principle of limiting investments to those with a high margin of safety not only is imposed on the companies by the system of state investment laws described presently; it has long been recognized as a paramount consideration by insurance companies themselves. In order to carry out their role as managers and trustees of policyholders' funds, life insurance companies place these funds in outlets in which the risk of loss through default is kept to a minimum, and the margin of safety is often greater than required under the limits of the investment laws governing their operations. At the same time, however, it is a mistake to assume that life companies are unwilling to assume reasonable risks in their lending. On the contrary, reasonable risks are assumed after careful evaluation, with the investment yield adjusted in accordance with the risk.

There are numerous ways by which the safety of investments by life insurance companies is assured. In the case of real estate mortgage loans the underlying security consists of unencumbered real property which could be sold after foreclosure in the event of default. Mortgage loans which are insured by the Federal Housing Administration or guaranteed by the Veterans Administration involve a high degree of safety. In the case of corporate obligations, many take the form of mortgage bonds representing first liens on physical assets of the borrower. In other instances the safety of the investments is assured by the high credit standing of the borrower as evidenced by his ability to meet interest payments or to provide a continuous flow of dividends to investors.

In the last analysis the safety and security of an investment depend not only upon the legal claims of the lender and the value of the underlying security but also upon the borrower's ability to manage his affairs efficiently and his willingness as well as ability to repay. Thus, the investment of life insurance reserves requires careful and continual attention both to the financial standing and to the character and integrity of the borrower.

The diversification of the investment portfolio is another important way in which the safety and security of investment assets is achieved. This process involves first of all a spreading of investments among various types of assets—mortgage loans, corporate bonds, corporate stocks, state and local government securities, U.S. Government securities, investment real estate, etc. Diversification also requires the spreading of investments among various types of business activity in order that a technological change or temporary difficulty in a single industry will not adversely affect a large portion of the investment portfolio. Thirdly, geographical diversification is important, most obviously for mortgage loans but also for loans to business corporations and to state and local governments. Finally, diversification according to scheduled loan maturities is necessary in order to stagger repayments over time and produce a fairly steady flow of funds to be reinvested in new outlets or to provide a constant source of liquidity.

Maximizing Investment Return. In placing policy reserves into various investment outlets within the limits of the safety of the principal, the objective of life insurance investment officers is to obtain the maximum rate of return available for these funds. The incentive to maximize yield on the investment portfolio is directly related to the net cost of insurance to the policyholder, since earnings above and beyond the assumed interest rates of policy contracts are a direct factor in the size of policyholder's dividends. To the extent that a particular life insurance company is able to produce a higher yield on its portfolio, it is in a position to reduce the net cost of insurance below that of its competitors.

Maximizing investment earnings depends both on the level of investment expenses and on the gross yield on a particular investment. For example, the cost of originating and servicing residential mortgage loans is relatively high as compared with the cost of investing in corporate bonds. Thus, it is the *net* yield after expenses, depreciation, and taxes which must be considered in making investment decisions. As shifts occur over time in the differential between net yields on bonds versus mortgages, for example, the yield-maximizing principle also brings about a shift in the flow of new investments toward the outlet with the higher net return. For life insurance companies with a national scope of investment operations, the yield-maximizing principle also tends to direct funds into those areas where demand is greatest and the rates are highest. As an illustration of this, the rapid growth of population in the Southwest and Far West has kept housing demands and mortgage loan rates there higher than in the longer-established areas of the country, and life insurance funds have moved in that direction during recent years.

It is difficult if not impossible to draw an exact line of demarcation between the objective of maximizing yield and the principle of maintaining the safety of the investment portfolio. The safest of investments is obviously U.S. Government securities, on which risk of default is at a minimum. To hold the bulk of the investment portfolio in this form, however, would be to forego opportunities to reduce the net cost of life insurance through higher yields on investments with a high degree of safety. The challenge to investment officers of life insurance companies is to seek out those investments which will produce the highest net return without impairing the security of the principal amount involved. The investment laws of the several states fix the boundaries of safety for investments, but the ultimate decision for investment policies within these limits must be made by the finance committees and officers of the companies themselves.

Liquidity Requirements. There are perhaps three basic reasons why life insurance companies, like any other business, would wish to have available at any given time a fund of liquid assets or a source of liquidity upon which to draw. The first and most obvious is the need to maintain working balances of cash and bank deposits in order to carry on the normal transactions of receiving payments and making disbursements. The second need for liquidity stems from the possibility of unforeseen contingencies. Among these are the possibilities of war, epidemics, economic crises, or other catastrophes which would sharply increase death benefits and other claims or lead to widespread withdrawals of cash values in life insurance through policy surrenders or policy loans. A third reason for maintaining some liquidity is to remain sufficiently flexible to take advantage of worthwhile investment opportunities which may arise.

The usual method of measuring liquidity is the size of holdings of cash and bank deposits and of short-term securities which may be liquidated quickly without substantial loss. By these standards, life insurance companies would appear to hold rather little in liquid assets, since cash and bank deposits at the end of 1959 amounted to 1.2 percent of total assets while an additional 0.2 percent of assets was in the form of short-term U.S. Government securities.

More important as a source of liquidity for life insurance companies is the volume of their cash flow becoming available from insurance operations [1] and from repayments from the investment portfolio. The contractual nature of life insurance premiums historically has provided a fairly stable inflow of funds even during times of economic adversity. In order to keep their insurance protection intact, policyholders continue to pay their premiums except during times of extreme financial stress. The outflow of benefits and expenses by life insurance companies also exhibits great stability and a comparatively high degree of predictability. As seen in Chapter 2, which deals with these flows through life insurance companies, the gross inflow of funds has exceeded the gross outflow in recent years by about $5 billion, representing net savings by policyholders and a net accretion to investible assets. In addition to these amounts, approximately $5 billion becomes available each year from the amortization or redemption of bonds and mortgages from the investment portfolio.

With a total annual cash flow in excess of $10 billion, life insurance companies have not found it necessary to maintain a large stock of liquid assets in the form of bank balances or of securities which may be liquidated quickly. While it is true that a sudden or unexpected drain on life insurance companies could result from the contingencies mentioned above, the effect of such drains would be a reduction in the flow of funds into the investment market, rather than an inability on the part of the companies to meet sharply rising claims or withdrawals of cash values. Not until cash flow actually became negative would it be necessary to liquidate invested assets in order to raise funds to meet such drains.

It may be helpful to examine the ways in which life insurance companies handle their needs for the three types of liquidity specified above; namely, for transactions, for unforeseen contingencies, and for invest-

---

[1] Roughly, this consists of premium income less benefits and expenses.

ment opportunities. The transactions referred to here are not only those between the company and its policyholders and employees, but also between the company and its borrowers. In order to make disbursements against payrolls, death claims, and other benefits, life insurance companies must maintain a working balance of cash and bank deposits. Such balances are also required in order to disburse funds for the acquisition of new investments. In this latter case, the schedule of disbursements is often arranged at the time the loan is negotiated and an advance commitment is made. It is therefore possible to hold funds in anticipation of these disbursements not only in the form of cash but also as short-term securities maturing close to scheduled disbursement dates.

In order to meet minor unforeseen contingencies, the size of holdings of these liquid assets is somewhat larger than absolutely necessary for transactions purposes. A second line of defense consists of intermediate term holdings of Government securities which may also be quickly converted into cash in the event this becomes necessary. A third line of defense lies in the fact that such drains would first reduce cash flow before forcing involuntary disposal of long-term investments such as bonds and mortgages.

The need to maintain a flexible position to take advantage of worthwhile investment opportunities is met through the control of forward commitments in relation to cash flow. As will be discussed more fully in Chapter 7, the process of making forward investment commitments involves the pledge to certain borrowers that funds will be disbursed to them in future months or years. The total of such commitments obviously cannot be allowed to exceed the total cash flow expected during the same period from net insurance operations and the return flow from investments. To the extent that the expected cash flow for a given period is not yet committed, the life insurance investment officer retains a margin of flexibility which can be used for the acquisition of investment assets coming to his attention during that period.

It is obvious that the liquidity requirements of life insurance companies have little similarity to other types of financial institutions such as commercial banks, savings banks, or savings and loan associations. Policy reserves are essentially a long-term liability rather than a short-term deposit, and the option available for withdrawals of cash values is used sparingly and infrequently by most policyholders. As mentioned earlier, voluntary withdrawals in the form of surrenders or policy loans amount to less than 20 percent of premium income. For these reasons, the need by life insurance companies for holdings of cash, short-term Governments and other types of very liquid assets is relatively small. Instead, life insurance companies concentrate their investments in assets which are generally long-term in nature with the expectation that they will be held to maturity, or until paid off by the borrower.

Other Factors. In addition to the factors cited above there are a number of other investment considerations which do not fit readily into the foregoing discussion. These include the size and location of the life insurance company, the use of mortgage correspondents or a mortgage field force, and the specialization of investment personnel in particular types of investments.

The basic preference for mortgages versus bonds [2] appears to relate to the asset size of life insurance companies. For example, at the end of 1959 companies with total assets of one billion dollars or more held 32.6 percent of their assets in mortgages and 52.9 percent in bonds, while a sample of those with assets ranging from $200 million to one billion dollars held 41.2 percent in mortgages and 42.6 percent in bonds. Breaking these percentages down further, the most notable difference in their mortgage portfolios occurred on FHA mortgage loans. Companies with assets of one billion dollars or more invested 6.2 percent in this form while the sample with assets ranging from $200 million to one billion dollars held 12.6 percent in the form of FHA loans.

A group of companies with assets ranging from $50 million to $200 million held an average of 38.9 percent of assets in mortgages, a slightly lower proportion than the next larger group; bond holdings were 45 percent of total assets, slightly more than the next larger group. Table 4-1 summarizes the percentage distribution of assets held by the three groupings mentioned above.

The geographic location of a life insurance company has some bearing on its investment acquisitions, although probably to a lesser extent than in earlier years. This factor stems from the frequent need for an investment officer to make a personal field trip to appraise properties on which mortgage loans are being considered or inspect business concerns to which direct loans are being considered. Since the cost of such inspection adds to the expense of making the investment, it is only natural that many companies tend to limit the geographic area over which they will carry out the necessary inspection. In the case of investments in bonds publicly offered by corporations with national credit standing, the location of a company provides no barrier.

The biggest single factor in reducing the influence of location in recent years has been the development of a national mortgage market in those mortgages insured by the FHA or guaranteed by the VA. The standard characteristics of insured and guaranteed mortgages, together with the development of mortgage bankers who originate and service such loans, make it possible for life insurance companies located in the East or Mid-

---

[2] In this context, the term "bonds" includes a small amount of securities with a maturity of less than one year, chiefly Treasury bills and certificates and short-term commercial paper.

TABLE 4-1
Asset Distribution by Size of Company
As of December 31, 1959

(In percent of total assets)

	Asset Size		
	$50 Million to $200 Million	$200 Million to $1 Billion	$1 Billion or Over
U.S. Government Securities	6.4	4.5	5.8
All Other Bonds	38.6	38.1	47.1
Stocks	1.9	2.6	3.2
Mortgages (Total):	38.9	41.2	32.6
Farm	(1.6)	(1.2)	(2.9)
Non-Farm: FHA	(12.1)	(12.6)	(6.2)
VA	(6.7)	(7.1)	(6.3)
Other	(18.5)	(20.3)	(17.2)
Real Estate	3.0	3.7	3.1
Policy Loans	6.0	5.5	3.7
Cash	1.3	0.9	0.9
Other	3.9	3.5	3.6
Total assets	100.0	100.0	100.0

Data are based on assets of forty-nine companies holding 84 percent of total assets of all United States companies.

west to lend on properties in Texas or California without the need for an extensive field trip for appraisal or credit purposes. However, where direct corporate loans or conventional mortgages are involved, except in the case of the very large companies, there is a natural tendency to look first to opportunities in nearby areas which can be reached at relatively little expense.

It should be noted that the location of the home office of a life insurance company does not always provide a sufficient guide to the effect of this location factor since many of the larger companies maintain regional offices or a field force throughout the United States.

As mentioned above, shifts in the differential on net yields on bonds versus mortgages typically are reflected in shifts in the direction of new investments. There is, however, an additional consideration which serves to limit a diversion of new investments away from the mortgage loan field. This arises from the necessity of maintaining a working field force of mortgage investment officers who are employees of the company, or as is more often the case, maintaining relationships with mortgage correspondents who originate and service mortgage loans in the company's portfolio. In the former case, where mortgage officers are employees of the company their salaries represent a form of fixed expense which would remain unchanged even though the dollar volume of mortgage acquisitions were to dwindle sharply. In economic terms, the marginal cost of originating an additional mortgage loan by the field force is close to zero, and the expense avoided in cutting back mortgage loans is also close to zero.

A somewhat similar situation prevails when mortgage correspondents are used to originate new mortgage loans. Although these correspondents are not employees of the company, they depend for their livelihood upon the volume of mortgages which they supply to the investment portfolio. There is therefore a resistance on the part of the life insurance company to cutting back mortgage loan operations to the point where relationships of long standing between the company and its correspondents are broken off and would require considerable effort to re-establish at a later date. As a result of these considerations there is a tendency to moderate somewhat any declines in the volume of mortgage lending even when the relative yields on alternative investments such as bonds increase in attractiveness.

A final factor which influences the direction of new investments by life insurance companies pertains to the qualifications and specialties of those on the investment staff. For example, the presence of an investment officer with considerable skill and experience in the field of farm mortgage loans or water works obligations or railroad equipment financing may lead to somewhat greater emphasis by a particular company in such a field although these forms of investment may not be actively sought after by other life insurance companies. Conversely, the absence of trained personnel equipped to assess loan opportunities in specialty fields may preclude the investment of funds in those forms.

Public Interest Aspects

In developing and implementing their investment policies, the primary responsibility of life insurance companies is to the policyholders whose reserve funds are being invested. The keynote of these practices, as discussed above, is to obtain maximum yield consistent with adequate safety and security of principal. As discussed in Chapter 11, the incentive of life companies to maximize investment yields leads to an allocation of capital funds to those investment outlets in our national economy in which the marginal efficiency of capital is highest and hence the demand for funds more urgent. Because life insurance company investment practices touch upon so many areas of the investment markets and of the financial life of the nation, the question of public interest aspects of these investment practices frequently arises. This section will illustrate a number of ways in which investment policies are affected by considerations of the broad public interest as an adjunct to serving the direct and immediate interest of the policyholders.

U.S. Government Securities. During the postwar period, long-term U.S. Government securities have not been an attractive investment outlet for life insurance companies relative to corporate bonds and real estate mortgage loans. As mentioned earlier, life companies have been substantial net sellers of Government securities during the postwar period reducing their holdings from 46 percent of total assets at the end of 1945 to 6 percent at the end of 1959. Nevertheless, life insurance companies have been active in taking up new issues of long-term Government bonds when they have been offered from time to time by the Treasury. In large measure, it has been the factor of public interest which has led to the acquisitions of such issues. This factor also has had a moderating effect upon the extent of net liquidation of Government bonds by life companies.

This attitude toward Government securities essentially stems from the deep concern among life insurance company officials about inflation and the harmful effect it has on life insurance policyholders. Life insurance companies, as the trustees of a large share of the accumulated savings of the public, have therefore felt that it is appropriate to cooperate with the Treasury in its efforts to pursue noninflationary debt management practices.

It is difficult to measure precisely the impact which this attitude has had upon the investment in Treasury bonds by life insurance companies. It is recognized that a U.S. Government obligation represents an investment with the smallest degree of risk and even today, in the rapidly fluctuating market for Governments, still provides the greatest liquidity of any security through its ready marketability. The inherent drawback in Government securities is their relatively lower yield which accounts for the necessity, especially in the early postwar years, of switching into corporate bonds with a higher rate of return. At a 2½ percent yield, Government bonds issued during and immediately after World War II did not provide a return sufficient to cover the assumed interest rate on many policy contracts.

Residential Mortgage Lending. Residential mortgage loans have long been an important outlet for life insurance funds. After a low level of residential construction during the depression and the war years, the need for more adequate housing gave residential mortgage credit a higher social priority during the early postwar period. In addition to the depression-created Federal Housing Administration, the federal government established a loan guarantee program in 1944 under the Veterans Administration to facilitate the flow of private mortgage credit to veterans. In this environment of a basic economic and social need for postwar housing to be financed under the aegis of the federal government, life insurance companies channeled an increasing share of their investment funds into mortgage loans. The result during the postwar period has been that gross new loans of approximately $45.5 billion have been made for home financing, of which $13.3 billion was FHA mortgages and $10.6 billion was VA mortgages. If the average mortgage size can be taken at around $10,000, these loans have provided the financing of 4,550,000 homes for the American public.

There is no question that the relative rates of return on mortgage lending provided a basic economic incentive toward home financing over these years, especially with the risk-reducing influence of the FHA insurance and the VA guarantee. Nevertheless, life insurance companies which have been most active in such lending stepped up their activity in the residential mortgage field with a deliberate and conscious attitude that such lending served the public interest and the basic needs of the economy, as well as the interest of policyholders in general.

Participation in the Voluntary Home Mortgage Credit Program represents another facet of the recognition by life insurance companies of the public interest aspects of the residential mortgage market. This program was established at the urging of the life insurance business and was passed as Title VI of the Housing Act of 1954. It is designed to channel mortgage funds to credit-worthy applicants in small communities and remote areas and to minority groups. The basic purpose of the program is not only to see that such applicants obtain a more adequate share of the existing supply of mortgage credit, but to eliminate any need for direct VA mortgage loans or mortgage purchases in this field by the Federal National Mortgage Association.

The lack of availability of mortgage credit in small communities and remote areas has arisen from the expenses involved in making such loans, including the need for appraisal of the property and checking the credit standing of the applicant. It is understood that life insurance companies participating in the program are not expected to make such loans unless sound credit standards are satisfied. Since the program was begun in early 1955, through March 1960, loans placed through VHMCP have amounted to $424 million for an average loan amount of $10,200. About 85 percent of these funds have come from life insurance companies, while the participation of mutual savings banks, commercial banks, and savings and loan associations has been more limited.

From the standpoint of the life insurance business, the public interest considerations which led to the VHMCP are twofold. First is a recognition that special efforts may be required to ensure that private mortgage market facilities are generally available to the public at large regardless of geographic location or other factors. Second is the belief that the direct intervention of the federal government in the private lending field, and the mortgage market in particular, is an inappropriate use of governmental powers and that such intervention should be discouraged.

Investment in Housing Projects. Somewhat similar to the public interest aspects of residential mortgage lending is the investment in multi-family housing projects, owned and managed by life insurance companies. Prior to 1938 investment in this type of asset was generally ruled out by state investment law such as that of New York, which limited the acquisition of real estate to ownership of home and branch office properties.[3] Legislation passed in New York State in 1938 opened the way for housing project investment while limiting the amount going into this form to 10 percent of total admitted assets.

A strong impetus to the construction of housing projects by life insurance companies came with the outbreak of World War II when rapid shifts of population, especially toward metropolitan areas, created a shortage of housing facilities. These conditions of urban housing shortage continued through much of the early postwar period. According to a study by Schultz, the period 1941 through 1952 witnessed the construction or purchase of twenty-seven separate housing projects by ten life insurance companies at a total cost of $346 million.[4] At the end of 1952 housing accommodation provided by this form of investment was sufficient to shelter approximately 200,000 people. Many of these projects were designed as part of slum clearance programs in cooperation with city, state, or federal government authorities.

The extent to which public interest aspects were important in fostering housing project investment is recognized directly by Schultz in his study. He cites the fact that "social considerations" were among the incentives to undertake such investment, aside from the considerations of safety and rate of investment return. Among his conclusions Schultz makes the following observation: "The equity nature of an investment in housing projects involves social and operational aspects which are not generally present in other life insurance company investments. Direct investment in housing by the life insurance industry performs an outstanding social service by providing adequate and desirable housing facilities, the social service being particularly pronounced in cases where this investment has resulted in slum clearance developments."[5]

In mid-1960 the life insurance companies of the nation had $414 million of direct investment in residential properties. In recent years the sharply rising building costs have militated against this form of investment.

Small Business Financing. Most observers agree that the emergence of new business enterprise and the opportunity for small business concerns to expand and realize their potential is a necessary condition of a competitive, healthy and growing economy. The subject of small business

---

[3] Following World War I there was a temporary relaxation of this restriction from 1922 to 1926 which allowed direct investment in housing projects in New York to alleviate an emergency housing shortage.

[4] Robert E. Schultz, *Life Insurance Housing Projects* (Richard D. Irwin, 1956). This study was published for the S. S. Huebner Foundation for Insurance Education of the University of Pennsylvania.

[5] *Ibid.,* pp. 99-100.

financing is, therefore, one in which there are strong overtones of the public interest and the long-run well-being of our free enterprise economy. In the initial stages, small or new business firms normally require equity capital furnished by the proprietors and other interested parties; at a later stage additional risk capital from outside sources facilitates the expansion of such concerns. Provision of long-term credit on a basis free of speculation or undue risk becomes possible only when a small business has become sufficiently established to demonstrate its profitability and the ability to repay borrowings over future years out of adequate earnings.

As a major provider of investment funds to the business community, life insurance companies recognized the public interest aspects of small business financing. Indeed, the experience of many life insurance companies has been that lending to relatively small business concerns often develops into mutually satisfactory relationships which lead to additional lending as the small business expands and matures. However, the willingness of life insurance companies to invest in small firms which are new and unproven is severely limited by the strong speculative element that such lending would involve. As mentioned above, the principle that investments be devoid of speculative elements underlies the investment policies of the life insurance business, and many small business loans therefore must be ruled out.[6]

The system of state investment laws governing life insurance operations also directly limits the volume and nature of small business financing. For example, as discussed more fully in Chapter 5, until very recently the investment laws of New York State did not allow unsecured loans to unincorporated business, thus ruling out perhaps 85 to 90 percent of the small business field. Moreover, loans to incorporated business are required to meet tests based on the corporation's earnings during the five years previous to acquisition of such obligations. As a result of these restrictions, many small businesses find that their access to life insurance company financing is limited largely to mortgage loans against real property. The passage in 1958 in New York State of a "leeway clause" permitting up to 2 percent of assets to be placed in investments not otherwise prohibited or limited has the effect of relaxing these restrictions in New York and may facilitate various forms of small business financing in the future. As shown in Chapter 5, "leeway clauses" also are present in other state laws governing life insurance investments. Never-

---

[6] For a more comprehensive exploration of the problem of small business financing by life insurance companies, see "A Study on the Necessity and Desirability of Amending Section 81 of the New York State Insurance Law to Provide More Adequately for Loans to Small Business," prepared by the Metropolitan Life Insurance Company in 1950.

theless, small business lending must meet the basic test that the principal amount of the loan be adequately secured.

To examine the actual practice of life insurance lending to small business, the Life Insurance Association of America conducted a special survey in 1957 at the request of the Select Committee on Small Business of the House of Representatives.[7] This survey covered sixty-seven reporting life insurance companies whose combined assets accounted for 77 percent of the total assets of the business. Lending reported through this survey included business and industrial bonds, public utility bonds and mortgage loans to business and industry classified by size of loan and by size of obligor. The results of this survey brought out the fact that a very substantial share of the total number of loans by life insurance companies to business concerns are made to those that fall into the "small business" category. During the period 1953 through 1956, almost three-quarters of life insurance loans were in amounts of less than $250,000 each. Such loans represented between 4.9 percent and 6.8 percent of the total amount of business loans authorized by the reporting companies during those years. Although the bulk of such lending was done through the mortgage departments, there was a sizable number of small loans made through the medium of industrial and public utility bond issues.[8]

The coverage of this small business loan survey did not extend to farm mortgage loans which essentially are a form of small business lending. Data from the U.S. Department of Agriculture indicate an average loan size of $17,000 on farm mortgage loans by life insurance companies in 1956, for a total that year of almost one-half billion dollars. Moreover, small business sometimes obtains loan capital from life insurance companies through the medium of residential mortgage loans, the proceeds of which are used for business purposes rather than for the purchase of residential properties. Still another form of funds going into small business is the policy loan, whereby businessmen often borrow against the cash value of their policies when the need arises.[9]

Evidence of the positive attitude of life insurance companies toward small business financing is also to be found in their participation in state development credit corporations. These development credit corporations have been established in a number of states during the past ten years, beginning with the New England states and spreading to New York,

---

[7] The complete text of this survey is contained in Hearings Before the Select Committee on Small Business, House of Representatives, 85th Congress, First Session, Part 1, pages 142 ff.

[8] More detail about life insurance lending to small business is included in Chapter 10.

[9] For example, a special survey in 1958 made by a leading mid-western company revealed that 35 percent of policy loans of $10,000 or more were for "funds needed in business."

North Carolina, Wisconsin, and other states. The basic purpose of such corporations is to assist worthwhile business enterprises by providing financial assistance in the form of equity capital and longer-term credit when such financing is not available from traditional channels. The development credit corporation serves as an intermediary, obtaining its funds largely from the private financial institutions such as mutual savings banks, commercial banks, and life insurance companies which elect to become members or stockholders in the credit corporation. These institutions are thereby able to provide funds to small business through the medium of a development corporation, although a direct loan might not meet legal or quality standards.[10]

The participation of life insurance companies in existing development credit corporations has been as stockholders and/or members. In the latter case, the typical procedure is to fix a maximum loan amount which may be called upon by the development credit corporation as the need arises. As of the early part of 1958, thirty-four life insurance companies were participating in the activities of development credit corporations in the following states: Massachusetts, New Hampshire, New York, North Carolina, Rhode Island, and Vermont.

There have been at least two attempts by life insurance companies to service the financing needs of small business through establishment of a special loan program or department. The first of these was announced by the Metropolitan Life Insurance Company in February 1950 as the Small Business Loan Plan, which was formulated for the purpose of (a) determining if there was in fact an unsatisfied demand for sound small business credit and (b) helping to supply such credit if needed. In order to avoid prohibitive expenses of investigating small loan applications in all parts of the country, the Metropolitan asked local banks throughout the country to forward loan applications for amounts up to $250,000 in which the bank would be willing to participate by 10 percent or more. Investigation, negotiation, and servicing of the loan would be handled by the local bank.

In its first eight years of operation through February 1958, the Metropolitan received 228 loan applications amounting to $28 million from banks located in thirty-six states and the District of Columbia. The company approved eighty-six loans totaling $12 million, but applications for twelve of these loans aggregating $2 million were withdrawn after approval. Interest rates on loans made under the Small Business Loan Plan

---

[10] For a fuller description of the activities of the New England development credit corporations, see the Federal Reserve Bank of Boston *Monthly Review,* July 1954 and August 1954, and the study by Paul S. Anderson, "State Development Credit Corporations," in *Financing Small Business,* Report to the Committee on Banking and Currency and the Select Committee on Small Business by the Federal Reserve System, April 11, 1958, pp. 336-354.

ranged from 4½ percent to 6 percent, and more than half of the loans were for a term of ten years.

Beginning operations in June 1956, The Prudential Insurance Company created its Commercial and Industrial Loan Department for the purpose of bringing the financial resources of The Prudential to small and moderate-sized businesses throughout the United States and Canada which ordinarily do not have connections with the public capital market, and of achieving the widest possible distribution of its funds in all parts of both countries. Loan operations are carried out by company staff in the regional home offices of The Prudential. The financing is mainly in the form of unsecured loans to corporations with a minimum term of ten years.

In its first three and one-half years of operation the Commercial and Industrial Loan Department made 238 loans of which 67 percent were in amounts of $1 million or less and 41 percent were for $500,000 or less. An additional thirteen loan approvals were cancelled when prospective borrowers withdrew their applications. The total dollar amount of loans was $291 million. At the end of 1959, borrowers from this Department consisted of firms located in 165 towns and cities in thirty-five states and six Canadian provinces. They were engaged in a wide variety of retail, wholesale, and manufacturing activities.

In brief, life insurance companies recognize that small business financing is clothed with a public interest aspect. However, many types of small business lending are ruled out for them because of legal restrictions or because the nature of such loans is not consistent with the principle of adequate security of principal. Nevertheless, a substantial volume of lending to small business is carried out within these limits, largely through the medium of mortgage investments secured by real property. Efforts have also been made to provide funds to small business through the medium of state development credit corporations. As providers of long-term capital to the business community, life insurance companies recognize that small and growing enterprises require outside financing to realize their potential for expansion, and the companies have been important suppliers of such funds within the limits of their basic obligations to their policyholders.

Summary

With regard to the financial, economic, and public interest factors governing life insurance company investments, it is pertinent that life insurance and annuity contracts are long-term in nature and are typically written on the basis of an assumed rate of interest at which earnings on policy reserves will be compounded over the course of time. This factor inclines investment policy toward the placement of reserves in those investments bearing a fixed rate of return, regular payments of interest over the life of the loan, and scheduled repayment in a fixed number of dollars. Thus, investment in long-term obligations provides a characteristic of stability over time which parallels the contractual obligations made by the life insurance company to the policyholder.

In order to carry out their role as managers and trustees of policyholders' funds, life insurance companies place these funds in outlets in which the risk of loss through default is kept to a minimum, and the margin of safety is often greater than required under the limits of the investment laws governing their operations.

In placing policy reserves in various investment outlets within the limits of the safety of the principal, the objective of life insurance investment officers is to obtain the maximum rate of return available for these funds. The incentive to maximize yield on the investment portfolio is directly related to the net cost of insurance to the policyholder, since earnings above and beyond the assumed interest rates of policy contracts are a direct factor in the size of policyholders' dividends. To the extent that a particular life insurance company is able to produce a higher yield on its portfolio than the rate assumed in policy contracts, it is in a position to reduce the net cost of insurance below that of its competitors.

In addition to the factors which lead life insurance companies to place their funds in longer-term obligations at the maximum investment yields consistent with safety of principal, there are also certain liquidity requirements governing life company investments. One is the need to maintain working balances of cash and bank deposits in order to carry on the normal transactions of receiving payments and making disbursements. A second need for liquidity stems from the possibility of unforeseen contingencies. Among these are the possibilities of war, epidemics, economic crises, or other catastrophes which would sharply increase death benefits and other claims, or lead to widespread withdrawals of cash values in life insurance through policy surrenders or policy loans. A third reason for maintaining some liquidity is to remain sufficiently flexible to take advantage of worth-while investment opportunities which may arise.

In addition to these, and other less important economic and financial factors, the life insurance companies have been motivated by direct public interest consideration in their investments. This has been especially true of their emphasis upon residential mortgage lending, their direct investment in housing projects, and their lending to small business concerns.

Chapter 5

STATE LAWS GOVERNING
INVESTMENT POLICIES

The investments of life insurance companies in the United States are governed by the investment laws of the fifty states and the District of Columbia. The purpose of these laws is to specify appropriate areas and to establish standards for the investment of life insurance company funds, with a view to ensuring the financial soundness of the company and protecting the interest of the policyholder by preventing improper practices or speculative excesses. Accordingly, life insurance investment laws take the form either of prohibiting certain investments or of prescribing the permissible categories of investments which may be made subject to certain limitations. For the major classes of investments the state laws typically stipulate the quality standards which must be met, together with the maximum percentage of assets which may be placed in a particular class of investment either in the aggregate or as issued by one issuer. A review of the more important investment law restrictions is presented later in this chapter.

It is worthy of note that the regulation and supervision of life insurance investments is carried out by state governments rather than the federal government. These investment laws are administered in each state by the state insurance department (headed by a commissioner or superintendent of insurance) or by the state department of banking and insurance. These departments are responsible for the licensing of companies to sell insurance in their respective states and require of such companies annual financial statements which include the details of their investment operations during the course of the year. For example, this annual statement includes a listing of every security acquired, held, and disposed of during the year, together with the particulars of each transaction. A triennial examination of each company also is conducted by the state insurance departments.

No discussion of life insurance investment regulation would be complete without mention of the Armstrong investigation which took place in New York in 1905. As a result of various practices which had come to light at that time in the operation of certain life insurance companies, a full-scale investigation was conducted by a committee of the New York State legislature, with Charles Evans Hughes as its counsel and dominant figure. Prior to the Armstrong investigation life insurance companies were allowed wide latitude in their investment policies. When it was disclosed that their investments had led to financial control of banks, railroads and other corporations in which company directors and officers had a financial interest, severe limitations were imposed on investment policy to correct this situation.

> [The investment laws enacted by the New York legislature following the Armstrong investigation] limited life insurance investments to public debt obligations, including those of the Federal Government, states, counties, and other political subdivisions, adequately secured corporate bonds, mortgage loans secured by improved and unencumbered real estate worth 50 per cent more than the amount loaned, and such real property as might be needed for company occupancy. Real estate acquired in satisfaction of debt had to be disposed of within 5 years from the time it was acquired, unless the Superintendent of Insurance granted an extension on the ground of hardship. Companies were also required to make loans to their own policyholders upon the security of their policies of sums not exceeding the legal reserve required on the policy. Investments were not permitted in stocks, in income producing real property, in unsecured corporate obligations, or in obligations of unincorporated organizations or individuals unless secured by real estate mortgage or by collateral in which investments could be made directly.[1]

With the passage of time and the changing characteristics of the economy, the range of permissible investments under the New York law has been broadened substantially since 1906. In 1928, unsecured corporate obligations and preferred stock were made eligible for investment in New York provided that they satisfied certain earnings tests. Mortgage loans insured by the FHA were added to the list of permitted investments in 1934, housing projects were added in 1938, and mortgages guaranteed by the VA were added at the end of World War II. In 1946, New York law was amended to permit investment in income-producing real estate. A most significant change came in 1951 when, after forty-five years of prohibition, the purchase of common stock was allowed subject to certain limitations. In 1958, a "leeway clause" was added to New York law, allowing up to 2 percent of assets to be invested in forms not otherwise permitted. These and other changes are summarized in Table 5-1, showing the date of the amendments.

---

[1] Haughton Bell and Harold G. Fraine, "Legal Framework, Trends and Developments in Investment Practices of Life Insurance Companies," *Law and Contemporary Problems*, Vol. 17, No. 1 (Winter 1952), p. 47. For a review of the scope and nature of the Armstrong investigation, see B. M. Anderson, "The Armstrong Investigation in Retrospect," *Association of Life Insurance Counsel Proceedings*, Vol. XI, 1952-53.

TABLE 5-1
Principal Classes of Investments
Permitted Under the New York Insurance Law
With Date of Permissive Law*

Type of Investment	Permitted under law of:
1. U.S. Government Obligations	1906
2. Obligations of States, Counties, and Other Political Subdivisions	1906
3. U.S. Corporate Obligations	
A. Secured by adequate collateral	1906
B. Qualified by earnings test	1928
4. Preferred and Guaranteed Stocks	1928
5. Common Stocks	
A. Other than insurer or bank stock	1951
B. Insurer or bank common stock	1957
6. Trustees' or Receivers' Obligations	1937
7. Equipment Trust Obligations	1906
8. Acceptances and Bills of Exchange	1926
9. Mortgage Loans	
A. On unencumbered real property	1906
B. Insured by the FHA	1934
C. Guaranteed by the VA	1945
D. On leasehold property	1951
10. Real Estate	
A. For own use	1906
B. Foreclosed	1906
C. Housing projects	1922-26, 1938
D. Income-producing	1946
11. Foreign Investments	1906
12. Policy Loans	1906
13. Collateral Loans	1906
14. Miscellaneous	
A. Certain federal agency issues	1933, 1945
B. Obligations of World Bank	1947
C. Savings and loan association shares	1949
D. Other specified investments	Various
15. "Leeway" (not expressly permitted)	1958

*Data are as of June 1960.

The status of New York investment law has been emphasized in this discussion for a number of reasons. First, life insurance companies domiciled in New York, and therefore falling directly under its laws, have represented a large share of the total business during the period under discussion, as measured by total assets. As may be seen in Table 5-2, New York companies held 58 percent of the total assets in 1906. The more rapid growth of companies in other states reduced this share to 34 percent by 1958. Secondly, the importance of New York as a market

TABLE 5-2
Admitted Assets of Life Insurance Companies
Domiciled in Six States*

	1906	1928	1940	1950	1958
	(In millions of dollars)				
New York	1,700	6,470	12,779	24,225	37,027
New Jersey	234	2,562	5,045	10,304	16,678
Massachusetts	178	1,265	2,635	6,269	11,109
Connecticut	223	1,198	2,595	6,029	10,814
Wisconsin	221	871	1,421	2,705	4,114
Pennsylvania	191	812	1,495	2,608	3,127
Total six states	2,747	13,178	25,970	52,140	82,869
Total all U.S. companies	2,924	15,961	30,802	64,020	107,580
	(As percent of total)				
New York	58.1	40.5	41.5	37.8	34.4
New Jersey	8.0	16.1	16.4	16.1	15.5
Massachusetts	6.1	7.9	8.6	9.8	10.3
Connecticut	7.6	7.5	8.4	9.4	10.1
Wisconsin	7.6	5.5	4.6	4.2	3.8
Pennsylvania	6.5	5.1	4.9	4.1	2.9
Total six states	93.9	82.6	84.3	81.4	77.0
Total all U.S. companies	100.0	100.0	100.0	100.0	100.0

*Data are as of June 1960.

Source: Institute of Life Insurance.

for life insurance sales has meant that out-of-state companies have sought licensing in New York; life insurance companies licensed to do business in New York at the end of 1958 accounted for 81 percent of the total assets of the business at that date. Thirdly, New York has long served as a model state for the investment laws in other states. Changes initiated in New York often are followed quickly by similar changes elsewhere.

As may be seen in Table 5-2, companies domiciled in the states of New York, New Jersey, Massachusetts, Connecticut, Wisconsin, and Pennsylvania traditionally have held a major share of the total assets of the life insurance business, although the share represented by these companies has declined with the passage of time and the growth of companies in other states. Accordingly, the investment laws of these six states may be considered of major importance because of their impact on companies under their direct jurisdiction.

However, most life insurance companies are licensed to do business in many states other than their home state. Table 5-3 presents a state-by-state breakdown for 291 life insurance companies that are members of the American Life Convention or the Life Insurance Association of America, showing the number that are domiciled in each state and the number of out-of-state companies (from this same group) that are licensed in each state. In these circumstances, the question naturally arises as to which investment laws apply. Do the provisions of the most restrictive state in which a company is licensed serve to fix the limits of investments? Or do the investment laws of the state of domicile apply exclusively without regard to the laws of other states in which a company is admitted to do business? Current practice and interpretation lie somewhere between these two extremes.

In a number of states, there are statutory or constitutional provisions that an out-of-state corporation may not do business on a more favorable basis than a domestic corporation, or that foreign corporations shall be subject to the same regulations as like domestic corporations. Moreover, the insurance laws of several states make specific reference to the investments of out-of-state life insurance companies; a summary of these references is shown in Appendix Table 5A-1. Two basic patterns emerge from these latter provisions. The first is that the investments of foreign companies shall be of the same general character, or of a quality substantially as high, as that required of domestic insurers, or both. Another approach, found in New York and North Carolina, gives the superintendent of insurance discretion to require that the investments of out-of-state companies "comply in substance" with the requirements imposed on domestic insurers.

Such provisions are subject to varying interpretation, as might be expected. In the words of one authority on these matters:

> Literal compliance with the laws of one or more foreign states would in general be impossible without giving up the benefit of at least some of the investment powers afforded by the home state, and in some situations there would be a direct conflict between the provisions required of it by its own state and those required of insurance companies under

TABLE 5-3
Licensing of Member Companies of the American Life Convention and the Life Insurance Association of America, By State or Jurisdiction

State or jurisdiction	Domestic companies	Out-of-state companies	Total licensed
Alabama	4	121	125
Alaska	0	60	60
Arizona	2	143	145
Arkansas	4	136	140
California	8	145	153
Colorado	4	165	169
Connecticut	5	90	95
Delaware	2	120	122
District of Columbia	4	136	140
Florida	6	153	159
Georgia	4	129	133
Hawaii	0	87	87
Idaho	2	124	126
Illinois	19	141	160
Indiana	11	159	170
Iowa	10	130	140
Kansas	8	130	138
Kentucky	5	136	141
Louisiana	5	134	139
Maine	1	75	76
Maryland	5	135	140
Massachusetts	10	66	76
Michigan	5	142	147
Minnesota	7	141	148
Mississippi	3	122	125
Missouri	9	147	156
Montana	1	106	107
Nebraska	11	121	132
Nevada	0	119	119
New Hampshire	1	77	78
New Jersey	4	94	98
New Mexico	0	132	132
New York	20	47	67
North Carolina	8	117	125
North Dakota	5	103	108
Ohio	9	142	151
Oklahoma	4	135	139
Oregon	1	138	139
Pennsylvania	9	136	145
Rhode Island	1	68	69
South Carolina	2	107	109
South Dakota	3	114	117
Tennessee	6	141	147
Texas	29	134	163
Utah	2	126	128
Vermont	1	73	74
Virginia	3	150	153
Washington	7	140	147
West Virginia	1	127	128
Wisconsin	6	92	98
Wyoming	1	117	118
Total U.S.	278	6,123	6,401
Canada	13	37	50
Grand Total	291	6,160	6,451

Data are as of June 1960.

the law of the foreign state. Fortunately, literal compliance by the out-of-state company with the laws of the foreign state was evidently not contemplated when these statutes were enacted and they have not been interpreted to bring about such an impossible and intolerable situation.[2]

In summary, the investment laws of the several states apply directly to the life insurance companies domiciled in the state and often have some application to out-of-state companies licensed to sell insurance in the state. Hence, each life insurance company must conduct its investment operations in accordance with the laws of the state of domicile and, in many cases, with due regard also to laws of other states in which it sells insurance.

Standards of Investment Selection Required by State Law

The investment laws of almost every state set forth specific standards which must be satisfied in the purchase of investment assets by life insurance companies. This section will outline in general terms the nature of these standards in the various states; detailed summaries of the actual regulations in nineteen representative states are contained in the tables presented in the appendix of this chapter.

Standards for Corporate Bonds. Investment laws in a large number of states set forth the type and amount of collateral required on secured corporate obligations purchased by life insurance companies. For example, several states provide that not more than one-third of the required collateral shall be in the form of stock other than preferred stock eligible for acquisitions by life companies. Other states require that the obligation be secured by a mortgage on assets of a value ample to exceed the debt secured; in some states the value of collateral must be worth 50 percent more than the par value of the bond issue.

Even when these provisions as to ample security have been met, there are a number of states which call for additional standards in the form of earnings requirements. Such requirements include the availability of earnings to meet interest payments during perhaps five years preceding the loan, plus the actual payment of interest in full during any three (including the last two) of these five years, plus a ratio of net earnings to annual fixed charges of $1\frac{1}{4}$ or $1\frac{1}{2}$ times, depending on the state. It is typical also to require that the issue purchased not be in default as to principal or interest at the time of acquisition. This latter requirement often must be satisfied by the borrowing corporation for a prior period of five years.

When a bond is unsecured and its eligibility is based entirely on earn-

---

[2] Willis H. Satterthwaite, "Regulation of Life Company Investments and the Rule of Comity," *Association of Life Insurance Counsel Proceedings,* Vol. XIII (1956-57), p. 404.

ings rather than on collateral or a combination of earnings and collateral, somewhat similar tests are applied. There is usually a provision that earnings must have been available for five years (seven in some states), with interest requirements fully met in the most recent years, and with a ratio of net earnings to annual fixed charges of 1½ times or even 2 times. Again, the issue must not be in default as to principal or interest according to requirements in many of the states.

In a few states separate standards also are stipulated for the acquisition of contingent interest bonds, with requirements as to the number of years earnings have been available, the number of years interest requirements have been fully met, and the ratio of net earnings to average annual fixed charges.

Further detail as to standards for corporate bond selection under the investment laws of nineteen representative states is contained in Appendix Table 5A-2.

Standards for Mortgage Loans. The principal eligibility standard for mortgage loans by life insurance companies is the loan-to-value ratio. On conventional mortgage loans the vast majority of states have long set a maximum 66⅔ percent loan-to-value ratio, i.e., the amount of the loan cannot exceed two-thirds of the appraised value of the property. Quite recently, however, a number of states have amended their investment laws to permit a 75 percent loan-to-value ratio on one- or two-family dwellings, sometimes with additional restrictions as to size of loan and amortization period. The occasion for these recent amendments has been the relaxation of loan-to-value ratios imposed by state or federal laws upon other institutions which compete with life insurance companies in the residential mortgage field, namely, the savings banks, the savings and loan associations, and the commercial banks. It has been recognized that somewhat higher ratios are justified today because of changes which have taken place in mortgage lending, notably the widespread adoption of the amortized loan.

The purpose of fixing a maximum loan-to-value ratio on mortgages is to prevent a decline in real estate values from reducing the value of the mortgaged property below the outstanding amount of the loan. In the case of mortgage loans insured by the FHA or guaranteed by the VA, the risk for the life insurance company is reduced by the existence of such insurance or guaranty, and state investment laws have allowed the basic loan-to-value ratios to be exceeded in the case of FHA and VA mortgage loan acquisitions. It is the maximum loan-to-value ratios fixed by federal authorities which become operative in the case of such loans.

State laws often contain restrictions as to the type of property and the location of property which may be used to secure a mortgage loan. The traditional approach as to type of property has been to require that the real estate be held in fee simple, that is, owned outright by the borrower. Many states now allow mortgages on property under long-term leasehold if the unexpired term of the lease exceeds the term of the loan. Location of the mortgaged property is usually limited to the United States or to the United States and Canada, thereby ruling out mortgages on properties in foreign countries other than Canada.

Further detail as to standards for mortgage loans under the investment laws of nineteen representative states is contained in Appendix Table 5A-3.

Standards for Preferred Stock. The eligibility requirements for preferred stocks purchased by life insurance companies are broadly similar to those on corporate bonds in that they involve earnings tests in most states.

About half the states require that issuers of eligible preferred stocks must have had earnings available for the payment of dividends for a stated number of years (usually five) before purchase. Actual payment of dividends for a specified number of years is required in a number of states. Another requirement, imposed separately in some states and additionally in others, is that minimum earnings in preceding years be equal to a certain percentage (usually 4 or 5 percent) of the par value of stated value of the preferred stock. A variation of this last requirement is that net earnings shall have been a certain number of times the sum of (a) average annual fixed charges, (b) maximum contingent interest, and (c) preferred dividend requirements.

The aim of these requirements, of course, is to ensure that investments made in preferred stock shall yield a fairly reliable and sufficient rate of return, insofar as this can be determined from the history of the corporate issuer. Many states stipulate that the stock be paying dividends at the time of acquisitions; others rule out its purchase if dividends have been in arrears for ninety days within the preceding five years.

Other restrictions that are sometimes placed on preferred stock purchases involve prohibited classes of stocks. Among these are preferred stock of the life company itself (except for mutualization purposes), preferred stock of other insurers, assessable stock, and preferred stock of real estate companies.

Further detail as to standards for preferred stock purchases under the investment laws of nineteen representative states may be found in Appendix Table 5A-4.

Standards for Common Stock. The vast majority of states now permit investment by life insurance companies in common stocks. However, they place restrictions as to the quality or type of stock that may be acquired.

A number of states require that common stock be listed on a recognized securities exchange or that the stock be quoted in established over-the-counter markets or be regularly traded with quotations readily available. Among the classes of common stock that are prohibited in several states are assessable stock, and stock of real estate companies. A few states do not permit investment in insurance company stock, and some prohibit the purchase of common stock of companies with total earnings or net worth below stipulated amounts.

The other types of eligibility standards for common stock relate to various earnings tests. These may require that the stock has paid dividends for a certain number of years or that earnings have been available for a specified number of years. Earnings as a percent of par value or stated value must exceed specified minimums in several states, with an averaging provision or a "best three out of five years" provision often included.

Further details on common stock requirements in nineteen representative states are summarized in Appendix Table 5A-5.

Standards for Income Real Estate. Another form of direct equity investment by life insurance companies is income-producing real estate, which is now permitted by nearly every state. There are, however, provisions pertaining to such investments which govern the type of real estate which may be acquired. For example, the law in several states limits income real estate to property for industrial or commercial purposes; other states grant broader authority to include residential property—apartment houses or housing projects. Acquisition of property which is primarily for agricultural or mining purposes is specifically prohibited under the law in a number of states because of the greater risk often associated with such properties. In some cases, investment in hotels or amusement properties also is ruled out for life insurance companies.

In addition to the laws governing direct acquisition of income-producing real estate, provision is sometimes made for the transfer or reclassification of real estate holdings from other categories into the income-producing real estate category. Real estate acquired through foreclosure, for example, could be shifted under such provisions to the income real estate category, rather than being liquidated as normally required.

State laws also prescribe standards for the amortization or annual depreciation of income-producing real estate held by life insurance companies. Sometimes this write-down requirement is set at a certain percentage (usually 2 percent) per year; another approach is to require a write-down to zero at the end of the lease or by a fixed number of years, whichever is sooner.

Further detail as to the income real estate provisions in nineteen representative states is shown in Appendix Table 5A-6.

Statutory Limits on Holdings of Various Classes of Investments

As a means of ensuring diversification of life insurance portfolios and avoiding the risks of undue concentration in a single class of assets or in the obligations of a single borrower, state investment laws impose a variety of limits to the maximum holdings of particular assets by life insurance companies. This section will describe the nature and application of these limits in the various states; detailed summaries of the actual limitations in nineteen representative states are contained in the appendix to this chapter.

Limits on Corporate Bond Holdings. A typical limit to be found in state laws pertains to the maximum percentage of total assets which may be held in the form of corporate bonds, notes, and other forms of indebtedness. These limits apply, of course, to bonds which are eligible for purchase under the investment standards set forth in the respective statutes (shown in Appendix Table 5A-2 and summarized in the preceding section). As may be seen in Appendix Table 5A-7, these limits are often applied to a particular category of bonds rather than the entire corporate bond portfolio; for example, the law may set a maximum of 30 percent of assets in utility bonds, 10 percent in railroad bonds, and 20 percent in other corporate bonds. Another variation is to fix such limits in terms of a maximum percent of capital and/or surplus, or legal reserves, rather than total assets of the life insurance company.

Another common statutory limit on corporate bond holdings is the maximum percentage of assets which may be invested in the obligations of one issuer. The percentages under this limit are frequently applied not to bonds alone but to all securities of a single issuer, including preferred and common stock. When this is the case, the percentage is usually higher than the limit applied solely to fixed-income obligations. A third form of limitation is the percent of total assets that may be held in any single bond issue; the typical limit is not more than 2 percent of assets in any one issue of one issuer.

In addition to the limits imposed on corporate bonds which life insurance companies are expressly authorized to purchase, bonds may also be purchased under "leeway" provisions in the state investment laws. As will be discussed in greater detail at a later point, these "leeway" clauses allow companies to acquire investments not otherwise eligible under other provisions of the law, up to a certain percent of total assets. In states where such leeway clauses allow further corporate bond investment beyond limits otherwise specified, this has been noted in Appendix Table 5A-7.

Further detail on the limits on corporate bond investments in nineteen representative states is set forth in Appendix Table 5A-7.

Limits on Mortgage Holdings.   Three types of statutory limits on life insurance mortgage holdings are to be found in the state investment laws. The first type imposes a limit on total mortgage holdings, expressed as a percent of total assets or of legal reserves. Only a few states apply limits of this type, however, and they range upwards of 40 percent of total assets in those states where they appear. The second type of limitation is applied to the percent of total assets which may be placed in mortgages of a single borrower. Most of the states applying this limit set a maximum of 10 percent; some fix the percentage at 4 or 5 percent. A third form of mortgage loan limitation sets a maximum for the amount which may be invested in a single parcel; this usually is expressed as a certain dollar amount or a certain percent of assets, whichever is the greater.

Further detail on such limitations in nineteen representative states may be seen in Appendix Table 5A-3.

Limits on Preferred Stock Holdings.   Limits on holdings of preferred or guaranteed stock are similar in form to those imposed on corporate bonds. First, a limit is often imposed on total holdings of preferred stock in relation to the total assets, or total legal reserves, or total capital and/or surplus. Second, a limit on the percent of assets which may be invested in the preferred stock of any one issuer is also quite common. However, limits on the percent of assets which may be placed in any one issue of preferred stock are imposed far less frequently than in the case of corporate bond issues. Finally, limits are frequently imposed as to the percentage of the outstanding preferred stock of a single issuer which may be held by a life insurance company.

As noted above for corporate bond issues, the existence of a leeway clause in the investment law sometimes has the effect of allowing further purchases of preferred stock beyond the limits directly applied, or outside the eligibility standards usually required. Such provisions have been noted in Appendix Table 5A-8, which sets forth the details of statutory limits on preferred stock holdings in the nineteen representative states.

Limits on Common Stock Holdings.   In those states authorizing the purchase of common stock, limits are often applied in one or more of the following forms. First, the aggregate holdings of common stock must not exceed a specified percentage of total assets, or of the surplus of the life insurance company. Second, the holdings of common stock of any one corporate issuer are often limited to a specified percentage of total assets, or of surplus. Third, the holdings of common stock must not exceed a specified percentage of the outstanding common stock of a single corporate issuer. The first two types of limitations are aimed at preventing an undue concentration of assets in the form of common stock; the third type of limitation is aimed at preventing the acquisition of control of a corporation by a life insurance company through the ownership of voting shares.

Leeway clauses sometimes allow the purchase of common stock beyond the aggregate limits imposed on holdings, or outside the selection standards otherwise prescribed, or when the purchase of common stock is not specifically authorized. The leeway provisions applicable to common stock are noted in Appendix Table 5A-9 with the additional limits imposed under such clauses.

Further detail as to the statutory limits on common stock holdings by life insurance companies in nineteen representative states is summarized in Appendix Table 5A-9.

Limits on Holdings of Income Real Estate. Statutory limits on life company holdings of income-producing real estate typically set a maximum percentage of total assets that may be held in this class of investment. The most frequent limit is 5 or 10 percent of total assets, as may be seen in Appendix Table 5A-6; where a higher percentage is specified it usually applies to all forms of real estate including home office buildings and real estate acquired through foreclosure. In a few states, a limit on aggregate holdings is also expressed as a percentage of the capital and/or surplus of the life company.

Additional limitations also apply in many states as to the percent of assets, or of capital and/or surplus, which may be invested in a single parcel of income-producing real estate. Further details for nineteen representative states may be found in Appendix Table 5A-6.

Other Provisions of Investment Laws

This section is concerned with the other provisions of state investment laws which have a major bearing on life company investment practices or which constitute special problems not covered elsewhere. These include the "leeway" or "basket" clauses, the laws affecting small business financing by life companies, the laws governing foreign investments, and the compulsory investment law in the State of Texas.

Leeway or Basket Clauses. Because of the changing nature of the business economy and of practices in the financial markets, it is not always possible for the detailed provisions of state investment laws to keep pace with new developments that occur and new investment opportunities that arise. Although legislative amendments to existing investment laws are continually under consideration, such amendments are only enacted after careful study and the passage of considerable time. In order that innovations may be introduced, and that life insurance company investment practice may retain the flexibility required in a dynamic capital market, many states have enacted "leeway" or "basket" clauses in their investment laws.

These leeway clauses usually permit a specified percentage of assets (or capital and/or surplus) to be invested in forms not authorized under other sections of the law. In those states in which the investment laws take the form of a listing of permitted investments, such as New York, any investments not specifically authorized would be automatically ruled out were it not for such a leeway clause.

The nature of the leeway permitted under these clauses varies from state to state. Sometimes the leeway clause permits investments in forms not otherwise permitted, or not meeting the eligibility standards required, but does not allow an alteration of existing statutory limits on particular investment holdings as a percent of assets. In other states, the reverse is true; the leeway clause allows statutory limits to be exceeded, but only on classes of investments already permitted under other sections of the law. Of course, if a particular type of investment is expressly prohibited by the investment law, the leeway clause is not allowed to nullify such prohibition.

As may be seen in Appendix Table 5A-10, the amount that may be placed in leeway investments ranges from 2 percent of assets to funds in excess of three-fourths of reserves. With this degree of flexibility, it is possible for the life insurance companies affected to enter fields of investment otherwise closed to them or to innovate in their investment practices, without raising a serious danger of impairing the over-all quality of their investment portfolios.

Further detail as to the leeway clauses in nineteen representatives states is contained in Appendix Table 5A-10.

Small Business Financing. Because of the high element of risk involved, investment by life insurance companies in small or new business enterprises is generally ruled out by state investment laws, with the exception of mortgage loans. This section will discuss the ways in which state laws act to prohibit or severely limit life company financing of small business through investment in their stock or through unsecured loans based on their credit.

A precise definition of "small business" is difficult to find, but the term is generally applied to those concerns which are comparatively new or of moderate size in relation to competing firms engaged in the same lines of business. They are on the lower end of the scale in their industry, whether measured by net worth, total assets, gross sales, or number of employees. Often such small business is a family concern, built upon the efforts of one or two individuals who have ventured their own capital and efforts in making the business a going concern. It has been estimated that 85 to 90 percent of small businesses are unincorporated, operating as partnerships or sole proprietorships. In seeking to expand, these firms often find that their need for substantial amounts of outside capital, usually on a long-term basis, is a major impediment in their attempts to obtain "medium-sized" status. Frequently what these firms need is more equity capital, but they prefer to sell debt in order to prevent diluting ownership.

At the same time, it must be recognized that small business of this type often is quite risky in terms of its long-run potential. As a family or individually controlled enterprise, the death or incapacitation of a single individual could adversely affect its ability to continue operations. Sudden shifts in market demand or supply factors could quickly alter the profitability of such concerns, based as they often are on the manufacture or distribution of a single product or a limited number of related products. For these and other reasons, a large element of risk is present when the future of such a concern is appraised. In these circumstances, investments by life insurance companies in the small business field may be considered inappropriate when it is recalled that the underlying philosophy of life company investments is that they be long-term in nature with close attention to the safety and security of the principal amount.

State investment laws, through their various requirements for selection of assets, reflect this concern for the safety of the principal amount invested. Mortgage loans may be made to small business, just as to individuals, since the loan is secured by property with a value considerably above the amount loaned. Unsecured loans, based on earnings rather than collateral, usually are allowed only for incorporated business, thus ruling out the bulk of those concerns usually considered as small business. Only one state expressly permits unsecured loans to be made to "solvent persons" or unincorporated business.

Even when the small business is incorporated, it must satisfy a number of state investment law requirements in order to sell its stock or place its bonds or notes with life insurance companies. In the case of stock, a common requirement is that the stock be listed on a recognized securities exchange. As noted earlier, the investment laws of many states require, for either stocks or bonds, that certain earnings tests be satisfied. These involve the number of years that earnings have been available to pay dividends or interest, or the number of years that dividends or interest have actually been paid, or specify the minimum ratios of earnings to annual fixed charges (see earlier section). Many small businesses, although organized as corporations, are unable to meet these investment law requirements.

This is not to say that life insurance companies have not been providers of capital to the small business field. As noted above, small business may obtain life insurance funds through mortgage loans and the amount of these has been substantial.[3] Although unsecured loans to small business

---

[3] See Chapter 4, "Some Basic Factors Governing Investment Polices," section on Small Business Financing; also, see Chapter 10, section on Loans to Small Business and Industrial Concerns.

may not satisfy the eligibility standards cited above, life companies in many states may lend to small business directly through "leeway" clause provisions, where such standards are waived, if the loan satisfies the investment requirements of life company financial officers as to its soundness and safety. Appendix Table 5A-11 sets forth the leeway clauses which may be applied to unsecured loans to unincorporated business in nineteen representative states.

An indirect form of life company investment in small business is also permitted through development credit corporations that have been established during the past ten years in a number of states. These development credit corporations serve as a pool of capital for making term loans in the state to businesses unable to secure capital through normal financial channels. Life insurance companies may contribute to this pool of capital by their purchases of stock in, or advances to, such credit corporations as allowed by state law. Appendix Table 5A-11 also indicates those of the nineteen representative states that permit participation by life insurance companies in state development corporations or similar organizations.[4]

Investments in Foreign Securities.   Most of the foregoing discussion of eligibility standards and limits on holdings of securities has applied implicitly to domestic securities, i.e., those issued by corporations domiciled in the United States and its territories and possessions. Investments may also be made, however, in securities issued by corporations or governmental units in foreign countries. This section will outline the manner in which state investment laws govern such foreign investments, with particular reference to the limitations placed thereon.

The majority of state insurance laws deal specifically with foreign securities as a class of investment. The usual form of such regulations is that investments in foreign securities be of the same quality or the same kind as permitted for domestic securities. However, many states permit such investments only in those countries in which the insurance company is admitted to do business. A number of states limit foreign investments to a particular class of securities; usually these are the securities of the foreign government and its political subdivisions, but sometimes only the corporate securities of foreign issuers are authorized. In a few states the only types of eligible foreign securities are those required by the foreign government in order to do business in that country. This refers to a common requirement by foreign countries that, as a condition of admittance to the country, United States insurers must maintain a certain portion of reserves against insured lives in prescribed securities, often held in the custody of the foreign insurance authorities.

Within this framework of the kinds of foreign securities permitted

---

[4] See Chapter 4, section on Small Business Financing.

under state law, limits on the aggregate holdings are usually stipulated. Such limits are usually tied to the requirements of foreign law or to the size of foreign business done by the life insurance company. A typical limitation is that such investments shall not exceed the amount required to conform with foreign law, or the deposit and reserve obligation incurred in the foreign country. In some states, such as New York and California, the upper limit is set up 1½ times reserves and other obligations incurred in the foreign country, unless a greater amount is required by foreign law. In only a few states are the limits on foreign security holdings related to the total assets of the life insurance company.

Leeway clauses also may be called upon for the authorization of life company investments in foreign securities, either beyond the limits stipulated or in classes of securities not otherwise permitted. Those states in which these leeway clauses may be applied to foreign securities have been noted in Appendix Table 5A-12.

Further detail as to the investment laws in nineteen representative states that pertain to foreign securities generally is contained in Appendix Table 5A-12.

In addition to these regulations bearing on foreign securities generally, the insurance laws of most states make provision for investment in the Dominion of Canada. This special treatment of Canadian investments stems, of course, from the recognition of the proximity and close economic relations between the United States and Canada, as distinct from other foreign countries.

As may be seen in Appendix Table 5A-13, authorization of investments in Canadian securities is made by reference to specific types of securities —Dominion bonds, provincial bonds, corporate bonds and stocks, etc. In a few states, only securities of the Dominion or its political subdivisions are permitted, but the vast majority of states allow investment in some or all classes of corporate securities. It should be noted that the authorization of Canadian securities in Appendix Table 5A-13 is in addition to the more general authorization of foreign securities summarized in Appendix Table 5A-12. Thus, an investment not expressly authorized for Canada might be permitted under the provisions applicable to foreign countries generally, so long as they meet the requirements imposed on such investments.

Limits on aggregate holdings of certain classes of Canadian securities are also shown in Appendix Table 5A-13. So close are the relations between the United States and Canada that these often take the form of limits applied simultaneously to the securities of both countries. In such cases, where a limit of 10 percent of assets is imposed on common stock holdings, for example, it is possible for a company to invest the full 10 percent in Canadian common stock if it so desires. In general, where such aggregate limits exist on U.S. and Canadian securities, they are applied to a particular class of security rather than to corporate securities in general.

In addition to the foregoing limitations on holdings of U.S. or Canadian securities, many states stipulate limits on Canadian securities specifically. As before, these are usually stated in terms of the percent of total assets that may be placed in particular types of Canadian securities. Further details on the regulations regarding Canadian investments in nineteen representative states are shown in Appendix Table 5A-13.

Geographic Limits on Investment. While the foregoing regulations of investments are intended primarily to protect the interests of policyholders, there has been public pressure to influence the type and amount of life insurance company investments so that they might serve the interest of special areas or public programs. On the state level, public leaders long have advocated laws which would require insurance companies to invest more in their own particular state.

The main purpose of such state proposals is usually to increase the supply of capital funds needed for the economic development and growth of the state. Often this has taken the form of an effort to obtain risk capital for new or young industries. A second and closely related goal is to lower interest rates in the state, either to encourage general economic expansion or to encourage some desirable goal such as increasing home ownership. Still another goal may be to encourage the formation of domestic insurance companies and to strengthen those already in existence.

The first two goals are based on the assumption that insurance companies from other states, through neglect or arbitrary policy, are withdrawing more capital funds from the state than they are putting into it. Almost invariably this is not the case, but to a state hungry for capital expansion, it may appear to be so. To correct this situation, two main legislative approaches have been tried by several states. The first is to allow reductions in tax rates paid by life insurance companies if their investments in the state come up to certain standards. The other is to require, as a condition for permission to write insurance policies on the lives of residents of the state, a certification that 75 percent of the reserves on such policies have been invested in the state.

Ten states currently have laws using the tax exemption approach.[5] Eight of these vary the tax rate in relation to the percentage of assets of the company invested in the state. The South Carolina premium tax rate depends upon the proportion of the reserves on policies issued in the state which is invested in certain designated South Carolina securities. Montana allows a deduction from the amount of the tax if a company has

---

[5] Alabama, Colorado, Georgia, Idaho, Louisiana, Montana, New Mexico, Oklahoma, South Carolina, and Texas.

50 percent of its capital stock invested in Montana securties. The other states vary the tax rate in relation to the proportion of total admitted assets invested in the state. They provide that the rate of tax levied on a life insurance company's premium income in a state depends on the percentage of the company's total admitted assets invested in specified securities.

It has been suggested that all of these tax abatement laws were not passed for the sole, or even major purpose of encouraging investments in the particular states but, instead for the purpose of giving comparatively lower taxes to domestic companies. Domestic companies usually have a larger percentage of their assets invested in their home state than do the out-of-state companies in that state.

The other type of law designed to encourage local investment is seldom enacted, but it has been frequently proposed. It requires life insurance companies to invest in a state as a condition for obtaining permission to do business within the state.

The first law of this kind was enacted by the state of Wisconsin in 1865 and the law was repealed in less than a year. The proponents of this type of legislation in Texas made a number of attempts to secure passage of such a law and in 1907 were successful in the passage of the "Robertson Law," which requires that 75 percent of the Texas reserves be invested in Texas securities as a basis for license to sell insurance in Texas. The premium tax was increased in Texas at this time and in 1909 a new law permitted a reduction in the premium tax on the basis of investments in Texas securities. While the requirement that 75 percent of Texas reserves be invested in "Texas securities," as a basis for admission to Texas, has been challenged, it is still in force.

At the time of the passage of the Robertson Law, the life insurance companies protested vigorously, and a number withdrew from Texas. In the fifty years since its passage, many have re-entered the state. There have been various motives, one important one being the ability to write coverage in every state in the country.

The great economic and industrial growth of Texas in the past half century cannot, of course, be attributed to the passage of the Robertson Law. The rapidly expanding economy offered such opportunities for investment that the companies soon had more than the 75 percent of the reserve held for the benefit of Texas residents invested in Texas. Many of the companies prior to re-entering the state had large investments in Texas.

The menace to sound investment practice in the Robertson Law lies not so much in the compliance with the law in Texas, but in any general adoption of the principle of compulsory investments by the several states. Any widespread acceptance would require that investments be shifted from one section of the country to another with the sale of insurance. In striving for the highest possible investment yield consistent with reasonable safety, the life insurance companies have directed their funds to the areas of greatest need and highest growth. Widespread adoption by states of legislation like the Robertson Law would greatly hamper the free market allocation of capital. It would inevitably deplete the capital supply available to certain sections of the country. The additional expense of maintenance of investments matching reserves in the various states would not be in the interests of the policyholders.

Since Texas adopted the compulsory investment law in 1907, similar bills have been introduced in the legislatures of forty-one other jurisdictions up to the end of 1959. In some of these states such a measure was introduced several times and at different sessions. It was considered by these forty-one jurisdictions 242 different times and without a single exception every one of these bills failed.[6]

---

[6] See the arguments advanced in *The Effects of State Investment Requirements for Life Insurance Companies* by Winston Beard, prepared for the Arkansas Insurance Commissioner by the University of Arkansas College of Business Administration, Industrial Research and Extension Center in cooperation with The Arkansas Industrial Development Commission, October 1958.

Appendix to Chapter 5

(Data for Tables 5A-1 through 5A-13 are as of June 1960.)

Statutes Regulating Investments of Out-of-State Life Insurers[1]

State	Type of Compliance Specified	Other Provisions
Arizona	Shall have assets of same general character and quality, and home office real property investment, all as specified for domestic insurers.	Director may recognize as assets investments authorized by domiciliary law.
Arkansas	Investments shall be of quality substantially as high as those required for like domestic insurers and shall be as permitted by domiciliary law.	
District of Columbia	Shall satisfy superintendent funds are invested in accordance with domiciliary law and in securities or property affording degree of financial security substantially equal to that required for similar domestic companies.	
Florida	Investment portfolio shall be as permitted by domiciliary law if of quality substantially as high as that required for like domestic insurers.	
Hawaii	Investments shall be of quality substantially as high as those required for like domestic insurers and shall be as permitted by domiciliary law.	
Idaho	Investments shall be of quality substantially as high as those required for like domestic insurers and shall be as permitted by domiciliary law.	
Kentucky	Shall have assets of same general character as specified for domestic insurers.	Commissioner may recognize as assets investments authorized by domiciliary law.
Louisiana	Investments shall be of quality substantially as high as those required for like domestic insurers and shall be as permitted by domiciliary law.	

(Continued)

Table 5A-1 (Continued)

State	Type of Compliance Specified	Other Provisions
Nebraska	Capital and funds shall be kept invested in same class of securities specified for domestic insurers.	Insurance Department may recognize as legal investments securities authorized by domiciliary law.
New York	Substantial compliance with investment requirements and limitations imposed on like domestic insurers.[2]	Investments deemed in substantial compliance, if noncomplying investments do not reduce surplus to policyholders below amount reasonable in relation to liabilities and adequate to financial needs but not below minimum surplus to policyholders.
North Carolina	Substantial compliance with investment requirements and limitations imposed on like domestic insurers.[2]	
Oklahoma	Investments shall be of quality substantially as high as those required for like domestic insurers and shall be as permitted by domiciliary law.	
Texas	Assets shall be invested in securities or property of same classes permitted by Texas laws as to domestic companies or by other Texas laws in other securities approved by Insurance Board as being of substantially the same grade.	
Utah	Investments shall be of quality substantially as high as those required for like domestic insurers and shall be as permitted by domiciliary law.	
Washington	Investments shall be of quality substantially as high as those required for like domestic insurers and shall be as permitted by domiciliary law.	

Table 5A-1 (Continued)

State	Type of Compliance Specified	Other Provisions
West Virginia	Shall have assets of same general quality as specified for domestic insurers.	Commissioner may recognize as assets investments authorized by domiciliary law.

---

[1]Refusal, suspension or revocation of license is the customary penalty for violation of the laws digested in this table.

Laws as to capital or deposit and local real estate or mortgage investments have been excluded. (A Kansas statute permits the same investments there as authorized for domestic life insurers. A Missouri law allows the same investments permitted domestic life companies. Neither act is to prohibit investments authorized by the foreign company's charter or domiciliary law. A Michigan statute permits investments in accordance with domiciliary law.)

[2]Discretionary in Superintendent or Commissioner to refuse license, if he finds investments do not so comply.

Principal Statutory Standards of Selection in Nineteen Representative

| | Eligibility Based on Security | | | | | | Fixed Interest Eligibility Based | |
| | Number of Last Fiscal | | Net Earnings Times Annual Fixed Charges[2] | Security Require-ments | Not in Default as to Princi-pal or Interest | Described as Fixed Interest Bonds | Number of Last Fiscal | |
State	Years Earnings Must Have Been Available	Years Require-ments Fully Met					Years Earnings Must Have Been Available	Years Require-ments Fully Met
California								
Connecticut								
Illinois								
Indiana							7[a]	Last 3[a]
							7[c]	Last 3[c]
Iowa				a	No		5	Last 1
Massachusetts							b 5	b 3, incl. Last 2

States as to Acquisition of Corporate Bonds by Life Insurance Companies[1]

Bonds on Earnings		Contingent Interest Bonds				
Net Earnings Times Average Annual Fixed Charges[2]	Not in Default as to Principal or Interest	Number of Last Fiscal Years Earnings Must Have Been Available	Number of Last Fiscal Years Requirements Fully Met	Net Earnings Times Average Annual Fixed Charges[2] and Maximum Contingent Interest	Not in Default as to Principal or Interest	Types Authorized, Miscellaneous, Notes, etc.
						Bonds must qualify as sound investment and be interest bearing.
						Bonds not in default as to interest within 5 years prior to purchase or during tenure of issue.
						Railroad or public utility (but not holding) corporation bonds, etc., not in default as to principal or interest during last 5 years or tenure.
						Other (but not holding) corporation bonds, etc., not in default as to interest.
						Domestic life insurer whose A&H premium income exceeds its life premium income may acquire bonds, etc., of corporations other than real estate corporations.
						Securities of corporation (other than another insurer, bank or real estate corporation) having prescribed earnings as to dividends.
2[a]	b					Corporate bonds, etc. a. Earnings averaged 2 times annual interest charges during preceding 7 fiscal years or equalled 2 times such charges during last 3 fiscal years. b. No interest obligation default for 90 days within last 5 years.
c	b					c. Earnings averaged 6% of par value of bonds, etc., of equal or greater security during preceding 7 fiscal years or equalled 6% of such par value during last 3 fiscal years.
1½	Yes	5	Last 2	1½	Yes	Corporate bonds, etc. a. Adequately secured and have investment qualities and characteristics wherein speculative elements not predominant.
b						b. Railroad bonds, etc., as prescribed.
1½						Bonds, etc., or mortgage bonds, of certain railroad corporations whose capital stock equals ⅓ funded indebtedness, which have paid regularly for last 5 years all interest charges on such indebtedness and 4% dividends on all issues of capital stock or have earnings record as indicated.
						Mortgage bonds of railroad corporation whose liens junior to such bonds equal ⅓ funded indebtedness secured by such bonds and prior bonds, and which has paid regularly for last 5 years all interest charges on funded indebtedness and 4% interest on such junior securities.
						Bonds, etc., of the American Telephone and Telegraph Company or its subsidiary or affiliated operating companies.

(Continued)

| State | Eligibility Based on Security | | | | | | Fixed Interest Eligibility Based | |
| | Number of Last Fiscal | | Net Earnings Times Annual Fixed Charges[2] | Security Require-ments | Not in Default as to Princi-pal or Interest | Described as Fixed Interest Bonds | Number of Last Fiscal | |
	Years Earnings Must Have Been Available	Years Require-ments Fully Met					Years Earnings Must Have Been Available	Years Require-ments Fully Met
Massachusetts (cont.)								
							5	Any 3, incl. Last 2
							5	Any 3, incl. Last 2
							5	Any 3, incl. Last 2
							7	
Minnesota								
							a	a
Missouri								
Nebraska								
							5	Last Year

| Bonds on Earnings | | Contingent Interest Bonds | | | | |
| Net Earnings Times Average Annual Fixed Charges² | Not in Default as to Principal or Interest | Number of Last Fiscal | | Net Earnings Times Average Annual Fixed Charges² and Maximum Contingent Interest | Not in Default as to Principal or Interest | Types Authorized, Miscellaneous, Notes, etc. |
		Years Earnings Must Have Been Available	Years Requirements Fully Met			
						First mortgage bonds, whose issue subject to regulatory body, of companies engaged directly and primarily in:
2						Telephone and telegraph systems or electric light or power companies;
2½						Gas companies;
1½						Water companies.
4						Bonds, etc., of corporations and of certain associations or trusts.
						Bonds, etc., of companies and of certain associations or trusts secured by assignment of certain leases.
						Evidence of indebtedness ineligible if assessable (other than for taxes). Leeway provision subject to this standard.
						Bonds, etc., of railway and other public utility corporations not in default as to principal or interest, and debentures of farm mortgage debenture companies.
	b					Bonds, etc., of other corporations. a. Earnings applicable to dividends averaged annually over last 5 fiscal years, and were during 3 of such 5 years, 4% of par or stated value of capital stock. b. No investment upon which interest obligation is in default or which has been in default for aggregate of 90 days within last 3 year period.
						Bonds, etc., of corporation if: (a) No default in principal or interest upon any outstanding indebtedness during prior 5 years, or; (b) Bonds, etc., not in default and net earnings for last 5 fiscal years averaged annually 1½ times fixed charges or 2 times yearly interest charges on all outstanding bonds, etc., of equal or prior lien.
						Railroad mortgage bonds, etc., if no principal or interest default during last 5 years or since issuance.
						Public utility mortgage bonds, etc., if no principal or interest default during last 5 years or since issuance.
1½	a					Mortgage bonds, etc., of other corporations. a. No principal or interest defaults thereon or on such obligations of equal or higher priority during last 5 yrs or since issuance.

(Continued)

103

State	Eligibility Based on Security						Fixed Interes Eligibility Base	
	Number of Last Fiscal		Net Earnings Times Annual Fixed Charges[2]	Security Require- ments	Not in Default as to Princi- pal or Interest	Described as Fixed Interest Bonds	Number of Last Fiscal	
	Years Earnings Must Have Been Available	Years Require- ments Fully Met					Years Earnings Must Have Been Available	Years Require ments Fully Met
Nebraska (cont.)								
New Jersey								
New York	5	Any 3 incl. 1 of Last 2	$1\frac{1}{4}$	a b	Yes	Yes	5	1 of Last 2
North Carolina								
Ohio							5	
							5	
							5	
							5	
Pennsylvania							5[a]	
Tennessee								
Texas								

Bonds on Earnings — Net Earnings Times Average Annual Fixed Charges[2]	Not in Default as to Principal or Interest	Contingent Interest Bonds — Number of Last Fiscal — Years Earnings Must Have Been Available	Years Requirements Fully Met	Net Earnings Times Average Annual Fixed Charges[2] and Maximum Contingent Interest	Not in Default as to Principal or Interest	Types Authorized, Miscellaneous, Notes, etc.
						Public utility revenue bonds, etc. Estimated net earnings available for debt service must show coverage equivalent to 1¾ times fixed charges.
						Mortgage or collateral trust bonds of railroads, bonds, etc., of Canadian public utility companies and of other corporations, not in default as to interest.
1½	Yes	5	1 of Last 2	1½	Yes	Corporate bonds, etc. a. Not over ⅓ of total value of required collateral to consist of stock other than eligible preferred stock. b. Adequately secured obligations having investment qualities and characteristics wherein speculative elements are not predominant.
						Other corporate obligations not qualifying under any paragraphs of §81(2).
						Corporate bonds, etc., not in default as to principal or interest.
1½ᵃ	b					First lien railroad mortgage bonds. a. Times average annual interest on mortgages, bonds and funded debts. b. Corporation must have been in business 10 years prior to purchase and must not have defaulted on interest or principal of any bonds or funded debts during last 5 years.
3ᵃ	b					Junior railroad mortgage bonds.
	b					Mortgage bonds, etc., of terminal companies assumed or guaranteed by 2 or more railroads whose bonds eligible above.
1½ᵃ	b					First lien utility company mortgage bonds.
3ᶜ	d					Corporate bonds, etc. c. Times interest on funded debt. d. No default as to interest or principal on bonds, etc., during last 5 years.
						Bonds, etc., of railroad or public utility corporations.
1½						Bonds, etc., of other corporations (capital and ¾ reserves). a. "Income available for fixed charges" for last 5 fiscal years.
						Corporate bonds, etc. (surplus and ¼ of reserves).
						Mortgage bonds of dividend-paying railway companies or other good and solvent securities, approved by Commissioner.
						First mortgage bonds of corporation not defaulting during last 5 years or debentures of such corporation with $5,000,000 capital stock where no prior lien exists at issuance.
						Bonds, etc., of corporation not defaulting during last 5 years.

(Continued)

Table 5A-2 (Continued)

State	Eligibility Based on Security						Fixed Interest Eligibility Based	
	Number of Last Fiscal		Net Earnings Times Annual Fixed Charges²	Security Requirements	Not in Default as to Principal or Interest	Described as Fixed Interest Bonds	Number of Last Fiscal	
	Years Earnings Must Have Been Available	Years Requirements Fully Met					Years Earnings Must Have Been Available	Years Requirements Fully Met
Texas (cont.)								5
Vermont							5ᵃ	Last 1
Virginia	5a		1½ᵇ	c	d	No		
								Last 3ᵉ
Wisconsin				a	b			
				c	d			

106

Bonds in Earnings		Number of Last Fiscal		Net Earnings Times Average Annual Fixed Charges² and Maximum Contingent Interest		Types Authorized, Miscellaneous, Notes, etc.
Net Earnings Times Average Annual Fixed Charges²	Not in Default as to Principal or Interest	Years Earnings Must Have Been Available	Years Requirements Fully Met		Not in Default as to Principal or Interest	
3a	b					Debentures of public utility corporation. a. 3 times annual interest charges. b. No default during last 5 years.
1½	Yes					Corporate bonds, etc. a. "Net income available for fixed charges" during last 5 fiscal years. Corporate or trust securities—earnings available for dividends for last 5 fiscal years averaged 4% of par or stated value of capital stock. Bonds, etc., of land companies which own, operate, etc., real estate foreclosed by life insurer. Bonds, etc., secured by first mortgage or other lien on terminal, depot or tunnel property used by railroads whose bonds, etc., eligible under (A) or (B)—no default within 5 years of investment or since issuance. Other corporate bonds, etc. (A) a. Average net annual income for last 5 fiscal years. b. 1½ times average annual interest on such bonds, prior obligations and obligations of equal rank. c. Secured by adequate collateral security, ⅔ of which is other than common stock. d. No interest default within last 5 years.
				2f		Other corporate bonds, etc. (B) e. Earned sum applicable to interest on outstanding indebtedness during last 3 fiscal years. f. 2 times annual interest due. Securities must be non-assessable (other than for taxes or wages). (A) Bonds, etc., of terminal, belt line, and railroad companies, approved by public authority if required at issue. a. Adequately secured by mortgage or pledge of property of issuer, or held in trust for it, or by adequate collateral so secured. b. No interest default within 3 years of investment or since issuance. (B) Bonds, etc., of public utilities, approved by public authority, if required at issue. c. Adequately secured by mortgage on, or pledge of, property and franchises of issuer or held in trust for it, or by adequate collateral so secured. d. No interest default during 3 years prior to investment.

(Continued)

State	Eligibility Based on Security						Fixed Interest Eligibility Based	
	Number of Last Fiscal		Net Earnings Times Annual Fixed Charges[2]	Security Requirements	Not in Default as to Principal or Interest	Described as Fixed Interest Bonds	Number of Last Fiscal	
	Years Earnings Must Have Been Available	Years Requirements Fully Met					Years Earnings Must Have Been Available	Years Requirements Fully Met
Wisconsin (cont.)							3	
				f	g			
							3	

---

[1]This table does not cover equipment trust obligations or receivers' certificates, investment company or trust securities, building and loan or savings and loan association securities, housing or redevelopment company securities, business development company bonds, or foreign securities, or capital and deposit provisions.

[2]Fixed charges are defined in the statutes of Iowa, Massachusetts, Nebraska, New York, Pennsylvania, and Vermont.

	Contingent Interest Bonds					
Bonds on Earnings						
Net Earnings Times Average Annual Fixed Charges²	Not in Default as to Principal or Interest	Number of Last Fiscal Years Earnings Must Have Been Available	Years Requirements Fully Met	Net Earnings Times Average Annual Fixed Charges² and Maximum Contingent Interest	Not in Default as to Principal or Interest	Types Authorized, Miscellaneous, Notes, etc.
1½	e					(C) Evidences of indebtedness of public utilities, in addition to (B), approved by public authority, if required at issue. e. No interest default during 3 years prior to investment or since issuance. (D) Bonds, etc., of other (but not holding) corporations, in addition to (A), (B), (C), and (E), approved by public authority, if required at issue. f. Adequately secured by mortgage on, or pledge of, property of issuer or held in trust for it, or by adequate collateral so secured. g. No principal or interest default during 5 years prior to investment or since issuance.
2	h					(E) Evidences of indebtedness of other (but not holding) corporations, in addition to (A), (B), (C), and (D), approved by public authority, if required at issue. h. No principal or interest default during 5 years prior to investment or since issuance.

Principal Statutory Provisions in Nineteen Representative States Regulating
(Capital and Deposit

State	Type of Property	Situs of Property	Loan to Value Ratio[1] (Percent)	Aggregate Limit
California	Fee		75[a] 66⅔[b]	
	Leasehold[c]		60	
Connecticut	Fee		66⅔	
	Leasehold		66⅔	
Illinois	Fee	Any of states of U.S., or D.C.	75[a]	50% of assets in mortgages and housing[2]
	Leasehold[b]		75[a]	
Indiana	Fee	U.S. or Canada	66⅔	
	Leasehold[a]	U.S. or Canada	66⅔	
Iowa	Fee	U.S., U.S. posses- sions, or Canada	75	
	Leasehold[a]	Same	75	
	Leasehold[b]	Same		10% of legal reserve
Massachusetts	Fee	Any of states of U.S., D.C., or Puerto Rico; Canada[c]	75[a]	
	Leasehold[b]		66⅔[a]	
		Canada[c]		
Minnesota	Fee	U.S.	66⅔	
	Leasehold[a]		50	
Missouri	Fee	U.S. or U.S. terri- tory or possession	66⅔	
	Leasehold[a]	U.S. or U.S. terri- tory or possession	66⅔	1% of assets
Nebraska	Fee	Any state of U.S., or D.C.	75	
	Leasehold[a]	Any state or territory of U.S., or D.C.	75	
New Jersey	Fee	States, D.C., or Canada	75[a] 66⅔	
	Leasehold[b]	States, D.C., or Canada	75[a] 66⅔	
New York	Fee	U.S.	75[a] 66⅔	40% of assets[2]
	Leasehold[b]	U.S.	75[a] 66⅔	

110

Conventional Real Estate Mortgage Investments by Life Insurance Companies
(Provisions Not Included)

Single Parcel Limit	Limit on Mortgages of One Mortgagor— % of Assets	Miscellaneous, Notes, etc.
		a. Of loan plus public bond, assessment, or tax liens, as to one-family dwelling.
		b. Of loan plus public bond, assessment, or tax liens, as to other than one-family dwelling.
		c. If loan is for 5 years, or for 20 years on one-family residence with monthly amortization.
Greater of $10,000 or 2% of assets		a. H.863, L.1959, but H.939, L.1959, retains 66⅔%. The Illinois Insurance Department has informally advised that 75% is the effective limit.
Greater of $10,000 or 2% of assets		b. Having unexpired term of at least 25 years.
		Loans on producing oil or gas properties, and participating loans, permitted as prescribed.
		a. Having unexpired term of at least 50 years.
		a. Having unexpired term of at least 50 years.
		b. Under lease or purchase contract to certain government bodies or corporations.
		a. Commissioner may establish minimum amortization schedule required on loans over 60% of value.
		b. Having unexpired term of at least 21 years. Loan to be amortized within ⅘ of unexpired term.
		c. Not exceeding premiums from insurance on Canadian lives and amounts from authorized Canadian investments.
		First lien on lessor's interest required as additional security for bonds, etc., secured by certain leases.
		a. If approved by Commissioner— to have unexpired term of at least 40 years.
Greater of 1% of assets or 10% of capital and surplus		
Greater of 1% of assets or 10% of capital and surplus		a. Having unexpired term of at least 50 years.
		a. Loan to be fully amortized within unexpired term.
		Participating loans permitted, as prescribed.
		a. If annual amortization and excess over 66⅔% carried as reserve by insurer.
		b. Loan to be fully amortized within 9/10 of unexpired term of leasehold.
Greater of $30,000 or 2% of assets	10[3]	a. If loan on one-family dwelling, not over $30,000, and fully amortized in 30 years.
Greater of $30,000 or 2% of assets	10[3]	b. Having unexpired term of at least 21 years. Loan to be fully amortized within lesser of unexpired term of leasehold or 35 years.
		Senior participation permitted, as prescribed.

(Continued)

Table 5A-3 (Continued)

State	Type of Property	Situs of Property	Loan to Value Ratio[1] (Percent)	Aggregate Lim
North Carolina	Fee	Any state, territory or possession of U.S., or D.C.	75	
	Leasehold[a]	Any state, territory or possession of U.S., or D.C.	75	
Ohio	Fee	Any state, D.C., or Canada	75[a] 66⅔	
	Leasehold[b]		60[c]	
Pennsylvania	Fee	Any state, district, or territory of U.S.	75[a] 66⅔[b]	
	Leasehold[c]	Any state, district, or territory of U.S.	75[a] 66⅔	
Tennessee	Real Property	Any state	66⅔[a] 60	
Texas	Fee		75	
	Leasehold[a]			
Vermont	Real Estate	Within borders of U.S.	80[a] 66⅔[b] 60[c]	
	Timberland	Vt.	40[d]	
Virginia	Fee	U.S. or Canada	75[a] 66⅔	
	Leasehold[b]	U.S.	50	
Wisconsin	Fee	U.S. or Canada	66⅔[a]	
	Leasehold	U.S. or Canada	66⅔[a]	

---

[1]Mortgages guaranteed or insured under the National Housing Act or the Servicemen's Readjustment Act of 1944 ar exempted, as prescribed, from the ratio requirements listed in this table.

[2]Limit on aggregate of fee and leasehold mortgages.

[3]Limit on all investments in securities of one corporation.

[4]Limit on all investments in, or loans on, property, securities, etc., of one person or corporation.

Single Parcel Limit	Limit on Mortgages of One Mortgagor— % of Assets	Miscellaneous, Notes, etc.
		a. Having unexpired term of at least 30 years. Loan to mature at least 20 years before lease expires.
		a. If loan not over $30,000, on one-family dwelling, and fully amortized within 30 years.
		b. For not less than 99 years, renewable forever.
		c. Ceiling on loan plus rent capitalized at 5%.
Greater of $10,000 or 2% of assets		a. If loan on improved real estate and fully amortized within 30 years.
Greater of $10,000 or 2% of assets		b. Mortgages on certain corporate or business trust leases excepted.
		c. Loan to be fully amortized within unexpired term of leasehold.
		a. If loan fully amortized in 20 years.
		a. Duration and amortization of loan not to exceed ⅘ unexpired term of leasehold, latter term to extend at least 10 years beyond term of loan.
		a. If loan on one or two-family dwelling and meets prescribed standards.
		b. If loan fully amortized within 20 years.
		c. If loan not amortized and payable on demand or one year.
		d. If loan on timberlands, mines, quarries, etc., with 5 year maturity.
	5^4	a. If loan on single family residence and fully amortized within 25 years.
	5^4	b. For term of at least 99 years with unexpired term of at least 50 years.
	10^3	a. Excess over 66⅔% may be deemed to be made under leeway clause.

113

Principal Statutory Standards of Selection in Nineteen Representative States as

Eligibility Requirements Based on Earnings[2] and

	Number of Last Fiscal			Minimum Earnings in Last Fiscal Years as % of Par or Stated Value
State	Years Stock Must Have Paid Dividends	Years Earnings Must Have Been Available	Years Earnings Requirements Must Be Fully Met	
California				
Connecticut	5[a]			
Illinois				
		3		4[b]
Indiana		7		5
Iowa			Last 5 years	
Massachusetts				
Minnesota		5	3 of last 5	5
Missouri		5	Last 2	
Nebraska	5[a]	5[a]		

114

to Acquisition of Preferred or Guaranteed Stock by Life Insurance Companies[1]

Dividends Net Earnings Times Average Annual Fixed Charges, Maximum Contingent Interest, and Preferred Dividend Requirements	Requirement That Stock Be Dividend Paying and Not in Default When Acquired	Prohibited Classes of Corporations or Prohibited Types of Stock	Types Authorized, Miscellaneous, Notes, etc.[3]
			Corporate stock—must qualify as sound investment.
		Mining companies.	Corporate stock. a. Must pay annual cash dividends of $3\frac{1}{4}\%$ of par or stated value (or that of eligible junior stock).
	a	Other insurers. Own (except for mutualization, employee plans, and as prescribed).	Corporate preferred or guaranteed stock. a. Not in default as to prescribed dividends.
		Other insurer, bank, or real estate corporation.	Corporate capital stock. b. Earnings must have totaled 12% during 3 out of last 5 fiscal years. Stock must be listed on recognized exchange.
		Real estate corporation.	Corporate capital stock. Authorized for life company whose A&H premium income exceeds its life premium income.
2	a	Own, except for mutualization.b	Corporate preferred or guaranteed stock. a. Stock ineligible if any dividend in arrears for 90 days within preceding 5 years. b. Leeway provision subject to this standard.
$1\frac{1}{2}$a,3	b	Own, or other insurers'.	Corporate preferred or guaranteed stock. a. Separate requirements specified for guaranteed stock—same as for corporate bonds whose eligibility is based on earnings (see Table 5A-2), with guaranteed dividends included as fixed charges. b. Not in default as to dividends.
		Assessable (other than for taxes).a Own, or other insurers' stock.a	Corporate stock. a. Leeway clause (see Table 5A-8) subject to this standard but excepts Massachusetts trust company or New England national banking association capital stock meeting prescribed dividend and surplus requirements.
			Stocks of banks and insurers.
2a	b		Preferred or guaranteed stock of other corporations. a. In the alternative. b. Stock ineligible if dividend in arrears 90 days within last 3 years.
$1\frac{1}{2}$a,3		Own, except with superintendent's prior approval.	Corporate preferred or guaranteed stock. a. Separate requirement specified for guaranteed stock—net earnings of assuming or guaranteeing corporation for last 5 fiscal years shall average $1\frac{1}{2}$ times annual fixed charges, with guaranteed dividends or covering rental included as fixed charge.
		Own or other insurers' shares except may invest up to 50% of surplus to policyholders in other insurers' stocks, as prescribed.b	Corporate preferred stock. a. Or during such part of said 5 years next preceding it had preferred stock outstanding. Issuer or its predecessor shall earn dividends of at least $100,000 annually during such 5 year period. b. Leeway provision subject to these provisions.

(Continued)

Eligibility Requirements Based on Earnings[2] and

| State | Number of Last Fiscal | | | Minimum Earnings in Last Fiscal Years as % of Par or Stated Value |
	Years Stock Must Have Paid Dividends	Years Earnings Must Have Been Available	Years Earnings Requirements Must Be Fully Met	
New Jersey	5[a]			
New York		5	1 of last 2	
North Carolina				
Ohio		5		
		5		
Pennsylvania				
Tennessee				
Texas	a			
	a		Last 5	
Vermont		5	Last 2	

Dividends

Net Earnings Times Average Annual Fixed Charges, Maximum Contingent Interest, and Preferred Dividend Requirements	Requirement That Stock Be Dividend Paying and Not in Default When Acquired	Prohibited Classes of Corporations or Prohibited Types of Stock	Types Authorized, Miscellaneous, Notes, etc.[3]
		Own, except for retirement or as specifically permitted.	Corporate capital stock. a. Stock ineligible if dividends not paid during each of past 5 years preceding purchase, unless such stock represents majority in control of outstanding stock.
$1\frac{1}{4}$a,[3]	b	Own, except for mutualization.	Preferred or guaranteed stocks of institution. a. Separate requirements specified for guaranteed stock—same as for corporate bonds whose eligibility is based on earnings (see Table 5A-2), with guaranteed dividends or covering rental included as fixed charge. b. Must be income paying.
	a		Corporate stocks. a. Dividend on last preceding dividend date not to be passed.
2^a		Own, except for mutualization.	Preferred stock of public utility companies. a. 2 times dividend requirements of public utility companies, in which mortgages, bonds, debentures, funded debts and preferred stock shall not exceed 70% of total capitalization.
4^b			Preferred stock of other companies. b. 4 times dividend requirements of other companies, in which mortgages, bonds, debentures, funded debts and preferred stocks shall not exceed 60% of total capitalization.
		Assessable (other than for taxes or wages). Own or other like insurers' except, as prescribed, to acquire its business and assets.	Corporate stock.
	a	Real estate corporation.	Corporate preferred stock. a. Dividend paying. Commissioner's approval required.
	a	Own. Assessable (other than for taxes). Manufacturing corporation with capital stock less than $25,000 or oil corporation with capital stock less than $500,000.	Corporate capital stock. a. No default by it or predecessor as to any debts within last 5 years.
3^b	a		Public utility corporation preferred stock. b. 3 times annual dividend requirements. Stock must be entitled to first claim on net earnings after deducting sum necessary to service bonds.
			Stock of national or state banks that are FDIC members.
$1\frac{3}{4}$a,[3]			Preferred or guaranteed stock of institution. a. "Net income" used instead of "net earnings." Separate requirements specified for guaranteed stocks—same as for corporate bonds whose eligibility is based on earnings (see Table 5A-2), with guaranteed dividends or covering rental included as fixed charge.

(Continued)

Eligibility Requirements Based on Earnings[2] and

| State | Number of Last Fiscal | | | |
	Years Stock Must Have Paid Dividends	Years Earnings Must Have Been Available	Years Earnings Requirements Must Be Fully Met	Minimum Earnings in Last Fiscal Years as % of Par or Stated Value
Vermont (cont.)		5		4
Virginia			Last 3	
Wisconsin		5		
		3[a]		

[1]This table does not cover business development corporation stock, building and loan or savings and loan association stock, housing or redevelopment company securities, investment company or trust securities, or foreign securities; or capital or deposit provisions.

[2]Iowa, Missouri, New York, Texas, Vermont, and Virginia require that all senior securities, if any, pass earnings or other tests as a condition for eligibility of preferred or guaranteed stock.

[3]"Preferred dividend requirement" means cumulative or non-cumulative dividends, whether paid or not.

Dividends			
Net Earnings Times Average Annual Fixed Charges, Maximum Contingent Interest, and Preferred Dividend Requirements	Requirement That Stock Be Dividend Paying and Not in Default When Acquired	Prohibited Classes of Corporations or Prohibited Types of Stock	Types Authorized, Miscellaneous, Notes, etc.[3]
			Corporate securities.
3a,b		Own, except for mutualization. Assessable (other than for taxes or wages).	Corporate preferred or guaranteed stock. a. 3 times annual dividend requirements. b. Separate requirements specified for guaranteed stock—guaranteeing corporation shall earn during each of last 3 fiscal years 2 times annual interest and guaranteed dividend requirements.
2		Holding companies.	Corporate preferred stock, approved by public authority if required at issue.
1½a			a. Alternative set of requirements.

119

Principal Statutory Standards of Selection in Nineteen Representative

Eligibility Requirements Based on Earnings[2] and Dividends

| State | Number of Last Fiscal | | Minimum Earnings in Last Fiscal Years as % of Par or Stated Value | Requirement That Stock Be Listed on Recognized Exchange |
	Years Stock Must Have Paid Dividends	Years Earnings Must Have Been Available		
California				
Connecticut	5[a]			
Illinois				
		3[a]	4[a]	Yes
		3[b,c]	4[f],[c]	
Indiana		7[a]	6[a]	
Iowa				
Massachusetts				
Minnesota				
		5	6[a]	
Missouri	5	5		Yes[a]
Nebraska		7[a]		
New Jersey	5[a]			
New York	10	10	4	Yes[a]

Requirement That Stock Be Dividend Paying and Not in Default When Acquired	Prohibited Classes of Corporations or Prohibited Types of Stock	Types Authorized, Miscellaneous, Notes, etc.[3]
		Corporate stock that qualifies as sound investment.
	Mining and manufacturing other than gas and electric.	Corporate stock. a. Must pay annual cash dividends of $3\frac{1}{2}\%$ of par or stated value (or that of eligible junior stock).
	Own (except for mutualization, employee plans, and as prescribed).	
	Insurance, banking, and real estate corporations.	Corporate capital stock. a. Earnings must have totaled 12% of price paid during 3 out of last 5 fiscal years.
	Real estate corporation.	Corporate capital stock. b. Standards apply to life company whose A&H premium income exceeds its life income. c. Earnings on industrial corporation shares must have totaled 12% during 3 out of last 5 years or 4% annually during tenure.
	Own, except for mutualization.[b]	Corporate common stock. a. Inapplicable to primary-subsidiary relationship between life insurer and another insurer. b. Leeway provision subject to this standard.
		Common stock.
	Own or other insurers' stock.[a] Assessable (other than for taxes).[a]	Corporate stock. a. Leeway clause (see Table 5A-8) subject to this standard but excepts Massachusetts trust company or New England national banking association capital stock meeting prescribed dividend and surplus requirements.
		Stock of banks and insurance companies.
		Common stock of other corporations. a. 6% must have been earned annually during 3 out of last 5 fiscal years.
	Own, except with superintendent's prior approval.	Common stock of corporation whose net worth at end of last fiscal year at least $10,000,000. a. Or quoted in established over-the-counter markets.
		See footnote 2.
	Own or other insurers' shares except may invest up to 50% of surplus to policyholders in other insurers' stocks, as prescribed.[b]	Corporate common stock. a. Earnings available for dividends for last 7 years shall be $250,000 annually, except $25,000 annually where corporation has majority of operations in Nebraska. b. Leeway provision subject to these provisions.
	Own, except for retirement or as specifically permitted.	Corporate capital stock. a. Stock ineligible if dividends not paid during each of past 5 years preceding purchase unless such stock represents majority in control of outstanding stock.
b	Own, except for mutualization.	Common stock of institution. a. Requirement inapplicable to stock of bank, trust company, or insurer. b. Must be income paying.
		See footnote 2.

(Continued)

121

Table 5A-5 (Continued)

| State | Eligibility Requirements Based on Earnings[2] and Dividends | | | |
| | Number of Last Fiscal | | Minimum Earnings in Last Fiscal Years as % of Par or Stated Value | Requirement That Stock Be Listed on Recognized Exchange |
	Years Stock Must Have Paid Dividends	Years Earnings Must Have Been Available		
North Carolina				
Ohio				
Pennsylvania				
Tennessee				
Texas	a			
Vermont	5	4		
Virginia	3a	5a		
Wisconsin	3a,b			

[1]This table does not cover shares in building and loan or savings and loan associations, business development companies, housing and redevelopment companies, or investment companies or trusts, or foreign securities; or capital and deposit provisions.

[2]Missouri and New York require that all senior securities, if any, pass earnings or other tests as a condition for eligibility of common stock. Under Texas law, an eligible corporation must not have defaulted in paying obligations during the previous 5 years.

[3]California requires acquisition at a price not exceeding market value or fair value.

Requirement That Stock Be Dividend Paying and Not in Default When Acquired	Prohibited Classes of Corporations or Prohibited Types of Stock	Types Authorized, Miscellaneous, Notes, etc.[3]
a		Corporate stock. a. Dividend paying—dividend at last preceding dividend date not to be passed.
	Own, except for mutualization.	
	Assessable (other than for taxes or wages).	Corporate stock.
	Own or other like insurers', except as prescribed, to acquire its business and assets.	
a	Real estate corporation.	Corporate common stock. a. Must be dividend paying. Commissioner's approval required.
a	Own.	Corporate capital stock. a. No default by it or predecessor as to any debts within last 5 years.
	Assessable (other than for taxes).	
	Manufacturing corporations with less than $25,000 capital stock and oil corporations with less than $500,000 capital stock.	See footnote 2.
		Stock of national or state banks that are FDIC members.
		Corporate securities.
	Own, except for mutualization. Assessable (other than for taxes or wages).	Common capital stock of bank or trust company which is FDIC member. a. Must earn 5% on total capital accounts for each of preceding 3 years.
	Holding company.	Corporate common stock. a. Earnings during any 3 of last 5 completed fiscal years (with adjustment for capitalization changes) must total 10% of price paid per share, or b. In the alternative, during last 3 fiscal years average annual net earnings available for fixed charges and dividends must equal $1\frac{1}{2}$ times average annual fixed charges maximum contingent interest, and preferred dividend requirements.

Principal Statutory Provisions in Nineteen Representative States as[1]

| State | Limits Under Provision Specifically Authorizing Purchase of Income Real Estate | | | | Limits Under a Leeway or Similar Provision[4] | |
| | Limits on Total Holdings[2] | | Limits on One Parcel[2] | | Limits on Total Holdings[2] | |
	As % of Insurance Co. Assets	As % of Insurance Co. Capital &/or Surplus[3]	As % of Insurance Co. Assets	As % of Insurance Co. Capital &/or Surplus[3]	As % of Insurance Co. Assets	As % of Insurance Co. Capital &/or Surplus[3]
California	10[a]		1			
Connecticut					8	
Illinois	10					
Indiana	8					
					10[a]	100[a,b]
Iowa	10[a]					
Massachusetts	5[a]		1			
					b	b
Minnesota	5		½ of 1			
Missouri	8		1	10		
Nebraska	5					
					5	
New Jersey	5					

to Income Real Estate Investments by Life Insurance Companies[1]

Provision That Property Primarily for Agricultural, Mining, or Certain Other Purposes Excluded	Provision That Other Property May Be Held Under Income Real Estate Provisions	Annual Write-Down, Amortization, etc.	Types of Income Real Estate Authorized Under Specific Provisions, Miscellaneous, Notes, etc.
Yes			Real estate and leases thereof; for business or residential purposes. Unexpired term of lease at purchase must be at least 24 years. a. There is also a 10% of assets limit on all real estate, except that for home office or transaction of business or acquired by gift or devise.
		Investment with 3% interest to 0 at end of primary term of lease or 40 years, if sooner.	Real estate under lease.
	Yes	2% of initial investment plus excess of net rent over 6% of such investment.	Real estate for leasing located in United States or Canada or territory or possession thereof. Requirements as to term, lessee, and its securities, prescribed. a. Leases to 1 corporation limited to 2% of assets. Leeway provision is subject to this limit. b. Capital, surplus and contingency reserves.
Yes[a]		Recovery of investment and return within anticipated useful life of personal property.	Real property (including leasehold) or personal property located within continental limits of United States or Dominion of Canada. a. 10% of legal reserve. b. Exclusion provision inapplicable to such personal property.
Yes	Yes	2%.	Real property or any interest therein in any state of United States where insurer authorized to do business. a. Aggregate real estate investments not to exceed 20% of assets. b. Leeway provision deals with funds other than $^3/_4$ reserves.
Yes		2%, and as prescribed.	Real property.
	Yes		Real estate or any interest therein.
			Leases to one individual, partnership or corporation limited to greater of 1% of assets or 10% of capital and surplus.
			Investment limited to new business or new industrial properties or new residential properties or new housing purposes, insurance superintendent's approval first having been obtained.
			Authorized foreign life insurers may make investments permitted Missouri life insurers.
	Yes[a]	2%. To 0 within lesser of $^8/_{10}$ unexpired term or 40 years from acquisition.	Domestic insurer with policyholders' surplus or unassigned funds of $1,000,000 may acquire real estate (including leasehold having at least 20 years unexpired term) in cities or towns, essentially residential or commercial in character. a. If Insurance Department consents.
	Yes[a]	Investment to 0 within lesser of $^8/_{10}$ unexpired term or 40 years after acquisition or improvement.	Real estate (including leasehold having at least 20 years unexpired term) for business or residential purposes. a. If Commissioner approves.

(Continued)

Table 5A-6 (Continued)

	Provision Specifically Authorizing Purchase of Income Real Estate				Limits Under a Leeway or Similar Provision[4]	
	Limits on Total Holdings[2]		Limits on One Parcel[2]		Limits on Total Holdings[2]	
State	As % of Insurance Co. Assets	As % of Insurance Co. Capital &/or Surplus[3]	As % of Insurance Co. Assets	As % of Insurance Co. Capital &/or Surplus[3]	As % of Insurance Co. Assets	As % of Insurance Co. Capital &/or Surplus[3]
New Jersey (contd.)					2	
New York	5[a]		.005% of assets to 500 million, .0025% thereof over 500 million[a]			a
North Carolina	6[a]	50[a]				
Ohio	10					
Pennsylvania	10[a]					
					5[b]	
Tennessee	10[a]		2			
Vermont	10[a]					

Provision That Property Primarily for Agricultural, Mining, or Certain Other Purposes Excluded	Provision That Other Property May Be Held Under Income Real Estate Provisions	Annual Write-Down, Amortization, etc.	Types of Income Real Estate Authorized Under Specific Provisions, Miscellaneous, Notes, etc.
			Foreign or alien insurer transacting business in New Jersey may purchase, etc., real estate there but only for purposes and in manner permitted New Jersey insurers.
Yes	Yes	2%, and as prescribed.	Real property. a. Aggregate of income real estate held under leeway and specific authorization provisions is subject to limits in latter. Leeway limit on total holdings is 2% of assets.
		To ¼ of investment within lesser of normal term or 30 years.	Real estate for leasing. Requirements as to improvements prescribed. a. No investment in real property for leasing or employee facilities to cause total real property investment to exceed 10% of assets.
			Real estate, and personal property in connection therewith, for leasing within United States.
			Requirements as to lessee and its securities and earnings prescribed.
	Yes	2%	Real estate or any interest therein for renting for business, commercial or industrial use. a. Aggregate limit for income and housing real estate and stock of income or housing real estate corporations.
			With Commissioner's approval domestic life insurer may participate with other authorized insurers in ownership and control of income real estate. b. Authorized as to investment of surplus and last ¼ of reserves.
			Foreign or alien insurer authorized in Pennsylvania may acquire real property there, participate with other authorized insurers in ownership and control of real estate, and invest in capital stock and obligations of corporations organized to acquire Pennsylvania real estate, in same manner and subject to same limitations as Pennsylvania insurers.
			Real property. a. Aggregate limit on all real estate.
			No investments in hotels, clubhouses, garages, schools, factories for special purposes or agricultural properties without Commissioner's advance specific approval.
Yes[b]		Investment to 0 during lease.	Real property or any interest therein within U.S., or personal property or any interest therein, for leasing. a. 5% of assets limit on personal property.

(Continued)

Table 5A-6 (Continued)

| State | Limits Under Provision Specifically Authorizing Purchase of Income Real Estate | | | | Limits Under a Leeway or Similar Provision[4] | |
| | Limits on Total Holdings[2] | | Limits on One Parcel[2] | | Limits on Total Holdings[2] | |
	As % of Insurance Co. Assets	As % of Insurance Co. Capital &/or Surplus[3]	As % of Insurance Co. Assets	As % of Insurance Co. Capital &/or Surplus[3]	As % of Insurance Co. Assets	As % of Insurance Co. Capital &/or Surplus[3]
Vermont (contd.)						
					3	
Virginia	5a					
	5a,b					
					c	
Wisconsin	5					
					5	

[1]No pertinent statutory provisions were found for Texas.

[2]When figures appear in both columns under this heading, the smaller amount controls except in Missouri, where the larger amount is effective.

[3]The percentage figure usually refers to capital and surplus in the case of stock insurers, and to surplus, in the case of mutual insurers.

[4]These limits are additional to any limits on total holdings permitted under a specific authorization provision.

Provision That Property Primarily for Agricultural, Mining, or Certain Other Purposes Excluded	Provision That Other Property May Be Held Under Income Real Estate Provisions	Annual Write-Down, Amortization, etc.	Types of Income Real Estate Authorized Under Specific Provisions, Miscellaneous, Notes, etc.
			Requirements as to lessee, term and financial standing of lessee prescribed. b. Exclusion provision inapplicable to such personal property.
		Investment to 0 at end of lease or 50 years, if sooner.	Real property for leasing. a. Such income real property and all other real property not to exceed 15% of assets.
			Requirements as to term, improvements, lessee, etc., prescribed.
Yes	Yes	2%. Investment to 0 within lesser of $^8/_{10}$ unexpired term or 40 years after acquisition.	Real property (including leasehold on housing development). b. Aggregate income real estate investments during any 12 month period not to exceed 2% of assets.
			c. Capital and surplus in excess of minimum capital and surplus.
			Real estate (including leasehold) within continental limits of United States or Dominion of Canada.

129

Principal Statutory Limits in Nineteen Representative States as

Limits Under Provision Specifically Authorizing
Purchase of Corporate Bonds

State	Limits on Total Holdings[2]		Limits on Holdings in One Issuer[2]	
	As % of Insurance Co. Assets	As % of Insurance Co. Capital &/or Surplus[3]	As % of Insurance Co. Assets	As % of Insurance Co. Capital &/or Surplus[3]
California				
Connecticut				
Illinois	33⅓		a	
	33⅓		a	
	33⅓		a	
		100		
		b	2c	
Indiana			2a	
Iowa	a		b	
	c			
Massachusetts				
	a			
	5			
Minnesota				
Missouri			1	

to Acquisition of Corporate Bonds by Life Insurance Companies[1]

Limits Under a Leeway or Similar Provision[4]		
Limits on Total Holdings[2]		
As % of Insurance Co. Assets	As % of Insurance Co. Capital &/or Surplus[3]	Types of Corporate Bonds Authorized Under Specific Provisions, Miscellaneous, Notes, etc.
		Corporate bonds, etc.
8		Corporate bonds.
		Railroad (but not holding) corporation bonds, etc. a. Limit is 2% of assets in any one issue.
		Public utility (but not holding) corporation bonds, etc.
		Bonds, etc., of other (but not holding) corporations.
		Bonds, etc., of corporations, other than real estate corporations. (Authorized for domestic life insurer whose A&H premium income exceeds its life premium income).
		Securities of corporation other than another insurer, bank, or real estate corporation. b. Limit is 50% of excess of capital and/or surplus over minimum capital and original surplus. c. Limit as to shares and securities.
5		
		Corporate bonds, etc. a. Limit on bonds and capital stock of, and real estate leased to, one corporation. This limit inapplicable to bond investments in subsidiary insurer. Leeway investments are subject to this limit of 2% of assets as to bonds, etc., of one corporation.
10a	100a,b	b. Capital, surplus, and contingency reserves.
		Corporate bonds, etc. a. 50% of legal reserve. b. Limit on corporate bonds, preferred stock, and equipment trust obligations of one corporation is 2% of legal reserve.
		Railroad bonds, etc. c. 10% of legal reserve.
		Bonds, etc., or mortgage bonds, of certain railroad corporations.
		Mortgage bonds of railroad corporation whose liens junior to such bonds equal $\frac{1}{3}$ funded indebtedness secured by such bonds and prior bonds.
		Bonds, etc., of the American Telephone and Telegraph Company or its subsidiary or affiliated operating companies.
		First mortgage bonds, whose issue subject to regulatory body, of companies engaged directly and primarily in:
		Telephone and telegraph systems or electric light or power companies.
		Gas companies.
		Water companies.
		Bonds, etc., of corporations and of certain associations or trusts. a. Limit is $\frac{1}{2}$ reserve.
b	b	Bonds, etc., of companies and of certain associations or trusts secured by assignment of certain leases. b. Leeway provision deals with funds other than $\frac{3}{4}$ reserve.
		Bonds, etc., of railway and other public utility corporations, and debentures of farm mortgage debenture companies.
		Bonds, etc., of other corporations.
		Corporate bonds, etc.

(Continued)

Table 5A-7 (Continued)

State	Limits Under Provision Specifically Authorizing Purchase of Corporate Bonds			
	Limits on Total Holdings[2]		Limits on Holdings in One Issuer[2]	
	As % of Insurance Co. Assets	As % of Insurance Co. Capital &/or Surplus[3]	As % of Insurance Co. Assets	As % of Insurance Co. Capital &/or Surplus[3]
Nebraska				
			a	
New Jersey				10a
New York			5	
	½ of 1a,b			
North Carolina				
Ohio			a	
			a	
			a	
			a	
Pennsylvania				
Tennessee				
Texas			5	
		100a		
	5			
Vermont			2½	
	3a			

Limits Under a Leeway or Similar Provision[4]		Types of Corporate Bonds Authorized Under Specific Provisions, Miscellaneous, Notes, etc.
Limits on Total Holdings[2]		
As % of Insurance Co. Assets	As % of Insurance Co. Capital &/or Surplus[3]	
		Railroad mortgage bonds, etc.
		Public utility revenue bonds, etc.
		Public utility mortgage bonds, etc.
		Mortgage bonds, etc., of other corporations. a. Limit is 3% of assets in any one issue.
5		Mortgage or collateral trust bonds of railroads, corporate bonds, etc. a. Limit on bonds, equipment trust certificates and receivers' certificates of one corporation. Up to $50,000, par value, of bonds of any corporation may be held if none of its stock is held.
2		Corporate bonds, etc., meeting standards (see Table 5A-2).
1½b		Other corporate obligations not qualifying under any paragraphs of §81(2) (see Table 5A-2). a. Inapplicable to reorganization securities. b. Leeway clause expressly permits investment thereunder up to 1½% of assets in excess of ½ of 1% of assets limit in specific authority provision.
		Corporate bonds, etc.
		First lien railroad mortgage bonds. a. Limit is 1% of assets as to bonds, etc., and preferred stock of one issuer.
		Junior railroad mortgage bonds.
		Mortgage bonds, etc., of terminal companies assumed or guaranteed by 2 or more railroads whose bonds eligible above.
		First lien utility company mortgage bonds.
		Corporate bonds, etc.
5		Bonds, etc., of railroad or public utility corporations. (Capital and ¾ reserves).
		Bonds, etc., of other corporations. (Capital and ¾ reserves).
		Corporate bonds, etc. (Surplus and ¼ of reserves).
5		Mortgage bonds of dividend-paying railway or street railway companies or other good and solvent securities, approved by Commissioner.
		Corporate first mortgage bonds or debentures of corporation with $5,000,000 capital stock.
		Corporate bonds, etc. a. Capital, surplus and contingency funds over policy reserves.
		Public utility corporation debentures.
		Corporate bonds, etc.
		Corporate or trust securities. a. Limit on corporate or trust securities and registered investment company or trust shares.
		Bonds, etc., of land companies which own, operate, etc., real estate foreclosed by life insurer.
3		

133

(Continued)

| | Limits Under Provision Specifically Authorizing Purchase of Corporate Bonds | | | |
| | Limits on Total Holdings[2] | | Limits on Holdings in One Issuer[2] | |
State	As % of Insurance Co. Assets	As % of Insurance Co. Capital &/or Surplus[3]	As % of Insurance Co. Assets	As % of Insurance Co. Capital &/or Surplus[3]
Virginia			5[5]	
	10		5[5],a	
			5[5],a	
Wisconsin			10a	
			10a	
			10a	
			10a,b	
			10a,c	

[1] This table does not cover equipment trust obligations, receivers' certificates, investment company or trust securities deposit provisions.

[2] When figures appear in both columns under this heading, the smaller amount controls.

[3] The percentage figure usually refers to capital and surplus in the case of stock insurers, and to surplus in the case

[4] These limits are additional to any limits on total holdings permitted under a specific authorization provision.

[5] Limit on all securities, etc., of one issuer.

Limits Under a Leeway or Similar Provision[4]		
Limits on Total Holdings[2]		
As % of Insurance Co. Assets	As % of Insurance Co. Capital &/or Surplus[3]	Types of Corporate Bonds Authorized Under Specific Provisions, Miscellaneous, Notes, etc.
		Bonds, etc., secured by first mortgage or other lien on terminal, depot or tunnel property used by railroad whose bonds, etc., eligible under (A) or (B).
		(A) Other corporate bonds, etc. (Eligibility based on security—see Table 5A-2). a. Limit is 2% of assets in any one issue.
		(B) Other corporate bonds, etc. (Eligibility based on earnings—see Table 5A-2).
	100[b]	b. Excess of capital and surplus over minimum capital and surplus.
		(A) Bonds, etc., of terminal, belt line, and railroad companies. a. Limit on securities of one corporation.
		(B) Bonds, etc., of public utilities.
		(C) Evidence of indebtedness of public utilities, in addition to (B).
		(D) Bonds, etc., of other (but not holding) corporations in addition to (A), (B), (C), and (E). b. Limit is 2% of assets in any one issue.
		(E) Evidence of indebtedness of other (but not holding) corporations, in addition to (A), (B), (C), and (D), approved by public authority, if required at issue. c. Limit is 1% of assets in any one issue.

5

Principal Statutory Limits in Nineteen Representative States as to

Limits Under Provision Specifically Authorizing
Purchase of Preferred or Guaranteed Stock

State	Limits on Total Holdings[2]		Limits on Holdings in One Issuer[2]		
	As % of Insurance Co. Assets	As % of Insurance Co. Capital &/or Surplus[3]	As % of Insurance Co. Assets	As % of Insurance Co. Capital &/or Surplus[3]	As % of Issuer's Stock
California				25	30[a]
Connecticut					
Illinois	10		a		
		50[b,c]	2[c]		5
		100[d]	5[e]		5[e]
		50[f]			
Indiana	10[a,c,d]		2[b,c,d]		
Iowa	10[a]		2[a]		
Massachusetts					
Minnesota	7[b]				
	b				20[a]
	10[b]				
Missouri	5		1		5

Preferred or Guaranteed Stock Held by Life Insurance Companies[1]

Limits Under a Leeway or Similar Provision[4]		Types of Preferred or Guaranteed Stock Authorized Under Specific Provisions, Miscellaneous, Notes, etc.
Limits on Total Holdings[2]		
As % of Insurance Co. Assets	As % of Insurance Co. Capital &/or Surplus[3]	
		Corporate stock. a. Inapplicable as to purchase of stock of other insurers, as prescribed; 50% of capital and surplus limit as to such insurance company stock.
8		Preferred or guaranteed stock of corporation (except other insurer). a. 2% of assets limit as to any one issue. Capital stock of corporation (except other insurer, bank, or real estate corporation). b. 50% of excess of capital and/or surplus over minimum capital and original surplus. c. Limit on shares or securities of corporation. Capital stock of corporation (except real estate corporation). d. Authorized for life company whose A&H premium income exceeds its life premium income. e. Limit on industrial corporation stock. f. Limit on insurance company stock.
5		Corporate preferred or guaranteed stock. a. Limit on preferred, guaranteed, and common stock. b. Limit on bonds, etc., and capital stock of, and real estate leased to, one corporation. c. Inapplicable where investment, as prescribed, effects between life insurer and another insurer primary-subsidiary relationship or enlarges life company's investment in subsidiary insurer. Limit on investments in subsidiary insurers is 7% of assets. d. Aggregate of stock held under leeway and specific authorization provisions is subject to limits in latter. Leeway limit is lesser of 10% of assets or aggregate capital, surplus, and contingency reserves.
d[c]	d[c]	Corporate preferred or guaranteed stock. a. % of legal reserve, not assets.
a	a	Corporate stock. a. Leeway provision is subject to following limits: 10% of capital and surplus as to stock of 1 corporation and 10% of capital stock of 1 corporation. Excepted are Massachusetts trust company and New England national banking association capital stock meeting prescribed standards and limits. The leeway provision deals with funds other than $^3/_4$ reserve. Stock of banks and insurers. Preferred or guaranteed stock of other corporations. a. Limit on preferred and common stocks of other than bank or insurer is 10% of aggregate par or stated value of such stocks. b. Limit on all stocks is 10% of assets. Corporate preferred or guaranteed stock. With Superintendent's prior approval, domestic insurer may acquire and hold at least $^2/_3$ of other insurer's stock for purpose of common control.

(Continued)

137

Table 5A-8 (Continued)

| | Limits Under Provision Specifically Authorizing Purchase of Preferred or Guaranteed Stock | | | | |
| | Limits on Total Holdings[2] | | Limits on Holdings in One Issuer[2] | | |
State	As % of Insurance Co. Assets	As % of Insurance Co. Capital &/or Surplus[3]	As % of Insurance Co. Assets	As % of Insurance Co. Capital &/or Surplus[3]	As % of Issuer's Stock
Nebraska	10				5[a]
New Jersey			2[a]		5[b]
New York			2[a]		20[a]
North Carolina	10[a]		3[a]		20[b]
Ohio		100[a]			
		100[a]			
Pennsylvania			2[a]		
Tennessee		a	2[b]		c
Texas		100[a]		10[a]	
	2½				20[b]
Vermont	5				5

Limits Under a Leeway or Similar Provision[4]		
Limits on Total Holdings[2]		
As % of Insurance Co. Assets	As % of Insurance Co. Capital &/or Surplus[3]	Types of Preferred or Guaranteed Stock Authorized Under Specific Provisions, Miscellaneous, Notes, etc.
		Corporate preferred stock.
		a. Limit as to total issue of stocks of company inapplicable to common and preferred stock of insurer.
		Domestic insurer meeting asset requirements may acquire all or part of stock of another insurer up to 50% of total surplus to policy-holders.
		Corporate capital stock.
		a. Limit on stock.
		b. Applies only as to voting stock.
2		
		Preferred or guaranteed stock of institution.
		a. Aggregate of preferred or guaranteed stock held under leeway and specific authorization provisions is subject to limits in latter. Lee-way limit on total holdings is 2% of assets.
a		
		Corporate stock.
		a. Limit on stocks.
		b. Limit on voting stock of corporation not engaged solely in insurance business, except as Commissioner permits.
		Utility company preferred stock.
		a. Capital, surplus, and contingency funds.
		Preferred stock of other companies.
5b		b. Applies only to Ohio legal reserve life insurers.
		Corporate stock.
		a. Limit on stock.
		Domestic life insurer may acquire and temporarily hold majority of voting stock of another insurer transacting like classes of business but solely to acquire its business and assets.
5		
		Preferred stock of corporation (other than real estate company).
		a. Limit on preferred and common stocks is 50% of excess of capital and surplus over minimum capital and surplus, and 100% of such excess, if secured by reserves equal to 50% of such excess. Commissioner's approval required.
		b. Limit on stock.
		c. Limit on stock of bank or insurer is 5% of outstanding stock, but domestic life insurer may acquire over 75% of stock of another insurer where no monopoly, etc.
		Capital stock of corporation (other than manufacturing corporation with less than $25,000 capital stock or oil corporation with less than $500,000 capital stock).
		a. Capital, surplus, and contingency funds.
		Preferred stock of public utility corporations.
		Stock of state or national banks which are FDIC members.
		b. Limit as to such bank stock and insured building and loan or savings and loan association shares.
		Preferred or guaranteed stock of institution.

(Continued)

139

Table 5A-8 (Continued)

| State | Limits Under Provision Specifically Authorizing Purchase of Preferred or Guaranteed Stock | | | | |
| | Limits on Total Holdings[2] | | Limits on Holdings in One Issuer[2] | | |
	As % of Insurance Co. Assets	As % of Insurance Co. Capital &/or Surplus[3]	As % of Insurance Co. Assets	As % of Insurance Co. Capital &/or Surplus[3]	As % of Issuer's Stock
Vermont (contd.)	3a				
Virginia	10a		5[5]; b		
	10a		5[5]; b		
Wisconsin	5		½ of 1; 10[6]		

---

[1]This table does not cover business development corporation stock, building and loan or savings and loan association stock, housing, income real estate, or redevelopment company securities, investment company or trust securities, or foreign securities; or capital or deposit provisions.

[2]When figures appear in both the % of Assets and % of Capital &/or Surplus columns under this heading, the smaller amount controls.

[3]The percentage figure usually refers to capital and surplus in the case of stock insurers, and to surplus in the case of mutual insurers.

[4]These limits are additional to any limits on total holdings permitted under a specific authorization provision.

[5]Limit on all securities, etc., of one issuer.

[6]Limit on all securities of one corporation.

Limits Under a Leeway or Similar Provision[4]			
Limits on Total Holdings[2]			
As % of Insurance Co. Assets	As % of Insurance Co. Capital &/or Surplus[3]		Types of Preferred or Guaranteed Stock Authorized Under Specific Provisions, Miscellaneous, Notes, etc.
			Corporate securities.
			a. Limit as to certain investment company or trust shares and corporate or trust securities.
3			
			Corporate preferred stock.
			a. 20% of assets limit on preferred and guaranteed stock and common capital stock of bank or trust company which is FDIC member.
			b. Limit is 1% of assets in one issue.
			Corporate guaranteed stock.
		c	c. Excess capital and surplus over minimum capital and surplus.
			Preferred stock of corporation (other than holding corporation), approved by public authority, if required at issue.
5			

Principal Statutory Limits in Nineteen Representative States

Limits Under Provision Specifically Authorizing
Purchase of Common Stock

State	Limits on Total Holdings[2]		Limits on Holdings in One Issuer[2]		
	As % of Insurance Co. Assets	As % of Insurance Co. Capital &/or Surplus[3]	As % of Insurance Co. Assets	As % of Insurance Co. Capital &/or Surplus[3]	As % of Issuer's Stock
California				25	30[a]
Connecticut					
Illinois		50[a,b]	2[b]		5
		100[c] 50[e]	5[d]		5[d]
Indiana	10[a,c,d]		2[b,c,d]		
Iowa		a			
Massachusetts					
Minnesota	7[a] a 10[a]				10

as to Common Stock Held by Life Insurance Companies[1]

Limits Under a Leeway or Similar Provision[4]		Types of Common Stock Authorized Under Specific Provisions, Miscellaneous, Notes, etc.
Limits on Total Holdings[2]		
As % of Insurance Co. Assets	As % of Insurance Co. Capital &/or Surplus[3]	
		Corporate stock.
		a. Inapplicable as to purchase of stock of other insurers, as prescribed; 50% of capital and surplus limit as to such insurance company stock.
8		
		(A) Capital stock of corporation (except other insurer, bank, or real estate corporation).
		a. 50% of excess of capital and/or surplus over minimum capital and original surplus.
		b. Limit on shares or securities of corporation.
		(B) Capital stock of corporation (except real estate corporation).
		c. Authorized for life company whose A&H premium income exceeds its life premium income.
		d. Limit on industrial corporation stock.
		e. Limit on insurance company stock.
5f		f. Aggregate held under leeway provision and (A) not to exceed 50% of excess of capital, surplus, voluntary reserves, and reserves for security fluctuations over minimum capital and original surplus requirements.
		Corporate common stock.
		a. Limit on preferred, guaranteed, and common stock.
		b. Limit on bonds, etc., and capital stock of, and real estate leased to, one corporation.
		c. Inapplicable where investment, as prescribed, effects between life insurer and another insurer primary-subsidiary relationship or enlarges life company's investment in subsidiary insurer. Limit on investments in subsidiary insurers is 7% of assets.
d[c]	d[c]	d. Aggregate of stock held under leeway and specific authorization provisions is subject to limits in latter. Leeway limit is lesser of 10% of assets or aggregate of capital, surplus and contingency reserves.
		Corporate common stocks.
		a. Limit on investment from surplus is 5% of funds.
a	a	Corporate stock.
		a. Leeway provision is subject to following limits: 10% of capital and surplus as to stock of 1 corporation and 10% of capital stock of 1 corporation. Excepted are Massachusetts trust company and New England National banking association capital stock meeting prescribed standards and limits. The leeway provision deals with funds other than $3/4$ reserve.
		Stock of banks and insurers.
		Common stock of other corporations.
		a. Limit on all stocks is 10% of assets.

(Continued)

Table 5A-9 (Continued)

| | Limits Under Provision Specifically Authorizing Purchase of Common Stock | | | | |
| | Limits on Total Holdings[2] | | Limits on Holdings in One Issuer[2] | | |
State	As % of Insurance Co. Assets	As % of Insurance Co. Capital &/or Surplus[3]	As % of Insurance Co. Assets	As % of Insurance Co. Capital &/or Surplus[3]	As % of Issuer's Stock
Missouri	5	50	½ of 1		5[a]
Nebraska	10[a]				5[b]
New Jersey			2[a]		5
New York	5[b]	50[a,b]	⅛ of 1[b]		2[b]
North Carolina	10[a]		3		20[b]
Ohio					
Pennsylvania	5[a]	2[b]			
Tennessee		a	2[b]		c
Texas		100[a]		10[a]	
					20[b]

Limits Under a Leeway or Similar Provision[4]		
Limits on Total Holdings[2]		
As % of Insurance Co. Assets	As % of Insurance Co. Capital &/or Surplus[3]	Types of Common Stock Authorized Under Specific Provisions, Miscellaneous, Notes, etc.
		Common stock of corporation whose net worth at least $10,000,000. a. Limit on preferred and common stock. With Superintendent's prior approval, domestic insurer may acquire and hold at least $\frac{2}{3}$ of other insurer's stock for purpose of common control.
		Corporate common stock. a. Limit as to common stock and investment trust shares, etc. b. 5% of common stock and 5% of total issue of stocks of a company other than common or preferred stock of an insurer. Domestic insurer meeting asset requirements may acquire all or part of stock of another insurer up to 50% of total surplus to policyholders.
2		Corporate capital stock a. Limit on stock.
b		Common stock of institution. a. 50% of surplus to policyholders. b. Aggregate of common stock held under leeway and specific authorization provisions is subject to limits in latter. Leeway limit on total holdings is 2% of assets.
		Corporate stock. a. Limit on stocks. b. Limit on voting stock of corporation not engaged solely in insurance business, except as Commissioner permits.
5ᵃ		a. Applies only to Ohio legal reserve life insurers.
		Corporate stock. a. Limit is 5% of assets, or surplus plus $\frac{1}{4}$ of reserves, whichever is smaller. b. Limit on stock. Domestic life insurer may acquire and temporarily hold majority of voting stock of another insurer transacting like classes of business but solely to acquire its business and assets.
		Common stock of corporation (other than real estate company). a. Limit on common and preferred stock is 50% of excess of capital and surplus over minimum capital and surplus, and 100% of such excess, if secured by reserves equal to 50% of such excess. Commissioner's approval required. b. Limit on stock. c. Limit on stock of bank or insurer is 5% of outstanding stock, but domestic life insurer may acquire over 75% of stock of another insurer where no monopoly, etc.
		Capital stock of corporation (other than manufacturing corporation with less than $25,000 capital stock or oil corporation with less than $500,000 capital stock). a. Capital, surplus, and contingency funds.
		Stock of state or national banks which are FDIC members. b. Limit as to such bank stock and insured building and loan or savings and loan association shares.

(Continued)

145

State	Limits Under Provision Specifically Authorizing Purchase of Common Stock				
	Limits on Total Holdings[2]		Limits on Holdings in One Issuer[2]		
	As % of Insurance Co. Assets	As % of Insurance Co. Capital &/or Surplus[3]	As % of Insurance Co. Assets	As % of Insurance Co. Capital &/or Surplus[3]	As % of Issuer's Stock
Vermont	3a				
Virginia	5a		5[5]		10
Wisconsin	5		½ of 1, 10[6]		

---

[1]This table does not cover equipment trust obligations, receivers' certificates, investment company or trust securities, housing or redevelopment company securities, business development company bonds, foreign securities; or capital or deposit provisions.

[2]When figures appear in both columns under this heading, the smaller amount controls.

[3]The percentage figure usually refers to capital and surplus in the case of stock insurers, and to surplus in the case of mutual insurers.

[4]These limits are additional to any limits on total holdings permitted under a specific authorization provision.

[5]Limit on all securities, etc., of one issuer.

Limits Under a Leeway or Similar Provision[4]		
Limits on Total Holdings[2]		
As % of Insurance Co. Assets	As % of Insurance Co. Capital &/or Surplus[3]	Types of Common Stock Authorized Under Specific Provisions, Miscellaneous, Notes, etc.
		Corporate securities. a. Limit as to certain investment company or trust shares and corporate or trust securities.
3		Common capital stock of bank or trust company which is FDIC member. a. 20% of assets limit on preferred, guaranteed, and such stock.
	b	b. Excess capital and surplus over minimum capital and surplus.
5		Common stock of company (other than holding corporation), approved by public authority if required at issue.

147

TABLE 5A-10
Life Insurance Company Investments Under Leeway Statutes in Nineteen Representative States[1]

State	Nature of Leeway Statute			Aggregate Limit	
	Permits Loans or Investments	But Expressly Subject to Following Principal		% of Assets	% of Capital and/or Surplus
		Standards	Limits		
Connecticut	Not qualifying or permitted under charter or general statutes.			8	
Illinois	Without regard to restrictions in or provisions of main investment sections (§§737-737.15, incl., 740, Ch. 73, Smith-Hurd Ann. St.)		As to common stock: 50% of excess of capital, surplus, voluntary reserve, etc., over minimum capital and surplus.	5	
Indiana	Not conforming to preceding categories, standards and limits in section.	Own stock prohibited except as to mutualization.	2% of assets as to bonds, etc., and capital stock of, and real estate leased to, single corporation; 10% of assets as to preferred, guaranteed, and common stocks; these two limits inapplicable, as prescribed, to investment in subsidiary insurer.	10[2]	100[2]
Massachusetts	In any manner directors determine.	Own or other insurer stock prohibited, also assessable (except for taxes) stock or evidence of indebtedness, except certain Massachusetts trust company and New England national banking association capital stock, as prescribed.	10% of capital and surplus in stock of 1 corporation; 10% of capital stock of 1 corporation; except certain Massachusetts trust company and New England national banking association capital stock, as prescribed.	[3]	[3]

State				
Minnesota	Conforming to preceding categories and standards in section but exceeding prescribed limits.		10% of assets as to all stocks.	2
Nebraska	In property not otherwise qualified for investment, subject to directors' approval.	Own or other insurer shares prohibited, except as prescribed.	5% of common stock, and 5% of total issue of stock, of 1 company other than insurer; 10% of assets in preferred stock described in §44-309(9); 10% of assets in common stock and investment trust shares, described in §44-309(10) (11); 50% of surplus to policyholders in stock of another insurer, as prescribed.	5
New Jersey	Not qualifying or permitted under preceding subsections.			2
New York	Not qualifying under foregoing subdivisions.		Limits provided in other subdivisions and sections as to authorized types of investments, except additional 1½% of assets may be invested in bonds under §81(2) (last par.)	2
Ohio	Not permitted under main investment section.			5
Pennsylvania	Not qualifying or permitted under preceding subsections.			5
Vermont	Not qualifying or permitted under charter or other sections.			3

149

(Continued)

State	Nature of Leeway Statute		Aggregate Limit	
	Permits Loans or Investments	But Expressly Subject to Following Principal Limits	% of Assets	% of Capital and/or Surplus
		Standards		
Virginia	Directors or investment committee determine to be for best interest of insurer.		[4]	[4]
Wisconsin	Not qualifying or permitted under charter or other pro- visions or sections.		5	

[1] In the 19 states covered by these tables, no pertinent leeway provisions were found in California, Iowa, Missouri, North Carolina, Tennessee, or Texas.
[2] Lesser of 10% of assets or aggregate of capital, surplus, and contingency reserves.
[3] Leeway provisions deal with funds over $3/4$ reserve.
[4] Excess capital and surplus over minimum capital and surplus.

Statutes in Nineteen Representative States Permitting Unsecured Loans by Life Insurance Companies to Unincorporated Small Businesses

| | Directly Permitted | | Indirectly Permitted |
| | Leeway | | |
State	% of Assets	% of Capital and/or Surplus	Business Development or Credit Corporations and Other Organizations
Connecticut	8		Connecticut Development Credit Corporation.
Illinois	5		
Indiana	10^2	100^2	
Massachusetts			Massachusetts Business Development Corporation.
Minnesota	5		Development Corporations.
Nebraska	5		
New Jersey	2		Business Development Corporations.
New York	2		New York Business Development Corporation.
North Carolina			North Carolina Business Development Corporations.
Ohio	5		
Pennsylvania	5		Business Development Credit Corporations.
Tennessee			Development Credit Corporations. Small Business Investment Companies.
Vermont	3		
Virginia		[3]	Industrial Development Corporations.
Wisconsin	5		Business Development Credit Corporations.

[1] In the 19 states covered by these tables no pertinent statutory provisions as to such loans were found in California, Iowa, Missouri, or Texas.
[2] Lesser of 10% of assets or aggregate of capital, surplus, and contingency reserves.
[3] Excess of capital and surplus over minimum capital and surplus.

TABLE 5A-12

Statutory Provisions in Nineteen Representative States as to Investments by Life Insurers in Foreign Securities[1]
(Excluding those limited to Canada only)

State	Authorized Types	Limits on Holdings of Securities of or in Foreign Country[2]	Leeway Limits[2]
California	Securities in foreign country, where company admitted or its risks located, of substantially same kinds and grades as those eligible under code.	Aggregate investment not to exceed greater of (1) amount insurer required to invest there or (2) $1\frac{1}{2}$ times reserves and other obligations under such contracts.	
Connecticut			8% of assets.
Illinois	Investments required for deposit required by foreign country where insurer admitted.	Not exceeding deposit.	
	Securities of foreign country where life insurer (whose A&H premium income exceeds its life premium income) operating or of its political subdivision.	Not exceeding total unearned premium reserve of policies issued in foreign country or in amount required to transact business there.	5% of assets (special limitation as to common stocks).
Indiana	Investments legal for life insurers domiciled in foreign country or doing business there as alien companies.	May invest funds equal to obligations in foreign country.	Lesser of 10% of assets or 100% of capital, surplus and contingency reserves (subject to stock and real estate limitations).
Iowa[3]			
Massachusetts[3]			Funds other than $^3/_4$ of reserve— various restrictions as to stock and evidence of indebtedness.

152

(Continued)

Minnesota	Securities of foreign country where doing business, of kind authorized for investment in Minnesota.	May invest funds required to meet obligations incurred in foreign country.
Missouri	Bonds of foreign country required to do business there.	
Nebraska[3]		5% of assets, subject to stock limitations.
New Jersey	Securities of governing body or agency or corporation of foreign country where lawfully doing business, of character otherwise authorized.	May invest funds not exceeding value of outstanding policies issued or delivered in foreign country. 2% of assets.
New York	Securities and investments in foreign country, where admitted or risks resident or located, of substantially same kinds or grades as those eligible under foregoing subdivisions of §81.	May invest not exceeding greater of (1) 1½ times reserves and other obligations under such contracts or (2) amount insurer required to invest in foreign country.
	Securities and investments in foreign countries. Of substantially same kinds and grades as those eligible under foregoing subdivisions of §81.	1% of admitted assets.
Ohio[3]		5% of assets.
Pennsylvania	Securities of foreign government to comply with its laws and do business there.	Insurance Commissioner may permit investment of sufficient capital and reserves to so comply. 5% of assets.
Texas[3]		

153

Table 5A-12 (Continued)

State	Authorized Types	Limits on Holdings of Securities of or in Foreign Country[2]	Leeway Limits[2]
Vermont[3]			3% of assets.
Virginia	Securities of or in foreign country, where transacting insurance, of substantially same kinds and grades permitted in U.S.	May invest funds not exceeding deposit and reserve obligations incurred in foreign country.	Capital and surplus in excess of minimum capital and surplus.
Wisconsin[3]	Securities in countries other than U.S. and Canada of substantially same kinds and grades as those eligible under subsection (other than leeway).	2% of assets.	5% of assets.

[1] In the 19 states covered by these tables no pertinent statutory provisions as to such foreign securities were found in North Carolina or Tennessee. Statutory provisions dealing specifically with real estate mortgages (see Table 5A-3) are not covered by this table.

[2] The limit on aggregate holdings is given unless otherwise specified.

[3] Some statutory provisions in this state authorize investment in certain securities issued by a "corporation." It may be argued that literally "corporation," without restriction as to state or country of creation, includes corporations of another country, and hence, foreign securities. On the other hand, it may be contended that, because of the public policy and purpose behind such a regulatory law, "corporation" was intended to refer only to corporations created in the United States, and their securities, not to securities of any corporation anywhere.

[4] Investment under the New York leeway clause, which has a 2% of assets limit, would be subject to the limits set forth in the column adjoining on the left.

154

TABLE 5A-13

Statutory Provisions in Nineteen Representative States as to Investments by Life Insurers in Canadian Securities[1]
(Foreign securities limited to Canada only)

State	Authorized Types of Canadian Securities	Limits on Holdings of Securities[2] of or in	
		U.S. and Canada	Canada Only
California	Dominion or province obligations.		
	Political subdivision obligations.		
	Corporate obligations.		
	Corporate stocks.	10% of capital and surplus.	
	Equipment trust obligations.		
Illinois	Securities permitted like companies by Dominion or province (also applicable to life insurer whose A&H premium income exceeds its life premium income).		5% of assets.
Indiana	Dominion or province bonds, etc.		
	Political subdivision bonds, etc.		
	Corporate bonds, etc.	2% of assets in bonds, etc., of one corporation.	
	Corporate preferred, guaranteed, or common stock.	10% of assets. 2% of assets in capital stock of one corporation.	
Iowa	Dominion, province, or municipal bonds, etc.		
	Corporate bonds, etc.	50% of legal reserve.	

Iowa (cont.)	Corporate preferred or guaranteed stocks.	10% of legal reserve.
Massachusetts	Dominion, province, or political subdivision bonds, etc.	
	Corporate bonds, etc.	$\frac{1}{2}$ of reserve.
	Corporate bonds, etc. secured by assignment of certain leases.	5% of assets.
Minnesota	Dominion, province, or political subdivision bonds, etc.	
	Public utility and other corporate bonds, etc.	
	Equipment trust obligations.	
Missouri	Dominion bonds, etc.	1% of assets plus reserves and other accrued liabilities under contracts on Canadian risks.
	Dominion, province bonds, etc.	10% of assets plus reserves and other accrued liabilities under contracts on Canadian risks.
	Equipment trust obligations.	1% of assets.
Nebraska	Dominion, province, political subdivision bonds, etc.	
	Corporate bonds, etc.	
	Bonds, etc. of public utility operated by political subdivision, etc.	

(Continued)

157

Table 5A-13 (Continued)

| State | Authorized Types of Canadian Securities | Limits on Holdings of Securities[2] of or in | |
		U.S. and Canada	Canada Only
New Jersey	Dominion, province, political subdivision bonds, etc.		
	Railroad bonds	10% of assets in bonds, etc. of 1 issuer.	
	Public utility bonds, etc.		10% of assets in bonds, etc. of 1 issuer.
	Other corporate bonds, etc.	10% of assets in bonds, etc. of 1 issuer.	
	Corporate capital stock.	2% of assets in stock of 1 issuer.	
New York	Securities and investments in Canada of substantially same kinds and grades as those eligible under §81.		(a) 10% of assets or (b) 1½ times reserve and other obligations under contracts on Canadian risks, or (c) amount insurer required by law to invest in Canada, whichever is greater.
North Carolina	Dominion, province bonds, etc.		
	Corporate bonds, etc.		
Ohio	Dominion, province, municipal bonds, etc.		

158

Pennsylvania	Dominion bonds, etc.	
	Province, political subdivision, bonds, etc.)	
	Corporate bonds, etc.)	5% of assets.
	Corporate stock.)	
Texas	Dominion, province, city bonds.	
Virginia	Dominion, province, municipal bonds, etc.	10% of assets.
	Railroad terminal and other corporate bonds, etc.	10% of assets.
Wisconsin	Dominion, province, city, political subdivision, commission bonds, etc.	
	Bonds, etc., of public utilities owned by political subdivision.	
	Other corporate bonds, etc.	2% of assets in any 1 issue.
	Other corporate obligations.	1% of assets in any 1 issue.
	Corporate preferred stock.	5% of assets.
	Corporate common stock.	5% of assets.
	Equipment securities, equipment trust certificates.	2% of assets in 1 issue.

[1] In the 19 states covered by these tables, no pertinent statutory provisions as to Canadian securities were found in Connecticut, Tennessee, and Vermont. Statutory provisions dealing specifically with real estate mortgages (see Table 5A-3) are not covered by this table.

[2] The limit on aggregate holdings is given unless otherwise specified.

Chapter 6

REGULATIONS GOVERNING
VALUATION OF SECURITIES

Regulations governing the valuation of investments for statement purposes are set up by the state insurance departments and commissions to implement the state insurance laws. Under the guidance of the National Association of Insurance Commissioners they have become substantially uniform between the various states. These valuation standards are a basic factor in the formulation of the investment policies of life insurance companies. The majority of large life insurance companies are mutual organizations. Mutuals, in fairness to all generations of policyholders, return most of their excess premium deposits and investment income to their policyholders each year. In fact, the New York law limits the accumulation of surplus by mutual companies to 10 percent of net policy reserves and policy liabilities. The laws of a number of other states impose similar limitations. Competition from the mutual companies precludes the stock companies from accumulating large surplus. With surplus thus limited, valuation becomes a factor to be considered in everyday investment decisions. To aid in understanding the present system the history of valuation regulations will be reviewed.

History of Valuation of Investments Held by
Life Insurance Companies

Prior to 1907 the valuation of investments held by life insurance companies did not play an important role in insurance regulation. The insurance codes of the various states on the whole were silent on the matter of valuation. There was little statutory guidance for the commissioners apart from Section 18 of the New York Insurance Law, which provided that no stocks owned by an insurance company should be carried in its statement at more than market value.[1] The companies and

---

[1] John Tatlock, "On the Proper Method of Valuation of Fixed Term Securities Owned by Life Insurance Companies," *Proceedings of the Association of Life Insurance Presidents*, 1907, pp. 71-72.

the commissioners assented in the use of market prices for both bonds and stocks for statement purposes.[2] Indeed, the annual statement contemplated that all investments except for mortgages would be valued at market. Thus mortgages were carried at book values, while bonds and stocks were converted to market values by adjustments reflecting the difference between market and book. In the case of real estate, book and market seem to have been construed to be the same, though the statements of some companies showed conversion adjustments similar to those used for bonds and stocks.

The National Convention of Insurance Commissioners (now the National Association of Insurance Commissioners) first became concerned about valuation in connection with the lack of uniformity in the market prices at which different companies were carrying the same securities. In 1907 they referred this problem to their Committee on Assets,[3] which recommended the next year that the Convention appoint a temporary Committee on Valuation of Securities to assemble uniform prices and make them available to each state department. The New York Department then advised the Convention that with the cooperation of the Massachusetts Department it had assembled prices for 1908 statements, and it offered to make these prices available to any department desiring to use them.[4] Uniform market prices thus became available to all state commissions in 1908. In 1910 the Committee on Valuation of Securities became a permanent committee of the Convention and assumed responsibility for the price lists.[5] These prices became "The Book of Valuations," which now is one of the major responsibilities of the Committee.

The commissioners had hardly begun to study the problem of uniform security prices when the question of stability of statement values arose— a question that continues to be the major concern of valuation policy today. The panic of 1907, involving a severe decline in the stock and bond markets, posed an immediate question of solvency for many companies. The commissioners recognized the seriousness of the situation and called two special conferences late in 1907. The conferences, agreeing that prices would have to be stabilized for statement purposes, produced the so-called "rule of thirteen" which defined market prices for 1907 statement purposes as the average of the prices prevailing on the first day of each month during the year and the last day of December. The New York Department had been advised during the summer by the State Attorney General that the Superintendent's authority to determine the

---

[2] *Proceedings of the National Convention of Insurance Commissioners*, 1908, p. 174.
[3] *Proceedings, NCIC*, 1907, pp. 97-98.
[4] *Proceedings, NCIC*, 1908, pp. 131-133.
[5] *Proceedings, NCIC*, 1910, pp. 49, 169-170.

meaning of market price was broad, reasonableness being the principal criterion.[6]

New York adopted the "rule of thirteen." But in 1908 the New York Superintendent, having studied the problem of valuation at some length, advised the Convention that he would henceforth accept amortization for statement purposes of all fixed-term bonds, amply secured and not in default, and that affirmative legislation was being sought.[7] The necessary statutes were enacted in 1909 and thus New York became the leader in a movement to introduce stability and continuity into the valuation of investments of life insurance companies.[8] Some twenty-eight states accepted amortization for 1909 statements and during the ensuing years all states came to accept the principle of amortization although by 1920 there were still only twelve states having legislation on the subject.[9] At their December meeting that year the commissioners adopted a recommendation of their Committee on Laws and Legislation for a uniform amortization bill for life insurance companies and early in 1921 action was undertaken to sponsor a model bill in the various state legislatures.[10] With but four exceptions all jurisdictions now have legislation permitting amortization of amply secured bonds having a fixed term and fixed rate of interest.[11]

The amortization of amply secured bonds was a major achievement in statement making. It meant that 80 percent or more of the assets of most companies would be valued on a stable basis. However, a substantial amount of assets in relation to surplus continued to be valued at market. Moreover, there was no guarantee that an uncomfortable volume of bonds would not become non-amortizable in subsequent financial crises, thus compelling the commissioners to adopt new standards of valuation in order to protect company surpluses, and this proved to be just what happened. The continued use of market for non-amortizable securities

---

[6] *New York Insurance Report, Part V,* 1907, pp. 122-126; *Part I,* 1908, pp. 11-12; *Proceedings, National Association of Insurance Commissioners,* 1940, p. 158.

[7] Otto Kelsey, "The Amortization Plan of Valuing Fixed Term Securities and Proper Method of Valuation of Other Securities," *Proceedings NCIC,* 1908, pp. 174-180.

[8] New York Insurance Law, §18, amended Ch. 301, Ins. L. 1909. This law was permissive and applied to all insurance companies subject to the supervision of the New York Department but was amended in 1910 to require amortization by all life companies doing business in New York (or, alternatively, permitting the use of market or book values if lower than amortized values) and to vest in the Superintendent the power to require amortization by other insurance companies. Ch. 634, Ins. L. 1910. (See *New York Insurance Report, Part V,* 1909, pp. 22-23; 1910, pp. 40-41.)

[9] These twelve states were California, Connecticut, Maine, Maryland, Massachusetts, Minnesota, New Jersey, New York, Oregon, Pennsylvania, Virginia, and Wisconsin.

[10] *Proceedings, NCIC,* 1921, p. 5.

[11] These four states are Georgia, Louisiana, Oklahoma, and Texas.

caused the valuation standards to break down in every financial crisis after 1907.

The first action taken by the commissioners after 1907 to establish stable prices of non-amortizable securities for statement purposes occurred when war in Europe broke out in 1914. Market prices, particularly those of active securities, declined sharply in the last week of July. In order to avert a panic the stock exchanges were closed and, as it turned out, remained closed for four months. Because of the uncertainty as to whether year-end market prices would be available and because of the inequities that would exist if the latest available quotations were used (since inactive securities had not suffered the July declines) the Commissioners' Committee on Valuation proposed that June 30th prices be used for 1914 statements. This proposal was adopted.[12] Year-end market values came back into use in 1915, but in 1917 the commissioners once again provided stabilization to protect company surpluses. This time a mean of the market prices of November 1, 1916, February 1, May 1, August 1, and November 1, 1917 was adopted.[13] In 1918 the formula was adjusted to reflect the average of the 1917 authorized values and November 30, 1918 prices, with the provision that December 31 prices could be used if higher. This procedure was continued with minor modifications until 1922, when year-end market prices again were adopted.[14]

During the long period of prosperity in the 1920's market values worked well for the companies. Stock investment had been prohibited for New York companies by the Armstrong legislation of 1906, and by the middle 1920's such holdings had been greatly reduced. But in 1928 the New York companies were permitted to buy preferred stocks. Moreover, the railroads accounted for a large proportion of the demand for funds during the 1920's, and the railroads, of course, encountered grave financial problems once the depression began. Many railroad bonds became non-amortizable, and the prices of other bonds, as well as of stocks, declined sharply. Thus valuation again became a problem for the commissioners. In 1931 they authorized the use of June 30th prices. In 1932, as the depression deepened, the commissioners authorized the use of the values permitted in 1931.[15] In 1933 the companies were allowed to average the November 1, 1933 prices and the values approved for 1932 statements.[16]

---

[12] *Proceedings, NCIC,* 1915, Adjourned Meeting, pp. 11-13.

[13] *List of Securities Held by Insurance Companies with Valuations to be Used in the Companies' Annual Statements,* December 31, 1917, p. v.

[14] *Ibid.,* for years ended December 31, 1918-22.

[15] *Proceedings, NCIC,* 1932, p. 6 and 1933, p. 8.

[16] *Proceedings, NCIC,* 1934, p. 8. Bonds of governments, states, and subdivisions were allowed to be carried at the 1932 Convention values (i.e., June 30, 1931 prices) except that those in default for longer than one year were to be carried at 1931 Convention values less 30 percent of the difference between such values and the market prices as of November 1, 1933.

In 1933 the commissioners adopted a rule which permitted life insurance companies to value their stock holdings in the aggregate at the lower of cost or book value provided income from such stocks in each of the preceding five years was at a rate sufficient to meet reserve requirements. A further proviso required the companies to earn enough on their ledger assets to cover reserve requirements.[17] Thus a life company could adopt statement values that would produce the necessary rate of earnings and at the same time be substantially higher than the approved market prices. Apparently little used by the companies, this ruling nevertheless continued in effect until 1939 when the commissioners ruled that all stocks acquired subsequent to June 30th should be valued at market.[18] Stocks already owned by the companies continued under the 1933 ruling until 1945.[19]

These of course were major departures from year-end market and they caused both the companies and the commissioners to look again at the whole theory of asset valuation for insurance companies. The need for stabilization was evident, but at the same time the New York Department, apparently concerned about the large number of bonds falling into default, concluded that more attention should be paid to the requirement of the New York Law that bonds must be "amply secured" to be amortizable.[20] In 1932 the Superintendent notified all companies doing business in the state that henceforth corporate bonds would be amortizable only if they fell within the first five rating grades of one of the four rating agencies.[21] This brought into use the rating tests, which with occasional modifications have continued to be an integral part of the valuation rules up to the present time. The prices of securities failing to pass the rating tests were stabilized by the Convention values used in 1932 and 1933, but after 1933 these securities, except for direct and guaranteed Governments, and states and municipals secured by full faith, credit and taxing power, became valued at year-end market. The adoption of the rating tests thus added to the need for some form of stabilized valuation system.

In 1938 the NAIC Committee on Valuation of Securities, under the Chairmanship of Superintendent Pink of the New York Department

---

17 *Ibid.*, pp. 8-9.

18 *Proceedings, NAIC,* 1939, p. 128.

19 Cf. *Proceedings, NAIC,* 1944, p. 238 and 1946 pp. 26-33.

20 In the 1914 Proceedings of the NCIC it is indicated that the Valuation Committee's contract with Marvyn Scudder, who assembled the necessary market prices required him to furnish any state commissioner, on request, with an opinion as to whether any bond yielding more than 6 percent was amply secured. By and large however, all bonds paying full interest and not in arrears were regarded as amply secured by most state commissions.

21 Circular letter addressed "To Companies under the Jurisdiction of the New York Insurance Department," July 19, 1932.

eported to the Association on studies it was making on the valuation
problem. The report made it clear that the Committee was not contemplat-
ng an outright departure from the use of market values, but rather a
ystem of stabilized values reflecting an average of several prices.

It is interesting that twelve out of thirty-one of these volumes (i.e.
Book on Valuations) have contained values other than the December
31 market quotations. In three instances average values were confined
to some classes of bonds, while actual market quotations for other classes
of bonds and for all stocks were used. The record, therefore, lends itself to the conclusion that in the judgment of this Association, actual
market quotations as of December 31 do not necessarily represent the
true or fair basis of security values.

          *   *   *

We have become so accustomed to the use of some formula for arriv-
ing at the fair value of securities that it is wise to consider the adoption
of a permanent formula. While those companies which are in danger
do not hesitate to make strenuous pleas for relief in times of extreme
economic disturbance, no one is sufficiently interested on the part of
policyholders and the public to object to the use of market values when
securities are inflated and are selling far beyond their intrinsic worth.
It is obvious that if some plan of fixing fair value is adopted, those affected must accept the disadvantages, as well as the advantages.

          *   *   *

Twenty-three states responded to the questionnaire inquiring whether
or not some plan of average values would be desirable. Eleven of these
states were in favor of the plan. Six states were definitely opposed. Three
states indicated that they would accept the plan if it met with the approval of the Convention. Three other states were doubtful.

This Committee is therefore of the opinion that there is sufficient merit
in the proposal for permanent use of average values to require further
study. It asks that it be instructed to continue its consideration of this
matter and determine whether a system of average values is feasible and
advisable from the standpoint of the general welfare. The Committee
should endeavor to work out a plan for such values which it deems just
and equitable, surround it with every possible safeguard against abuses,
and report its conclusions at the December meeting.[22]

The report was approved and the Committee settled down to complete the study. It developed a system of stabilized market values, which
averaged the previous years' values with the average of the high and low
quotations between January 1 and November 1 of the current year,
giving a weight of four to the previous years' values and a weight of one
to the current year's values. The proposal was conceived primarily as a
stock plan, but the companies were asked their opinions as to the
feasibility of applying the plan to bonds as well. The companies failed to
support the proposal with any enthusiasm, and some opposed it strongly.

---

[22] *Proceedings, NAIC,* 1938, pp. 105-107.

While no report is available on the reactions of the commissioners, it is evident from the Proceedings that they also had reservations. The Committee recommended continuing the use of year-end market prices for non-amortizable securities.[23]

In 1939 Ernest Howe, Chief Financial Advisor of the Insurance Section of the Securities and Exchange Commission and the principal Government witness on insurance before the Temporary National Economic Committee, criticized the companies for amortizing certain bonds for statement purposes when they were selling at low prices in the market place. The New York Department responded to this criticism by adding to the rating test a further requirement that to be amortizable a bond must have sold for more than 50 in each of the months of September, October, and November.[24] Thus the definition of "amply secured" was further refined, and the importance for statement purposes of stabilized market values became increasingly apparent.

In 1940 the NAIC adopted a modification of the New York requirements for amortization. Bonds were to be amortizable if they were rated in the first four grades by two of the agencies, in the first five grades by three of the agencies, or in the first five grades by two of the agencies and in addition were priced at 55 or better in each of the months September, October, and November.[25] In 1942 the price test was abandoned and a "yield" test was adopted as an alternative to the rating test. The yield test rendered all bonds amortizable if their yields based on Association values for the current and preceding year did not exceed the corresponding yield on comparable maturities of taxable United States Governments by more than 3.90 percent.[26] Thereafter the spread was reduced from time to time until it amounted to 1.50 percent in 1950.[27]

The introduction of the rating tests in 1932 and the subsequent adoption of these tests by the NAIC in 1940 led to an increasingly heavy volume of work in preparing the Book on Valuations. In 1940 the NAIC published as a special pamphlet a list of all the corporate bonds held by life insurance companies, indicating which of these bonds were amortizable. Two years later the list was extended to include municipal securities and was incorporated as part of the Book on Valuations for 1942.[28] The amount of work thus involved in the preparation of the Book led Moody's Investors Service, which had been doing the work, to review its commitments and to conclude that it could not undertake to compile the Book in 1943. The NAIC was so notified, and the commissioners

---

[23] *Proceedings, NAIC*, 1939, p. 28.
[24] *New York Insurance Report*, Vol. I, 1940, pp. 34a-36a.
[25] *Proceedings, NAIC*, 1941, pp. 66-67.
[26] *Proceedings, NAIC*, 1942, p. 125.
[27] *Proceedings, NAIC*, 1950, pp. 561, 567.
[28] *Proceedings, NAIC*, 1941, pp. 124, 127; 1942, p. 47.

thereupon delegated the task to its recently formed Subcommittee of the Committee on Valuations of Securities. An Executive Secretary was retained, and the Subcommittee and the Executive Secretary undertook to prepare the Book.[29]

The task of preparing the Book did not diminish under the new system. Furthermore, the valuation system itself was becoming obsolete. Relying as it did upon ratings and market prices, the system could not cope with the development of direct placement of corporate bonds, which came to be an increasingly important channel of investment for many companies. Direct placements are not rated by independent investment agencies because these securities are not underwritten and of course they generally have no market price. For the years 1938 through 1940 the NAIC had decided that direct placements should be carried at issue price.[30] But as the volume of direct placements increased, and notations as to amortizability and market valuations had to be made, the Committee finally concluded that a staff of security analysts would have to be retained.

A cumbersome and increasingly costly system of valuation had evolved. There was no assurance that this system would not become more costly as the years went by. There was no assurance that it would stand up under depression conditions. The commissioners therefore sought a better system, one more in tune with the needs of the insurance business.

Development of the Going-Concern Theory of Valuation for Life Insurance Companies

Throughout the years that valuation has been an important phase of insurance regulation, the commissioners have sought the development of a uniform system for all insurance companies. Different values for the same security simply because it was held by different kinds of insurance companies seemed fundamentally indefensible to the commissioners. At the same time the heavy cost of the valuation work troubled both the companies and the commissioners and caused them to seek a simpler, less expensive system. Accordingly in 1948 an All-Industry Committee, composed of representatives from different branches of the insurance business, was established to study the valuation problem from the standpoint of insurance generally. It was understood that the All-Industry Committee would report its findings to the commissioners.

The All-Industry Committee proceeded to make a careful study of the insurance business and its investments in bonds and stocks. They considered the actual performance of these investments over a long period of time and compared the investment experience of the business with the over-all corporate bond experience revealed by the Corporate Bond

---

[29] *Proceedings, NAIC,* 1942, pp. 126, 127; 1943, pp. 46-47, 155-159.
[30] *Proceedings, NAIC,* 1959, p. 28; 1940, pp. 183-184.

Research Project of the National Bureau of Economic Research. They concluded that market values behaved poorly as valuation standards for bonds and preferred stocks, and that insurance companies should value their assets primarily on a "going concern basis." The basic reasoning was that life insurance companies, because of the long-term nature of their contracts, and the high degree of liquidity in their operation, typically hold their fixed-interest investments until maturity, so that it is illogical to value these securities on a market or "liquidating" basis.

The plan developed by the All-Industry Committee proposed valuing all bonds not in default as to principal or interest at amortized cost, and proposed corresponding stabilization for dividend-paying preferred stocks.[31] Bonds and preferred stocks in default and all common stocks would continue to be carried at market price.

In order to cushion in advance the effect of losses and security depreciation and appreciation, the plan proposed accumulating a securities reserve, against which realized losses and write-downs of unstabilized bonds and preferred stocks would be charged. For this purpose securities were divided into five classes, as follows:

Class 1—(a) All United States and Canadian Government direct or guaranteed bonds.

(b) United States and Canadian political subdivision bonds secured by full faith, credit and taxing powers.

(c) Special revenue bonds of United States political subdivisions, and United States and Canadian corporate bonds which fall in one of the first four rating grades of one of the accredited rating agencies, or pass a prescribed yield test.

(d) United States and Canadian bonds which are not rated but which are certified by the insurance company in-

---

[31] An interesting part of the All-Industry Committee thinking was a proposal to amortize preferred stocks. Preferred stocks having a fixed sinking fund sufficient to retire the entire issue in fifty years or less would be amortized in the same manner as a bond bearing interest equivalent to the dividend rate and having a maturity equal to the final retirement date. Thus an issue having a fifty-year sinking fund bearing a 5 percent dividend rate purchased at 110 would reflect a yield of 4.50 percent, and would be carried for statement purposes at diminished prices each year until at retirement its book value would be par.

All other preferred stocks purchased on a current yield basis of less than 5 percent would be amortized to a price producing 5 percent current yield at the end of a fifty-year period. (Thus a 3½ percent preferred stock having a par value of 100 would have to sell for 70 in order to yield 5 percent. Hence if the purchase price were 100, it would be necessary to write off 30 points within a fifty-year period and the actual return on the investment, after amortizing the write-off, would be 3.26 percent.) Finally all preferred stocks purchased on a current yield basis of more than 5 percent would be carried at cost as long as they were not in default.

volved to be of a quality equivalent to bonds in one of
the first four rating grades.

(e) Preferred stocks which as of December 1 of the statement year were selling to yield not more than 0.5 percent in excess of the average yield on a selected list of
non-callable preferred stocks and preferred stocks not
publicly quoted but certified as being of equivalent
quality.

Class 2—All other United States and Canadian bonds and preferred
stocks not in default.

Class 3—Bonds and preferred stocks in default.

Class 4—Common stocks.

Class 5—Common or capital stocks of insurance companies.

Regular annual accruals, amounting to one-twentieth of 1 percent and
1 percent on Class 1 and Class 2 securities, respectively, were to be
credited to the reserve until the reserve reached a maximum of 1 percent
and 20 percent respectively. Companies desiring to do so were to be
permitted to accrue the entire reserve at once. During the initial period
of reserve accumulation, limitations on the use of the reserve and supplementary accruals were provided. Only 50 percent of the realized
losses on bonds and preferred stocks were to be charged to the reserve,
the remaining 50 percent to be charged to surplus. The same rule was to
apply to declines in the market value of bonds and preferred stocks in
default. All realized gains and all increases in the market values of
unstabilized bonds and preferred stocks were to be credited to the reserve,
as was the accrual of discounts on Class 2 bonds. But when the reserve
had once reached the maximum, all realized losses on bonds and preferred
stocks, as well as the entire decline in the market value of unstabilized
bonds and preferred stocks, were to be charged to the reserve, while all
realized gains were to be credited to surplus. Increases in market value
of unstabilized bonds and preferred stocks, however, were to be credited
to the reserve whenever it was below the maximum.

In respect to common stocks, the plan proposed a fluctuation reserve
to absorb any gains or losses in statement value.

The All-Industry Committee approach did not meet with success because it was soon realized by both the insurance industry and the
regulatory authorities that there were basic differences between the life
insurance companies and the property insurance companies which
militated against a uniform basis for valuation and reserves for both
branches. The plan which had been developed was consistent and logical
in terms of the economics of the life insurance business, but not the
property branch. As a result, the Committee on Valuation of Assets of the
life insurance business resumed work on the "All-Industry" plan and in

the spring of 1951 recommended a slightly amended plan to the NAIC for their consideration to be applied solely to life companies. This was the "Hubbell Plan," named after the chairman of the industry committee.

The Hubbell Plan proposed the same stabilization formulas as the All-Industry Committee Plan and the same classes of securities for reserve purposes. However, it provided that supplementary accumulations should come into play not only in the initial build-up period but whenever the reserve was below the maximum. Thus net profits on sales or disposals of securities, as well as increases in market values of bonds and preferred stocks in default and the increase in book value of Class 2 bonds, would be credited to the reserve, in addition to the regular annual accruals, whenever the reserve fell below its maximum. No provision would be made for a common stock reserve. (The proposals with respect to preferred stocks were withdrawn later in order to facilitate progress with respect to bonds.)

The NAIC Subcommittee on Valuation of Securities held hearings on the Hubbell Plan in the fall of 1951. The Subcommittee agreed to consider a separate valuation system for life companies only.[32]

Early in December 1951 the NAIC Subcommittee on Valuation of Securities invited industry views on a modification of the Hubbell Plan which would extend reserve proposals to preferred and common stocks for 1951 and 1952. The commissioners' proposals required the accumulation of reserves at a rate of one-twentieth of 1 percent per year on bonds amortizable under the then existing resolutions, and at 1 percent on all other bonds, all preferred stocks, and all common stocks. Net capital gains on bonds and stocks, both realized and unrealized, were to be credited to the reserve, while only 50 percent of any net capital losses were to be chargeable to the reserve. A maximum of 1 percent of the statement value of amortizable bonds plus 20 percent of the statement value of all other securities was placed on the reserve. The question of extending the principle of stabilized values, the commissioners indicated, required further exploration and discussion by industry representatives with the commissioners' technical staff. In 1951 the NAIC adopted the reserve plan outlined above.[33]

In 1953 the NAIC adopted two tests for determining amortizability of corporate bonds. The first was designed to dispose for examination purposes of the great body of high-grade bonds that are unquestionably entitled to amortization. Without going into all the ramifications and details of the tests, certain basic features can be briefly outlined. All bonds in the first four rating grades of any one of the accredited agencies automatically pass test 1. Also passing test 1 are bonds reflecting maximum

---

[32] *Proceedings, NAIC,* 1952, pp. 211-219; pp. 222-223; pp. 225-226.
[33] *Proceedings, NAIC,* 1952, pp. 208-217.

ebt ratios varying from 50 percent to 75 percent of total capitalization, verage earnings coverage of at least 1½ times before taxes over the receding five years, and actual coverage of 1½ times in either of the st two years. Amortizable bonds other than corporate and test 1 and quivalent corporate bonds require annual reserve accruals of one-ventieth of 1 percent.

Test 2 is designed to measure more carefully the risk likely to be ncurred on bonds failing to pass test 1. This test sets lower coverage andards but broadens its inquiry into cash flow, current position, and her more detailed financial analysis. Bonds passing test 2 are amor-zable for life companies but not for fire and casualty companies. For fe companies they require a 1 percent annual reserve accrual.

Bonds failing to pass test 2 and other bonds ineligible for amortization including of course bonds in default) continue to be carried at market alue in the annual statement and require annual reserve accruals of 1 ercent. The maximum reserve limits were set at 1 percent of test 1 and quivalent bonds (including amortizable bonds other than corporates) us 20 percent of all other securities. In order to prevent the reserve from eing depleted, the commissioners ruled that the reserve through the sorption of capital losses might not be reduced below the sum of 20 ercent of the statement value of test 2 bonds, one-twentieth of 1 per-nt of the statement value of test 1 and equivalent bonds, and any-rite-up resulting from the amortization of test 2 bonds.[34]

In 1954 the commissioners amended the provision that only half of the et capital losses on bonds and stocks in any year (realized and un-alized) could be charged to the reserve. This provision was adopted in)51 as a temporary measure to accelerate the accumulation of the serve. The commissioners believed that its purpose had been served. ock values were still unstabilized and with the rising securities market rge unrealized gains were being added to the reserve. They recognized e risk to surplus of adding all the net gains to the reserve but deducting llf of the net losses from surplus when the market reversed itself. The w rule permitted the companies to deduct all of the net capital losses securities in any year (realized and unrealized) from the reserve ovided it was not reduced below the minimum. The minimum was anged in 1954 to 20 percent of test 2 bonds plus four-twentieths of 1 rcent of test 1 and equivalent bonds.[35] An additional one-twentieth 1 percent of the statement value of test 1 and equivalent bonds has en added each year since 1954 to the bond component of the minimum serve requirement. At the end of 1959, it was 20 percent of the state-

[34] *Proceedings, NAIC,* Vol. II, 1953, pp. 650-652; pp. 658-674.
[35] *Proceedings, NAIC,* Vol. I, 1955, pp. 154-155.

ment value of test 2 bonds plus nine-twentieths of 1 percent of the state
ment value of test 1 and equivalent bonds.[36]

The formula for accumulating the reserve and absorbing capital gain
and losses was virtually unchanged from the end of 1954 to 1959 excep
for one amendment. Under the Federal Income Tax Act of 1959 a lev
was imposed for the first time on the net capital gains realized by lif
insurance companies. The companies believed that since they were re
quired to add all of their net gains on securities to the reserve, the
should be allowed to deduct the tax. The commissioners complied wit
their recommendation by adding the following item to the formula.

> 6. Less the amount of any United States Federal Income Taxes incurred
> on net long-term capital gains realized in 1959, on bonds and stocks,
> pursuant to Section 802 (a) (2) of the Life Insurance Company Income
> Tax Act of 1959.[37]

The valuation tests adopted for bonds in 1953 operated in an effecti
fashion. Almost all bonds held by life insurance companies were amo
tizable and the reserves were rapidly approaching the maximum fc
many companies. But the industry and the commissioners both continue
to be concerned about the position of companies having relatively larg
amounts of non-amortizable bonds, preferred stocks, and common stocl
in their portfolios. Moreover, while the tests had been carefully devise
with a view to their performance under varying economic condition
there was some concern in the minds of investment officers that a su
stantial increase might occur in the volume of test 2 bonds in depressic
times, thus compelling many companies to increase their reserves at a
accelerated rate at the very time when a free flow of life insurance fund
into the economy should be most encouraged.

Stabilization of Statement Values
Extended to Preferred Stocks

In 1957 the NAIC adopted provisions for stabilization of the value
qualified preferred stocks. It did so under the "one-fifth rule," in whi
the year-end value of qualified preferred stocks was to be the stateme
value for the prior year (cost if purchased during the year) plus or min
one-fifth of the difference between this value and year-end market pric

To qualify for stabilization under the new rules preferred stocks mi
meet certain earnings and dividend requirements. Cumulative preferr
stocks must have a coverage after income taxes of at least $1\frac{1}{4}$ times f
the last three years and must be paying full dividends. Non-cumulati
preferred stocks must meet the same earnings requirements and mi

---

[36] *Valuations of Securities as of December 31, 1959*, NAIC, p. 18.
[37] *Report of the Committee on Valuation of Securities*, NAIC, December 1959.

have paid full dividends for the last three years. Preferred stocks not meeting these requirements must be valued at year-end market (association) values.

Qualified directly placed as well as publicly traded issues may be valued by the one-fifth rule. Association value for directly placed preferred stock shall equal the lesser of current call price or an amount that will make the yield equal to that of a comparable publicly traded preferred stock of the same issuer. When no comparable publicly traded preferred stock of the same issuer exists, association value shall equal the lesser of current call price or an amount that will make the yield equal to that of the average at year-end market prices of a selected group of high-grade preferred stocks.[38]

The new regulations retained the single reserve against bonds, preferred stocks, and common stocks but added a factor for preferred stocks to the minimum requirement.

University of Wisconsin Valuation Research Project

Despite the improvements made in recent years in the system of valuing life insurance assets and the valuation reserves, both the regulatory authorities and the companies are giving further study to the problem in the light of changing conditions. Toward this end, in the autumn of 1958 work was begun on the "Study of Valuation of Securities by Life Insurance Companies and the Mandatory Securities Valuation Reserve." This study is being conducted by the School of Commerce of the University of Wisconsin through a grant from the Life Insurance Association of America. It is under the direction of Dr. Harold Fraine. Guiding the project is an advisory committee consisting of representatives from the life insurance companies, commissioners and their staff technicians, and academic specialists in finance. The purpose of the study is to appraise the existing system of valuation rules and the valuation reserves and determine ways of improving and simplifying them. In particular the study is expected to cover various questions concerning the reserves—their purpose, whether they are adequate to meet this purpose, and whether they should be segregated into separate reserves for bonds, preferred stocks, and common stocks. In addition it will consider the question of extending stabilization to common stocks and other securities not now stabilized.

The project has made satisfactory progress. A large amount of useful data has been obtained from the companies and the NAIC Staff. Members of the project are now in the process of discussing the results of their research with the advisory committee. The final report is expected in 1962.

---

[38] *Proceedings, NAIC*, Vol. II, 1957, pp. 443-444; pp. 456-457.

Chapter 7

THE INVESTMENT PROCESS IN
LIFE INSURANCE COMPANIES

The Organization of Investment Operations

The Finance Committee. Responsibility for the investment activities of a life insurance company rests ultimately with the finance committee of its board of directors. This body is composed typically of five or seven members, but there are sometimes as few as three or as many as ten members. As might be expected, a background in banking or finance predominates among its members. In order that there may be a balanced representation, one or two members are likely to be executives of manufacturing or commercial concerns or public utilities, bringing a business viewpoint to the work of the committee. Lawyers are also to be found on the finance committees of life insurance companies, and a background in construction or in the real estate field is considered desirable in many appointments. Among medium-sized and smaller life companies, but less frequently in larger companies, the members of the finance committee will often include the president or the financial vice president of the insurance company.

Some variation as to the organization of the finance committee is to be found among life insurance companies. In the vast majority, a single committee oversees all investment functions of the company. Sometimes the parent committee will establish two smaller subcommittees to supervise activities in bonds and stocks and in mortgage loans, respectively. The organization sometimes found among larger companies is for two autonomous committees, one for bonds and stocks and the other for mortgages, to report directly to the board of directors.

However organized, the primary function of the finance committee is to make the final decisions regarding company investment policies, both general and particular. When dealing with more general policy, the committee reviews the distribution and quality of the investment portfolio, approves any basic changes in investment practices, or even fixes the al-

174

ocation of investment funds among different types of investments. When dealing with the particular, the committee considers each of the investment opportunities presented by the financial officers of the company for approval or rejection.

In performing these functions the finance committee necessarily works very closely with the top financial officers of the company, sharing responsibility with them or actually delegating to them authority (within limits) for making loans. An example of shared responsibility may be found in the fixing of the allocation of investment funds for the year. The initiative for such allocations may come from the financial officers, subject merely to the review and approval of the finance committee, but the latter may feel the final decision must be its own. As an example of delegated loan authority, the finance committee may adopt certain standards for mortgage lending but allow loan transactions to be approved by lending officers within these standards, without prior review of individual loans by the finance committee. Most companies permit loan officers to approve residential mortgage loans up to a maximum amount of perhaps $25,000 so long as these loans meet the company's current requirement as to minimum down payment, maximum term, rate of return, credit standing and income of the borrower, and basic construction and design of the dwelling. The size of loan which may be approved by loan officers for commercial and farm mortgages is likely to be somewhat larger, ranging up to $50,000 or $100,000 for some companies. Loans made under such delegated authority are then reported in a written presentation at the following finance committee meeting. Mortgage loans of more substantial amounts, and almost all purchases of bonds and stocks, typically require the prior approval of the finance committee.

In order that the financial officer may have some latitude in the timing of security acquisitions, however, many companies grant authority for bond purchases to be made up to a certain amount without prior approval (so long as they meet certain standards), or they may permit purchases to be made from an approved list of securities which has been reviewed by the finance committee. This discretionary authority allows the investment officer to move more quickly in taking advantage of market situations that may develop between meetings of the committee.

The degree of discretionary authority that is granted to investment officers for securities purchases depends partly upon the frequency of finance committee meetings. Again, practice among companies varies widely. The most common practice is to hold regular meetings every week or every two weeks, with additional meetings on call. Some companies hold finance committee meetings twice weekly, but on the other hand, a few companies schedule their regular meetings for once a month. The range of practices that is to be found in the matter of meeting dates is indicative of the range of prevailing practice regarding the delegation of loan authority by the finance committee to the investment officers of the company; those committees that meet quite frequently have less need to delegate authority, and vice versa.

In addition to specific investment decisions, the finance committee also concerns itself with the problem of portfolio distribution. Companies as a general rule carry out a comprehensive review of the entire portfolio each year or sometimes every three months, considering the distribution quality and investment return on the portfolio. Somewhat less directly the question of portfolio composition and quality also must be raised whenever the committee considers the possible liquidation of assets either U.S. Government securities or private securities, in order to acquire more attractive investments.

To generalize the situation, the finance committee carries the ultimate responsibility for investment activities of the life insurance company and controls the broad direction of these operations. To facilitate the administration of this broad investment policy and to allow flexibility in timing the committee quite often will delegate authority for loans of limited amounts; even these loans are subjected to later review by the committee. In the main, the bulk of new investments are approved only after individual scrutiny by the committee, based on the detailed analysis and recommendations presented by the financial officers of the company. While the financial officers concern themselves with the task of making investment selections, the finance committee is continually called upon to exercise its judgment in shaping the investment philosophy of the company and in making the final investment decisions.

Financial Officers and the Investment Departments. The typical practice among life insurance companies is for a single investment officer usually designated as the financial vice president, to have jurisdiction over all investment operations including both bonds and mortgages. This officer often is a member of the finance committee and serves as a direct liaison between that body and the investment staff. In a number of companies, however, there is no single investment manager with overall responsibility; instead, separate vice presidents head the securities department and the mortgage department, respectively, and report directly to the finance committee and to the company president. In such cases, it is more likely that the allocation of funds between securities and mortgages is fixed by the finance committee. Where a financial vice president exists, that officer normally has the authority to determine the allocation of investment flows between the departments under his charge, usually subject to ratification by the finance committee.

The bond department, sometimes called the investment department or securities department, is usually headed by a vice president and staffed by subordinate officers with specialties in particular fields. In large companies, with assets of over $1 billion, the volume of lending operations may require a staff of fifteen to thirty men, exclusive of secretarial and clerical staff. In the case of a smaller life insurance company, with total assets of less than $200 million, the bond investments will be supervised by perhaps two or three investment officers.

The work of the bond department includes the analysis, recommendation, and supervision of securities in the company's portfolio. As direct loan applications are made or as public issues come to market, security analysts examine each loan for possible investment interest. Upon recommendation to the vice president of the department, a potential loan will be studied further if it is a public offering or negotiations opened with the borrower if it is a direct placement. If still considered favorably, the proposed loan will be reviewed by the other investment officers, perhaps through informal conferences or through formal screening sessions conducted by the financial vice president. The next step is the presentation of the loan for the approval of the finance committee (or bond committee). Written materials describing the terms of the loan, the financial history and the capital structure of the borrower, and other pertinent documents are submitted to finance committee members several days in advance of the meeting. At the meeting itself, financial officers will describe the proposed loan and answer questions that committee members may have. The effect of a loan upon the distribution and diversification of assets usually will be considered. A committee vote is taken and the official minutes record whether the loan was rejected or approved. As a matter of common practice the unanimous consent of the finance committee is usually sought, although a majority vote may be technically sufficient for approval in many companies. A strong dissent by any one member will lead in most instances to further negotiation or actual rejection of the loan.

Once a loan has been made or a stock purchased, the staff maintains a close supervision of its status. Quarterly financial reports are typically required of each borrower and any financial weaknesses or adverse developments are reported immediately to the finance committee. In the case of direct placements, the emergence of trouble spots may lead to direct consultation with the borrower or even to renegotiation of certain provisions of the loan agreement. In the case of public issues, poor performance may result in a recommendation to the finance committee that the issue be sold.

Little has been said of the preferred and common stock investment of life insurance companies, but a growing number of companies have become active in this field. Such transactions are usually carried out by specialists in the securities department. Many companies develop a list of stocks which are considered appropriate for investment and then acquire such stocks on a dollar-averaging or other formula basis. In the aggregate, such investments have not been large by comparison with investment in corporate and municipal bonds.

For the company with a large investment staff which can develop specialties and expert knowledge of particular lending fields, there is little occasion to seek outside assistance or advice on investment selections. But for the company with a limited investment staff, nevertheless seeking to maintain a broadly diversified pattern of investments, it has often been found desirable to call upon outside specialists for recommendations in certain fields. Selection of a common stock portfolio also is aided at times by outside investment counsel or advisory services utilized by smaller life companies investing in this field. Many companies, both large and small, also seek the advice of outside specialists on general economic conditions bearing on investments, but a number of companies include an economic research department within their own organization.

The mortgage department, headed usually by a vice president, is responsible for investments in residential, commercial, and farm mortgages. In some companies, usually of larger size, a division is made between city mortgages (residential and commercial) and farm mortgages, with a senior officer in charge of each department. The mortgage investment staff consists of fifteen to thirty members in most larger companies (except as noted below) and ranges down to two or three members in companies with a small mortgage portfolio. In the case of mortgage loans on commercial or farm properties or on multifamily dwellings, the investment officer deals directly with the borrower in arranging the terms of the loan and is usually a specialist in that type of lending.

For mortgages on one- to four-family dwellings, most insurance companies rely upon loan correspondents (also known as mortgage brokers or mortgage bankers) to originate mortgages meeting the prescribed standards currently required by company policy. For example, an investment officer may arrange for the purchase through a loan correspondent of perhaps 200 individual mortgages with similar characteristics of maturity, down payment, and interest rate, to be delivered in a single package. Such loans often are insured or guaranteed by the Federal Housing Administration or the Veterans Administration, although conventional mortgages are also acquired in substantial volume through loan correspondents. In most instances, the mortgage servicing (collection of monthly interest and amortization, taxes, and so forth) is handled by the loan correspondent rather than by the life insurance company.

A variation from this method is to be found in a few major companies and a few smaller companies which do not rely entirely upon loan correspondents to originate residential mortgages. Instead, these companies originate and service mortgage loans through a field force of company lending officers scattered throughout the country. There are, of course, a number of companies which acquire mortgages through a combination of field force activities and the use of loan correspondents.

A related type of investment that usually is handled by the mortgage department is investment real estate, principally through purchase-lease-back arrangements. This operation involves the purchase by the life insurance company of an office building, supermarket, filling station, or other commercial property, with immediate leasing to the seller on a long-term basis. Investment in housing projects owned by life insurance companies often is administered within the mortgage department, but there is sometimes a separate housing and real estate department that handles such transactions.

In summary, the process of selecting and supervising the investment of life insurance company funds is carried out by a staff of investment specialists, typically headed by a financial vice president or similar senior officer. In the selection of investment outlets, these officers make extensive use of mortgage loan correspondents and occasional use of outside investment specialists in stocks or bonds. Although the financial officers sometimes have the power to approve loans, under authority delegated by the finance committee, the bulk of their work consists of seeking out and recommending appropriate new investments to the finance committee for its final approval.

The Allocation of Funds. Since the ultimate objective of life company investment operations is to place its funds in the outlets with the highest return consistent with safety of the principal, the allocation of funds to various channels is of crucial importance in the investment process. The foregoing discussion has touched upon the question of responsibility for this allocation, but the topic is deserving of further consideration at this point.

The allocation process here considered refers to the channeling of funds into alternative forms of investment, including the entire array of assets in which life insurance companies are permitted to invest. For the sake of brevity, the problem will be simplified to that of bonds versus mortgages although it actually involves questions of corporate versus municipal bonds, corporate bonds versus common stock, commercial mortgages versus residential mortgages, FHA versus VA mortgages, and so forth.

When the allocation problem is one of entering investment areas in which the company has previously not been active, e.g., common stocks or foreign investments, it is likely that a fundamental policy decision by the finance committee will be required. The finance committees of most companies also make the final decision on the broad allocation of funds as between bonds and mortgages with a view toward maintaining the desired portfolio balance or moving toward some target of desired asset distribution. The targets are typically broad and flexible since market developments and changing yield patterns may call for subsequent modification.

One way in which flexibility may be maintained in the allocation process is to provide for a "discretionary fund" or unallocated amount which may be diverted into either bonds or mortgages as circumstances dictate. The decision as to eventual allocation of this fund is often left to the full discretion of the financial vice president. Some companies leave the problem of allocation of funds entirely in the hands of the financial vice president without the need for prior review or approval by the finance committee. Even when prior approval is required, it is often a case of ratifying the recommendations of the financial officers since it is the operating investment staff which is in closest touch with the various segments of the capital market and therefore in a position to perceive the advantages of re-channeling investments into the most favorable outlets.

It may well be asked why it is necessary for allocation of funds to be decided several months in advance of actual investment or disbursement of funds. The answer is that the normal process of investing in bonds and mortgages involves a substantial lead time through the forward commitment of investment funds, which will be described at length in a later section. In order that each department may have a close working approximation of the funds available for investment during the subsequent eight or twelve months, it is necessary for an allocation to be made on which that department may base its negotiations and loan commitments. The size of this allocation will depend also upon the expectation as to the gross inflow of investible funds, known as the "cash flow," which is discussed in the following section. The problem of the interrelations among future cash flow, the allocation of funds, and the issuance of forward commitments has become one of the critical areas of investment management in life insurance companies today.

Cash Flow Available for Long-term Investment

The Origin and Composition of Cash Flow.   Approximately $11 billion annually flows into the investment departments of life insurance companies. This section will examine the origin and composition of the cash flow becoming available for long-term investment and will describe some of the influences affecting its magnitude.

The sources of cash flow may be classified into three groupings. The first of these is the "new money" arising from the net savings by policyholders in life insurance companies; this source provides, on a cash basis, over \$4½ billion per year.[1] The second source is the return flow from invested funds arising from amortization, maturities, and other repayments of bonds and mortgages, currently (1960) running at just under \$5 billion. Finally, funds for new investment may be obtained through the outright sale of long-term assets from the investment portfolio or the drawing down of cash and short-term security holdings; the amounts from this source are more variable but have exceeded \$1 billion in recent years.

The new money portion of cash flow is made up of the inflow from premiums, investment income, consideration for annuities, and other types of income, *less* the outflow of funds for death claims and other benefits, commissions, expenses, taxes, and other disbursements. These flows and the influences which affect their magnitude have been discussed at length in Chapter 2. In simplified terms, new money is roughly equivalent to the net saving by policyholders in life insurance. More technically, the new money portion of cash flow is made up of net investment income plus net income from insurance operation, less the net increase in policy loans. The latter are, of course, investment assets but do not represent investments under the control of the financial officers. Hence, a rise in policy loans means a decline in cash flow available for long-term investment in the capital market.

The return flow of funds from amortization and repayments of previous investments constitutes an important source of funds available for new investments. In the case of mortgage loans, the bulk of this flow is fairly stable since it is derived from contractual amortization payments which are typically on a monthly basis for residential mortgage loans but often on an annual or semi-annual basis for commercial, industrial, and farm mortgages. A more variable return flow of mortgage funds arises from prepayments in full which remove the loan from the company's books. Prepayment of the entire mortgage usually arises from sale of the underlying property by the previous owner. When the volume of new construction is rising, the resale market in existing homes becomes more active since many families are moving from older homes into new housing and paying off their mortgages in the process. Another reason for prepayment in full of a mortgage loan occurs when a substantial decline in mortgage rates induces the home owner or other mortgagor to refinance his mortgage (with another lender) at the lower interest rate. Finally, a small portion of mortgage repayments represent "partial" or "privilege" prepayments, typically when the mortgagor decides to accelerate his repayment because of a rise in income or a financial windfall.

The greater part of the return flow from bond investments represents

---

[1] The concept of saving employed here differs from that in Chapter 2, which accounts for the somewhat lower figure.

contractual redemptions through fixed sinking funds and scheduled maturities; the trend in this form of cash flow depends upon the scheduling of maturity dates at the time the bonds are added to the portfolio. Somewhat more variable is the cash flow from contingency sinking funds, based on the borrower's right to prepay the loan at a faster rate in the event of higher earnings or other contingencies; arrangements for this form of repayment are usually stipulated in the terms of the loan agreement. A highly variable, and usually undesirable, form of cash flow arises from the early call of a bond issue in order that the borrower may refund the loan at a lower interest rate. Since the cash flow from this source must be reinvested at interest rates substantially lower than the original yield, life insurance company investment officers have tended to avoid purchase of bonds containing this potential disadvantage and have insisted whenever possible upon protection against early refunding through security calls.

The above-listed forms of cash flow may be considered as the *basic* cash flow against which investment officers may design their future investment programs and issue forward investment commitments. These forms of cash flow are beyond the direct control of investment officers since they depend upon the decisions of policyholders to save through life insurance, or upon the scheduled repayments of bonds and mortgages, or upon certain repayment options made available to the borrower. The investment officers themselves, however, are able to sell long-term assets from portfolio, reduce holdings of short-term securities, or draw down cash in order to make new investments. Outright sales and the adjustment of cash position, therefore, constitute a third major form of cash flow.

Outright sales of long-term Government securities represented a substantial portion of cash flow during the early postwar years but have become less important during the recent past. The incentive to liquidate holdings of long-term Governments derives from the more attractive investment yields normally available on private investments. The sale of Governments, however, may often involve the taking of capital losses. A switch from Governments into private bonds or mortgages, therefore, requires a sufficiently higher rate of return to recoup the loss incurred on sales below par. Many of these same considerations apply to outright sales of other securities such as corporate and municipal bonds and preferred stock. Decisions to liquidate these securities, however, are likely to involve additional factors such as the desire to broaden the diversification of the bond portfolio or to move out of securities in which the borrower's credit standing has deteriorated. For example, if it were considered desirable to purchase a new bond being offered on the market, the only source of available funds might be the liquidation of present holdings which are relatively less attractive for a variety of possible reasons. In recent years, the dollar volume of outright sales of private securities has slightly exceeded sales of long-term Treasury securities which were formerly a major source of cash flow for new investment.

A small amount of mortgages, transportation equipment (such as leased railway cars or automobiles), and real estate holdings are also sold outright and contribute to cash flow. Although the cash flow derived in this way may be of some importance to particular companies, such sales are of minor proportions for the life insurance business as a whole.

Adjustments in cash position represent the other means by which investment officers may control their total cash flow. Cash position, in this context, comprises holdings of short-term Government securities, commercial paper, and similar kinds of temporary investments, as well as holdings of cash and bank deposits. When the cash position of a life insurance company is decreased, a larger volume of new long-term investments is possible than would otherwise be the case; conversely, a rise in cash position must necessarily be at the expense of new acquisitions of long-term investments. Because of the difficulty in coordinating exactly the aggregate cash flow from other sources with the aggregate investment acquisitions during a given month or quarter, variations in cash positions are necessary to balance out these opposing flows. As noted in a previous chapter, certain holdings of cash or short-term securities may be earmarked for acquisition of a particular bond issue or mortgage loan, in which case a company's cash position may build up steadily for several weeks and then decline sharply, through design, at the time funds are disbursed to the borrower in question. In a broader sense, maintaining a flexible cash position provides a necessary cushion to absorb the shifts in gross flows which are bound to occur during the course of the year.

It may be noted that a few companies prefer to hold their cash position to a minimum level and meet seasonal or temporary needs for cash through borrowing at commercial banks for short periods. Since such borrowing is repaid rather quickly there is little or no carryover of this seasonal form of cash flow from year to year, and the amounts involved are quite small.

Trends in Cash Flow, 1957-59. A reliable basis for gauging the origin and composition of cash flow through the investment departments of life insurance companies has become available only in the past few years. Early in 1957 the economic research department of the Life Insurance Association of America began the collection of cash flow data from representative companies throughout the business. Table 7-1 shows the annual cash flow data for the years 1957, 1958, and 1959 estimated on the basis of reports received from thirty-nine companies holding over

TABLE 7-1
Estimates of Investment Funds (Cash Flow) of
U.S. Life Insurance Companies

	Millions of dollars			Percent of total		
	1957	1958	1959	1957	1958	1959
Net new money—cash basis	4,300	4,600	4,600	46.2	44.1	42.2
Mortgages (total):	(2,800)	(3,180)	(3,460)	(30.1)	(30.5)	(31.8
Amortization and partial prepayment	1,960	2,110	2,240	21.1	20.2	20.6
Other cash repayments in full	810	1,060	1,200	8.7	10.2	11.0
Outright sales	30	10	20	0.3	0.1	0.2
Securities (total):	(2,190)	(2,710)	(2,370)	(23.5)	(26.0)	(21.8
Bond maturities	710	900	1,000	7.6	8.6	9.2
Contingency sinking funds	120	100	90	1.3	1.0	0.8
Other security calls	230	300	250	2.5	2.9	2.3
Outright sales: Treasury securities	430	620	380	4.6	6.0	3.5
Other securities	700	790	650	7.5	7.6	6.0
All other sales and repayments	120	150	140	1.3	1.4	1.3
Net increase (-) in cash and short-term investments	-100	-220	320	-1.1	-2.1	2.9
Total available for long-term investments	9,310	10,420	10,890	100.0	100.0	100.0

Data are estimated from reports to the Life Insurance Association of America on the actual cash flow of thirty-nine life insurance companies (holding over 56 percent of the total assets of all U.S. life companies) except that changes in cash and short-term investments are from tabulations of the LIAA and the Institute of Life Insurance for all U.S. life insurance companies.

56 percent of the total assets of United States life insurance companies.

As may be seen in Table 7-1, net new money on a cash basis totaled $4.6 billion in both 1958 and 1959, somewhat above the 1957 level. As a percentage of total cash flow, however, new money has declined from 46 percent in 1957 to 42 percent in 1959. Mortgage repayments constitute roughly 30 percent of life insurance company cash flow, with $2.2 billion coming from scheduled amortization and partial prepayments and $1.2 billion from "paid in fulls" which remove the loan from the company's books. A negligible amount of cash flow came from the outright sale of mortgages.

Despite the fact that bond holdings are much larger than mortgage holdings in life company portfolios, the cash flow generated by bond maturities (including fixed sinking funds) is much smaller than from the amortization of mortgages, amounting to only $1 billion in 1959. The reason for this is not hard to find. Most important is the monthly amortization feature of residential mortgages, which automatically reduces the outstanding balance and roughly cuts in half the average life of a mortgage loan. Although many bonds carry fixed sinking fund provisions, which also reduce the outstanding balance with the passage of time, this feature is far less common than the monthly amortization of mort-gages. Contingency sinking funds have not been of much importance in recent years, generating only about $100 million in cash flow. Security calls ran considerably higher, with a temporary increase to $300 million during the decline of interest rates in 1958. The relatively high level of long-term rates throughout the 1957-59 period has precluded the large volume of calls for refunding which would be almost certain to occur, in the absence of call protection, if interest rates dipped substantially.

Table 7-1 shows a rise in 1958 in outright sales of both Treasury securi-ties and other securities, apparently facilitated by the rise in bond prices that year and the ability to liquidate certain bond holdings at a smaller capital loss than in 1957. As interest rates rose and bond prices declined in 1959, however, the volume of outright sales of securities declined from $1.4 billion to $1.0 billion, and the amount of funds available for new long-term investments was thereby reduced.

The data on other sales and repayments shown in Table 7-1 represent largely the cash flow realized from miscellaneous assets such as real estate and transportation equipment. They also include the net effect of small amounts of bank borrowing and repayment. This type of cash flow has amounted to barely more than 1 percent of the total. Adjustments in cash position, taken over a twelve-month period, have not been important in total cash flow, as may be seen in Table 7-1. In 1958, cash position was increased by $220 million, reducing by that amount the funds available for long-term outlets. In 1959, the reverse was true; cash position was reduced by $320 million, thus adding to the volume of available funds.

The Forward Commitment Process

The practice by life insurance companies of making forward invest-ment commitments has its foundations in the relative stability of their cash flow available for investment, as reflected in Table 7-1, the objective of maintaining a fully invested position, and the need of borrowers to know that funds will be forthcoming when required. A forward invest-ment commitment may be defined as a binding agreement on the part of the company to lend a specified amount of money at a given interest rate for a certain number of years, within an agreed upon time period. The process thus enables borrowers to plan their capital expenditures with assurance that external funds will be available and enables lenders to schedule disbursements to balance, as closely as possible, with their expected inflow of funds.

A commitment agreement may be oral or written, but in either case is regarded as binding on the part of the lender. Almost all life insurance companies issue a written commitment in connection with applications for residential or commercial mortgage loans, usually employing a simple printed form for home mortgage loans and a commitment letter for commercial mortgages. In the case of directly placed corporate bonds, however, the use of a written commitment varies. Although probably the majority of companies indicate in writing their intent to make the requested loan, there are a number which customarily have no signed commitment agreement for direct placements until details of the transaction and indenture terms are settled and the loan agreement is signed. The oral commitment is nevertheless as firm as a written one.

Because of the varying practice among companies in the use of written commitments and in the delegation of authority, and because of the variety of borrowers served, the point at which a commitment is considered to have been made also varies. The approval of the finance committee or, when there is delegation of authority, the approval of the authorized lending officer serves as the effective commitment action in the case of corporate bonds much more frequently than in the case of residential mortgages where, as noted, a signed commitment agreement is almost always provided.

The time period ahead covered by a forward commitment generally runs from one month to two and a half years. When circumstances require, a longer forward period would be provided but in actual practice most borrowers do not seek funds for further ahead than about two and a half or three years. The forward period varies by type of investment, size of borrower and lender, and also depends upon whether new construction is involved. On existing homes a typical mortgage commitment is for three months, while for new construction commitments are usually in effect from six to twelve months. Those for apartment houses, loans which most often are made by larger insurance companies, may be made for two or two and a half years. In the corporate bond field in which the bulk of commitments are made in connection with direct placements,[2] the effective life of a commitment varies with the size of lending company somewhat more often than it does in the field of home mortgage lending. The maximum time period for which large life insurance companies commit their funds generally ranges between a year to two and a half years, or longer. Smaller life companies are more often found to have a forward period of a year or less for their bond purchases. These

---

[2] In the statistical series of forward investment commitments compiled by the Life Insurance Association of America, commitments to buy publicly offered securities are also included. The reporting companies provide figures on commitments made during the month that were still outstanding at the end of the month and the total backlog of commitments at month end. Thus the amount of any unfilled orders at the end of a month for publicly offered securities would appear in the data.

time periods are not so much a matter of fixed policy on the part of lenders as they are a reflection of the needs and customary practices of their borrowers. It appears that large borrowers, who because of the size of their requirements must deal with lenders of sufficient size to accommodate their needs, plan capital expenditures further ahead than smaller borrowers.

The delayed takedown of commitments may serve to provide an additional flexibility in the lending operation of insurance companies. The making of new commitments is carried on within the limits of the allocations of funds into the various outlets open to life insurance companies. These allocations are not necessarily rigid, as noted earlier, and may be modified in the light of capital market developments. Even without an increase in the allotment of investible funds, however, the delayed takedown may permit the authorization of some loans which could not otherwise be considered. For example, if the securities department had used its allocation for the year, through actual investments already made and through commitments almost certain to be taken down within the year, it would be expected that a borrower seeking funds at this point would have to be turned away. Where the need for funds, however, is a few months in the future when a new year's allocations of funds would be available to the securities department, the application could be considered.

The commitment process is, of course, very closely bound to the steady inflow of cash available for investment and is in a sense a counterpart of cash flow. A measure of the relationship of commitments to cash flow available for investment (as defined in the preceding section) is provided for a large sample of companies by reports made to the Life Insurance Association of America. Although commitment data have been reported monthly beginning with April 1951, cash flow reporting on a quarterly basis was not initiated until 1957, so that the relationships of commitments to cash flow are available only from the later date.

Table 7-2 provides data on the amount of commitments outstanding at the end of calendar quarters, the annual rate of cash flow prevailing over the year ended with the quarter, and the ratio of the backlog of commitments to cash flow. (Commitments are for *forward* investment and the cash flow figures here is for the *past* year. The ratio is computed on this basis on the ground that when reviewing their commitment position companies are probably influenced by their experience with cash flow of the immediate past.) It may be seen that for these companies the backlog of commitments generally accounted for between 55 percent and 65 percent of their annual volume of investible funds.

From an operating viewpoint particular attention must be paid to data on the expected takedowns of commitments and the cash flow expected over the same forward period. Information on expectations for

TABLE 7-2
Ratio of Commitments Outstanding to Annual Rate of Cash Flow

Quarter ended	(1) Total commitments outstanding	(2) Annual rate of cash flow	(1) ÷ (2)
	(In millions of dollars)		(In percent)
1957 Dec. 31	3,305	5,366	62
1958 March 31	3,304	5,184	64
June 30	3,451	5,398	64
Sept. 30	3,793	5,605	68
Dec. 31	3,454	5,869	59
1959 March 31	3,486	6,078	57
June 30	3,537	6,079	58
Sept. 30	3,342	6,079	55
Dec. 31	3,072	6,031	51
1960 March 31	3,344	5,969	56
June 30	3,404	5,805	59
Sept. 30	3,480	5,715	61
Dec. 31	3,365	5,582	60

Data are for identical companies reporting commitments and cash flow consistently over the period. The companies account for 56 percent of the assets of all life insurance companies.

Annual rate of cash flow equals investible funds as reported in the four quarters ended with the quarter indicated.

six months ahead at various calendar quarters is set forth in Table 7-3. For the purpose of showing the relationship of expected takedowns and cash flow, the latter is shown in two ways: one includes funds from the sale of securities and the adjustment for change in cash position, and the second excludes these items. Since sales of securities and changes in cash position provide a means for bringing into balance the demand for and supply of funds, the exclusion of these items permits a closer measure of the commitment position. On this basis, the volume of commitments expected to be disbursed during the ensuing six months have generally averaged from 75 percent to 85 percent of the cash flow expected for the period. These ratios are, of course, averages for the group, and individual companies may vary widely from the average. Some companies prefer to work closely to the cash flow expected, and some acquire a volume of securities in the public market (which do not usually require forward commitments as defined here), while others invest almost entirely in direct placements.

Summary

Responsibility for the investment activities of a life insurance company rests ultimately with the finance committee of its board of directors. This body is composed typically of five or seven members, but there are some-

TABLE 7-3
Ratios of Expected Takedowns of Commitments to Expected Cash
Flow During Ensuing Six Months

Quarter ended	Takedowns of commitments expected in six months	Cash flow expected in six months		Col. (1) Col. (2)	Col. (1) Col. (3)
		Sales of securities and adjustment for change in cash position			
		Included	Excluded		
	(1)	(2)	(3)	(4)	(5)
	(In millions of dollars)			(In percent)	
1957 March 31	1,972	2,532	2,329	78	85
June 30	1,892	2,576	2,434	73	78
Sept. 30	1,822	2,594	2,400	70	76
Dec. 31	1,721	2,259	2,110	76	82
1958 March 31	1,687	*	*	72*	80*
June 30	1,955	*	*	72*	82*
Sept. 30	2,201	2,937	2,541	75	87
Dec. 31	1,953	2,615	2,398	75	81
1959 March 31	1,969	2,717	2,507	72	79
June 30	2,126	3,129	2,728	68	78
Sept. 30	2,000	2,837	2,705	71	74
Dec. 31	1,855	2,496	2,430	74	76
1960 March 31	1,965	2,712	2,472	72	79
June 30	2,013	2,813	2,642	72	76
Sept. 30	2,114	2,854	2,607	74	81
Dec. 31	2,019	2,768	2,543	73	79

*One company did not provide projections of expected cash flow; ratios are based on data of companies reporting both commitments and cash flow.

Data are for identical companies reporting commitments and cash flow consistently over the period. The companies account for 56 percent of the assets of all life insurance companies.

times as few as three or as many as ten members. As might be expected, a background in banking or finance predominates among its members. In order that there may be a balanced representation, one or two members are likely to be executives of manufacturing or commercial concerns or public utilities, bringing a business viewpoint to the work of the committee. Among medium-sized and smaller life companies, but less frequently in larger companies, the members of the finance committee will often include the president or the financial vice president of the insurance company.

The finance committee carries the ultimate responsibility for investment activities of the life insurance company and controls the broad direction of these operations. To facilitate the administration of investment policy and to allow flexibility in timing, the committee quite often delegates authority to investment officers for loans of limited amounts. Even these loans are subject to later review by the committee. In the main, the bulk of new investments are approved only after individual scrutiny by the committee, based on the detailed analysis and recommendations presented by the financial officers of the company. While the financial officers concern themselves with making investment selections, the finance committee is continually called upon to exercise its judgment in shaping the investment philosophy of the company and in making the final investment decisions.

The typical practice among life insurance companies is for a single investment officer, usually designated as the financial vice president, to have jurisdiction over all investment operations including both bonds and mortgages. This officer often is a member of the finance committee and serves as a direct liaison between that body and the investment staff. In a number of companies, however, there is no single investment manager with over-all responsibility; instead, separate vice presidents head the securities department and the mortgage department, respectively, and report directly to the finance committee and to the company president. In such cases, it is more likely that the allocation of funds between securities and mortgages is fixed by the finance committee. Where a financial vice president exists, that officer normally has the authority to determine the allocation of investment flows between the departments under his charge, usually subject to ratification by the finance committee.

Approximately $11 billion annually flows into the investment departments of the life insurance companies of this country. The sources of this cash flow may be classified into three groupings. The first of these is the "new money" arising from the net savings by policyholders in life insurance companies. This source provides over $4.5 billion per year. The second source is the return flow from invested funds arising from amortization, maturities, and other repayments of bonds and mortgages, currently running at just under $5 billion. Thirdly, funds for new investment may be obtained through the outright sale of long-term assets from the investment portfolio or the drawing down of cash and short-term securities holdings. The amounts from this source are more variable but have exceeded $1 billion in recent years.

The practice by life insurance companies of making forward investment commitments has its foundations in the relative stability of their cash flow available for investment, the objective of maintaining a fully invested position, and the need of borrowers to know that funds will be forthcoming when required. A forward investment commitment may be defined as a binding agreement on the part of the company to lend a specific amount of money at a given interest rate for a certain number of years, within an agreed upon time period. The process thus enables borrowers to plan their capital expenditures with assurance that external funds will be available and enables lenders to schedule disbursements to balance, as closely as possible, with their expected inflow of funds.

Chapter 8

INFLUENCE OF FEDERAL GOVERNMENT POLICY MEASURES ON LIFE INSURANCE COMPANY INVESTMENTS

The purpose of this chapter is to consider the various ways in which Federal policy measures influence life insurance company investments. Chapters 5 and 6 discussed the ways in which state laws and regulatory measures have their impact upon the investments of life companies.

It is sometimes asserted that the investment policies and activities of life insurance companies are largely unaffected by federal policy measures, and particularly unaffected by monetary policy. The argument advanced is that, although Federal Reserve policy has a direct impact upon the lending and investing of commercial banks, the effect of monetary policy on life insurance companies, and nonbank financial intermediaries generally, is very limted and indirect. This view is not substantiated by the facts, at least so far as life insurance companies are concerned. As will be developed in this chapter, life insurance company investments are affected in many important ways by government policies having an impact on the money and capital markets. Both the *direction of flow* of life insurance funds and the *volume* of these funds are influenced by Federal policy actions.

The discussion will cover the following areas of government policy action as they affect life insurance company investments: (1) monetary policy; (2) federal debt management policy; (3) other federal policy actions such as government insurance and guaranty of home mortgage loans, regulation of maximum terms on government-underwritten mortgages, and the control of redemption features in public utility bond issues by the Securities and Exchange Commission and the Federal Power Commission; and (4) taxation.

The Influence of Monetary Policy

In beginning consideration of the influence exerted by monetary policy on life insurance company investments, there are three characteristics of the investment operations of life insurance companies which are pertinent. First, as seen earlier, the life companies invest their funds in a wide variety of outlets, and thus there are many points of exposure to Federal Reserve policy actions. They are the largest investor in corporate bonds, covering the business and industrial, as well as the public utility and railroad areas. Their purchases of "direct placements" of corporate bonds bring their lending operations into an area closely akin to the term loans of commercial banks. Some companies are also active in the preferred and common stock markets. They have been the biggest factor in commercial and industrial mortgage lending, and in mid-1960 they had a combined FHA-VA residential mortgage portfolio larger than any other investor group. In addition, they are a major lender in the conventional residential mortgage field; they are the biggest factor in the purchase-leaseback field; and they have in the past been a large investor in U.S. Government securities. The securities of state and local government units do not bulk large in life company investment holdings, but even here the insurance companies have been highly important in revenue bond financing. Although life insurance companies are primarily long-term lenders, their purchases of Treasury bills and commercial paper are substantial. The point is that life insurance company funds as a whole flow into almost every area of investment. This is quite different from other institutional investors such as the mutual savings banks, savings and loan associations, and uninsured pension funds, where by law or custom the range of investment channels is much more limited. Because the flow of life company investments is so diversified, spreading virtually throughout the entire national market for loanable funds, there are many points at which Federal Reserve policy actions can and do exert their influence.

A second characteristic of life insurance company investments which is noteworthy in this connection is that the great bulk of their funds are placed in long-term, fixed-income obligations—bonds and mortgages. The obligations held by life companies are therefore subject to wide swings in market price occasioned by changes in long-term interest rates. Thus, as will be developed more fully later, the ability of life companies to convert existing assets into cash is seriously affected by changes in the level of long-term interest rates.

The third characteristic of life insurance company investing which is pertinent here is the great sensitivity which life companies have to changing differentials in investment yields. Life companies are keenly competitive with one another with respect to the rate of investment return. As noted earlier, the higher the rate of investment return, the greater the possibilities for reducing the cost of life insurance to policy-holders, and thus the more favorable competitive position of a company. Moreover, the higher the rate of investment return, the better the chance for life companies to meet the competitive challenge of other institutions such as mutual funds and uninsured pension funds. It is not surprising, therefore, that the investment officers of life companies are alert to changing yield differentials and are quick to take advantage of such changes. This sensitivity to changing yield spreads is an important factor in the effect which the monetary authorities can have on life company investments.

General Discussion. Keeping in mind these three characteristics of life insurance company investments, what are the ways in which monetary policy measures are brought to bear on life insurance companies? It will perhaps be helpful to consider this question first in broad terms and then to go into details with supporting documentation. The impact of *general* credit control measures on life company investments, as differentiated from *selective* credit controls which are discussed presently, has made itself felt in the following manner. When monetary policy has been directed to increasing the net free reserves of the commercial banking system, and thus to expanding the availability of loanable funds from the commercial banks, one of the prompt results has been increased competition for commercial loans and lower rates on such loans. Another result has usually been an expansion of commercial bank purchases of shorter-term Government securities and, depending upon the degree of ease in the bank reserves, a resulting decline in yields of shorter-term Governments.[1] With the decline in yield of shorter-term Government securities, increased availability of funds for commercial bank loans quickly acts to bring down the entire structure of short-term loan rates. As short-term rates decline, there is a natural tendency for commercial banks to reach out for the longer-term, higher-yielding Government securities and municipal bonds, thus bidding up their prices and reducing yields. Moreover, as shorter-term rates decline, the banks tend to become more competitive in the term-lending field, and accordingly the force of their competition acts to reduce the yields on direct placements of corporate securities. In addition, with a decline of short-term interest rates, and a tendency for long-term rates to soften, prospective long-term borrowers are encouraged to make greater use of short-term commercial bank financing in anticipation of lower long-term borrowing costs.

---

[1] The process described here has been true of periods of credit ease prior to 1960-61, but it is less true of this latter period because of the efforts made by the authorities to avoid too great a decline in short-term rates because of the gold outflow problem.

One effect of these various forces is that the yields on new offerings of corporate bonds decline. This is particularly true of new offerings of publicly-offered bonds where the response to monetary ease is most prompt. It is also true of the yields on direct placements, but the impact here is likely to be somewhat slower in being felt. In turn, the decline of yields in the corporate bond area leads some investors, notably life insurance companies, to shift their investment emphasis to mortgages, and thus the credit-easing effect is transmitted to the mortgage market by the increased availability of funds in that area. The speed with which the entire process works depends not only on demand and supply forces but also on the expectations of investors. When the monetary authorities create the expectation of a trend toward greater credit and capital market ease, the increased willingness of investors to commit their funds while rates are still comparatively high strengthens the market forces toward ease. Likewise, when borrowers expect credit and capital market conditions to ease, they hold back on their borrowing to take advantage of the anticipated lower rates.

The life insurance companies, being a vital part of the supply of long-term capital funds, are naturally affected by the changes in interest rates set in motion by a move toward credit ease by the monetary authorities.[2] As yields on corporate bonds decline, both on new public offerings and direct placements, there are several important effects on life company investment operations. One is that life companies become more willing to assume a fully committed position with respect to their cash flow as they expect rates to decline. This in itself exerts additional force toward declining interest rates. Another is that their investment emphasis shifts away from areas of the market where yields are declining to those areas where yields are slower to respond to monetary policy measures. In the main, this means shifting from corporate bonds to residential mortgages, particularly government-underwritten mortgages. Still another effect of declining interest rates is that the capacity of life companies to generate cash for investment is improved. As will be discussed in more detail later, as interest rates decline the cash flow of life companies from mort-

---

[2] In this discussion it should be borne in mind that it is *changing interest rates* which influence the investment policies of life insurance companies. Actually, as interest rates change in response to market demand and supply conditions (regardless of whether Federal Reserve policy measures are leading the way or merely following the change), the impact on life insurance investments will be as described here. In other words, under conditions of significant change in interest rates in response to changing market conditions, even with Federal Reserve policy neutral, the impact on life insurance investments outlined here would occur. Since the emphasis in this section is on the influence of monetary policy on life insurance investments, the discussion places the monetary authorities in a leading role with respect to interest rate changes. It should be recognized, however, that changes in market demand and supply forces have usually been the underlying forces.

gage repayments is increased, more funds tend to be left on deposit with the companies, refunding of debt at lower interest rates occurs, and as the market values of investment holdings rise it is possible to dispose of assets at smaller losses.

The reverse of this process takes place when the monetary authorities take action to tighten the reserve position of the commercial banking system and thus the general availability of bank credit.[3] In order to obtain funds to expand their loans, the banks dispose of shorter-term Government securities and thus set in motion a general rise of short-term interest rates. This rise is, of course, also the product of expanding demand for business and industrial loans. With an expanding commercial loan demand and rising short-term rates, the commercial banks tend to reduce their term-lending and their purchases of municipal bonds, thus contributing to lesser availability of long-term financing. As short-term rates rise there is a natural tendency for borrowers to move into longer-term borrowing, which acts to set in motion a general rise of long-term rates. This rise is reinforced and accelerated by expectations of borrowers and investors. As borrowers come to expect increasing interest rates, they tend to seek financing promptly in order to avoid the expected higher rates. Similarly, as investors anticipate rising rates, they tend to be less willing to commit fully their anticipated cash flow. Thus, the initial impulse of a tightening of commercial bank credit, by means of arbitrage, and accelerated by expectations speedily is transmitted throughout the longer-term capital market. The more sensitive long-term interest rates, such as those on publicly offered corporate bonds, are prompt to turn upward, but the rise quickly spreads to direct placements of corporate bonds and to mortgages.

As the monetary authorities move to tighten the reserve position of the commercial banking system and the general availability of bank credit, the specific impact on life insurance companies is as follows. As yields on corporate bonds rise, both on new public offerings and direct placements, there are a number of important effects on life company investment operations.[4] One is that life companies tend to become less willing to assume a fully committed position with respect to their cash flow as they expect interest rates to rise. This in itself serves to reinforce the tightening in availability of long-term funds. Another effect is that their investment emphasis shifts toward areas where yields are sensitive and are rising and away from areas where yields are slower to change. In the

---

[3] Here again the prime consideration is rising interest rates, which may occur largely independently of monetary policy measures.

[4] It should be re-emphasized that these effects occur because of changing interest rates, which might take place even under a neutral credit policy by the monetary authorities.

main this means shifting emphasis toward direct placements of corporate securities and industrial and commercial mortgages. It likewise means shifting away from government-insured and guaranteed mortgages, where interest rates are rigid. Still another effect of rising interest rates is that the capacity of life companies to generate cash for investment is reduced. As will be discussed in more detail later, with interest rates rising the cash flow of life companies from mortgage repayments tends to decrease, less funds tend to be left on deposit with the companies, policy loans expand, and as the market values of existing holdings decline it is only possible to dispose of assets at larger and larger losses.

The discussion up to this point has referred exclusively to the impact of general credit controls. As will be considered later in this chapter, the life insurance companies have also been affected by selective credit controls, for example, by Regulation X and the Voluntary Credit Restraint Program. Before turning to that discussion, however, it would be helpful to analyze in greater detail and to document wherever possible the influence general credit control measures exert on: (1) the direction of flow of life insurance company funds; (2) the liquidity of assets held by life companies; (3) the cash flow of the companies; and (4) their policy with respect to forward commitments.

Direction of Flow of Funds. The best way to illustrate the effect of monetary policy measures on the direction of flow of life insurance funds is to trace the experience during recent changes in Federal Reserve policy. It will be recalled that in early 1953, in the face of a sustained rise in the level of general business activity, the monetary authorities were pursuing a policy of credit restraint. Chart 8-1 shows the heavy net borrowed reserve position of the commercial banking system at that time. Because of strong demands for loanable funds throughout the money and capital markets, plus the restrictive credit policy, interest rates on bank loans and corporate bond yields rose sharply through the first five months of 1953 (see Charts 8-2 and 8-3). As shown in Table 8-1 and Chart 8-4, new commitments of life insurance companies to purchase corporate bonds and commercial and industrial mortgages were comparatively high.[5] This was also true of conventional residential mortgages. This is what might have been expected because interest rates in these areas of the capital market are sensitive and had moved higher in response to market forces and monetary policy. On the other hand, as shown in Table 8-2 and Chart 8-5, new commitments by life companies to purchase VA-guaranteed mortgages in the first two quarters of 1953

---

[5] The commitment figures used throughout this chapter are compiled from reports submitted by life insurance companies holding about 65 percent of the total assets of all U.S. life insurance companies. It is believed that the companies not reporting would fit the general commitment pattern of those reporting.

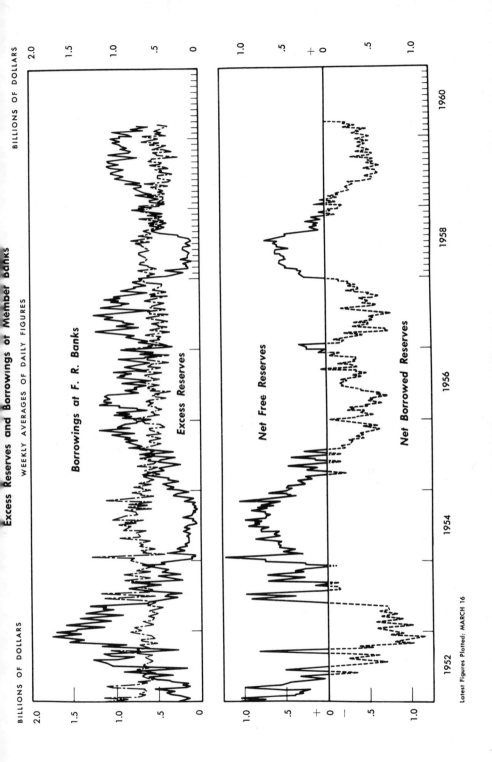

Excess Reserves and Borrowings of Member Banks

WEEKLY AVERAGES OF DAILY FIGURES

BILLIONS OF DOLLARS

Borrowings at F. R. Banks

Excess Reserves

Net Free Reserves

Net Borrowed Reserves

Latest Figures Plotted: MARCH 16

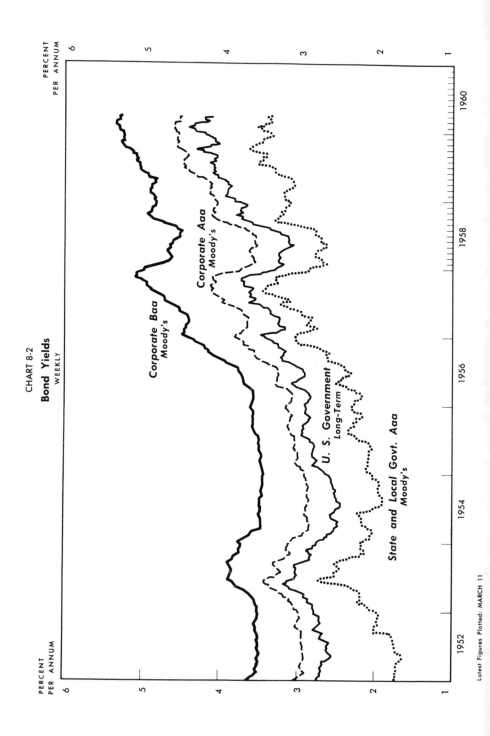

CHART 8-2

Bond Yields
WEEKLY

PERCENT
PER ANNUM

Corporate Baa
Moody's

Corporate Aaa
Moody's

U. S. Government
Long-Term

State and Local Govt. Aaa
Moody's

Latest Figures Plotted: MARCH 11

198

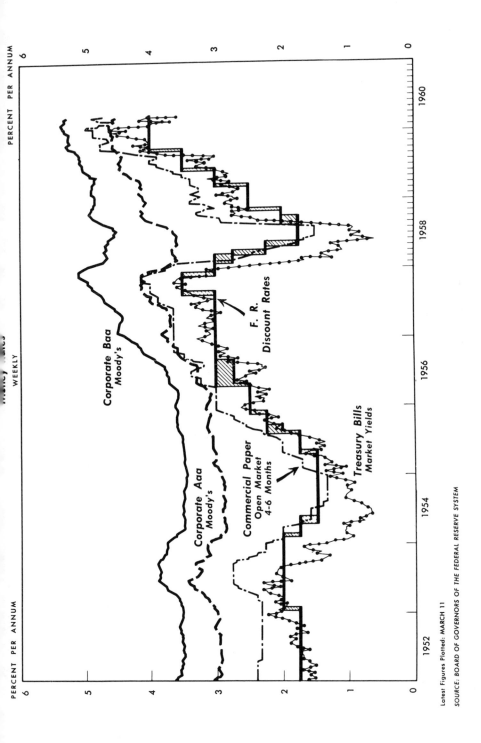

Money Rates

WEEKLY

PERCENT PER ANNUM

Corporate Baa
Moody's

Corporate Aaa
Moody's

Commercial Paper
Open Market
4-6 Months

F. R.
Discount Rates

Treasury Bills
Market Yields

1952   1954   1956   1958   1960

Latest Figures Plotted: MARCH 11

SOURCE: BOARD OF GOVERNORS OF THE FEDERAL RESERVE SYSTEM

CHART 8-4

**New Commitments of Life Insurance Companies for FHA and VA Residential Mortgages,
Corporate Bonds, and Commercial and Industrial Mortgages
4th Quarter 1952 - 4th Quarter 1959**

(In Millions of Dollars)

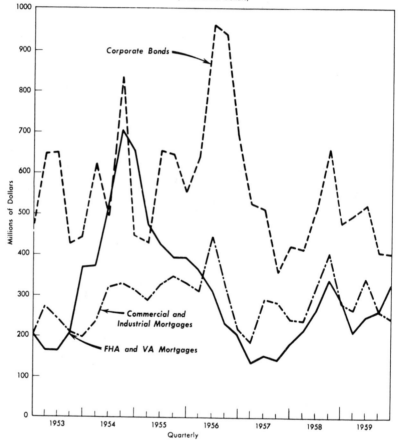

CHART 8-5

**New Commitments of Life Insurance Companies for
Residential Mortgages, 4th Quarter 1952 - 4th Quarter 1959**
(In Millions of Dollars)

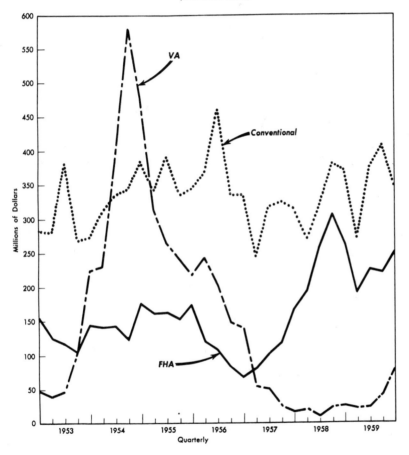

CHART 8-6

Net Uses of Funds in Selected Investments of Life Insurance Companies, 1947-1959
(In Billions of Dollars)

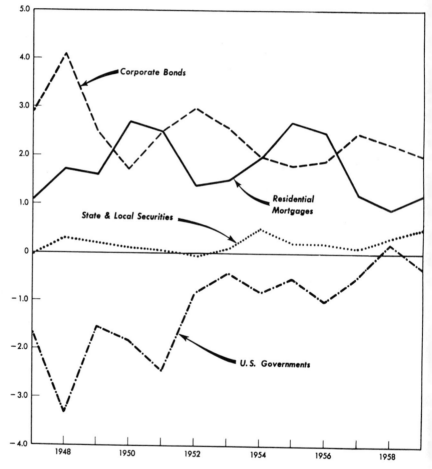

CHART 8-7

Index of Outstanding Commitments of Life Insurance Companies
1951 - 1959
(April 1951 = 100)

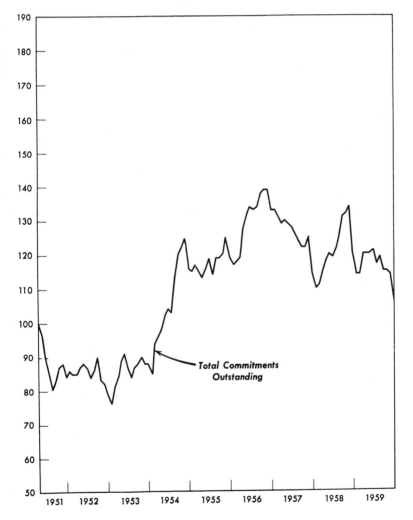

CHART 8-8

Index of Outstanding Commitments of Life Insurance Companies
1951 - 1959
(April 1951 = 100)

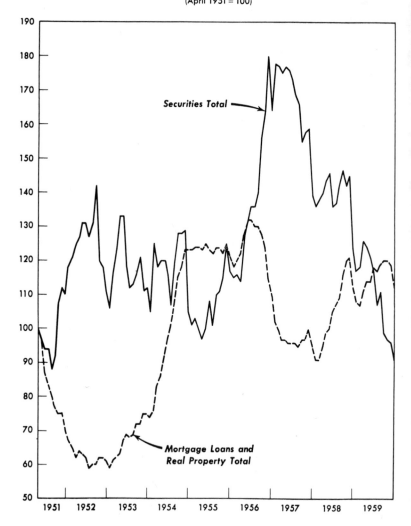

Securities Total

Mortgage Loans and
Real Property Total

TABLE 8-1
New Commitments of Life Insurance Companies
for FHA and VA Residential Mortgages, Corporate Bonds,
and Commercial and Industrial Mortgages
4th Quarter 1952 - 4th Quarter 1959

(In millions of dollars)

Quarter	FHA and VA mortgages	Corporate bonds	Commercial and industrial mortgages
1952 - 4th	203	457	205
1953 - 1st	165	648	275
2nd	166	650	245
3rd	210	428	211
4th	370	444	199
1954 - 1st	372	625	236
2nd	524	498	320
3rd	705	834	330
4th	654	445	315
1955 - 1st	476	430	290
2nd	427	656	327
3rd	394	649	350
4th	393	556	333
1956 - 1st	365	643	312
2nd	312	963	445
3rd	234	940	322
4th	209	693	220
1957 - 1st	134	529	187
2nd	152	516	292
3rd	144	360	286
4th	182	426	242
1958 - 1st	216	416	240
2nd	266	513	324
3rd	341	661	407
4th	290	479	286
1959 - 1st	212	498	267
2nd	250	523	345
3rd	264	408	265
4th	330	405	248

Life insurance companies reporting commitments represent about 65 percent of the total assets of all U.S. life insurance companies.

New commitments include only those made during a month that were still outstanding at the end of the month.

were at very low levels.[6] The reason for this is well-known, namely, that

[6] Data on new commitments of life companies are unfortunately not available for an earlier period than the fourth quarter of 1952, but the index numbers on outstanding VA commitments clearly show that the first two quarters of 1953 was a low point in new VA commitments.

TABLE 8-2
New Commitments of Life Insurance Companies
for Residential Mortgages,
4th Quarter 1952 - 4th Quarter 1959

(In millions of dollars)

Quarter	FHA insured	VA guaranteed	Conventional
1952 - 4th	154.7	48.1	283.0
1953 - 1st	125.5	39.4	279.1
2nd	118.2	47.5	381.6
3rd	105.5	105.0	268.1
4th	145.3	225.0	274.3
1954 - 1st	141.3	230.6	311.3
2nd	142.6	381.8	335.8
3rd	124.1	580.8	345.4
4th	176.0	478.0	383.2
1955 - 1st	161.5	314.0	340.9
2nd	162.7	264.2	393.2
3rd	153.4	240.5	334.5
4th	174.3	218.7	344.8
1956 - 1st	120.9	244.1	368.6
2nd	108.1	203.5	462.9
3rd	84.8	149.0	335.0
4th	68.5	140.1	335.8
1957 - 1st	80.4	53.5	243.3
2nd	101.4	50.5	318.8
3rd	119.3	24.7	324.2
4th	166.7	15.1	315.0
1958 - 1st	195.3	20.3	270.5
2nd	257.0	9.3	317.8
3rd	318.2	22.6	381.5
4th	264.8	25.7	372.3
1959 - 1st	192.3	20.1	273.5
2nd	226.6	23.1	377.3
3rd	221.6	42.1	409.3
4th	250.3	79.4	349.3

Life insurance companies reporting commitments represent
about 65 percent of the total assets of all U.S. life insurance
companies.

New commitments include only those made during a month
that were still outstanding at the end of the month.

the maximum rate on VA mortgages had been maintained rigidly at 4
percent, a level that was far out of touch with competitive yields in the
corporate bond and conventional mortgage markets. At this time it was
generally understood by investors that it was illegal to purchase VA

mortgages at a discount.[7] Although our concern here is primarily with life insurance companies, the same forces had reduced VA commitments of other institutional investors such as mutual savings banks, savings and loan associations, and commercial banks, as is borne out by the low level of VA housing starts in late 1952 and early 1953.

In the latter part of the spring of 1953, it will be recalled, the level of general business activity began to turn downward as a result of a cutback in business inventories, a sharp reduction in federal national defense expenditures, and other factors. At that time the monetary authorities shifted to an easier credit policy, and then in the second half of 1953 to active credit ease, with net free reserves of the commercial banking system rising sharply to a level of $500 million and over, as compared with net borrowed reserves of $500 million and over in the first five months of the year (Chart 8-1). In addition to this change in Federal Reserve policy, another most significant change occurred almost simultaneously. After several months of anguished indecision by the Congress and the Veterans Administration, as the availability of VA mortgage financing reached the vanishing point, action was finally taken to raise the VA maximum rate from 4 to 4½ percent, and the FHA maximum rate was increased from 4¼ percent to 4½ percent.

The combined effect of a lessened demand for business and industrial financing, as the national economy moved into recession, plus the move of the monetary authorities toward credit ease, and then "active ease," produced a prompt decline in money rates and corporate bond yields, as well as yields on conventional mortgages (Charts 8-2 and 8-3). The speed with which this occurred was made greater by investor and borrower expectations with respect to the outlook for business and monetary policy.

As might have been anticipated in the face of declining corporate bond yields, and the expectation of further declines, measured against the more attractive rate on VA mortgages, the life insurance companies promptly and sharply expanded their new commitments to purchase VA mortgages. Table 8-2 shows the spectacular rise of new VA commitments from $47.5 million in the second quarter of 1953 to $225 million in the fourth quarter. In the same period there was some tendency for FHA commitments to rise, but the sharp increase was in the VA area.

It was apparently true that in the second half of 1953 there existed a dammed-up demand for VA financing which absorbed the increased flow of funds without much effect on VA loan terms. However, in early 1954

---

[7] Throughout this discussion it should be recognized that life insurance companies have been reluctant to purchase government-insured and guaranteed mortgages, especially VA mortgages, at large discounts. As discounts have risen, therefore, the reaction has been to reduce such investments and to shift into other investment areas in which interest rates were not subject to government regulations.

the demand for VA-financed housing began to soften, and lending institutions further liberalized VA loan terms to the point that such credit became generally available on the maximum thirty-year, no-down payment basis. Various additional incentives were employed by builders to attract home purchasers, and hence the term "no no-down payment" came into the lexicon of the mortgage market.[8] With this type of financing, the demand for VA loans quickened, and new VA commitments of life insurance companies rose spectacularly to $580.8 million in the third quarter of 1954 and then started to decline.

The greatly expanded flow of life insurance funds into government-underwritten mortgages, which was induced in considerable measure by the easy credit policy of the Federal Reserve, as well as by the reduction in other credit demands, contributed much to the rising rate of home construction in 1954 and 1955, in which latter year private non-farm housing starts exceeded 1.3 million (old series). Although it is outside the purview of this discussion, similar forces operated with other lending institutions such as mutual savings banks and commercial banks.

By the latter part of 1954, outstanding commitments of life insurance companies had advanced 40 percent over the level of early 1953, resulting almost entirely from heavy new commitments for residential mortgages, particularly VA loans. In late 1954 and through most of 1955, the level of outstanding commitments registered a moderate decline as the backlog of prior commitments was worked off more rapidly than new commitments were made (Chart 8-7). As shown in Chart 8-5 the volume of new commitments for VA loans dropped sharply in this period, while new commitments for FHA and conventional residential loans and for commercial and industrial mortgages (Chart 8-4) continued to advance moderately through 1955. In the corporate bond field, the volume of new commitments declined in late 1954 and early 1955 (see Chart 8-4), reducing the level of outstanding commitments for securities during that period as shown in Chart 8-8.

Toward the end of 1955, business activity began to take on boom dimensions, with rising plant and equipment spending by industry and a build-up of business inventories coming on top of already high levels of consumer spending and residential construction. Demands for short and long-term financing mounted and interest rates began to move upward in early 1956 as shown in Charts 8-2 and 8-3. The Federal Reserve moved to a more restrictive credit policy and the net borrowed reserve position of the banking system returned to the $500 million level.

Analysis of their forward commitment position demonstrates that the response of life insurance companies to restrictive monetary policy and

---

[8] For example, it was a common practice for the builder to pay the closing costs on mortgages and in some instances the moving expenses for their customers.

changed market conditions was prompt. New commitments for corporate bonds rose sharply beginning in late 1955, responding to the more attractive yields available on such securities and to the quickened demands by corporations for capital funds to finance expansion of plant facilities (see Chart 8-4). Commercial and industrial mortgage commitments also advanced in response to the same type of demand. Meanwhile, statutory rates on FHA and VA mortgages were rigidly maintained and became less attractive to life insurance companies by comparison with yields available on bonds; the result was a further reduction during 1956 in the volume of new commitments for insured and guaranteed mortgages.[9] The net effect of these shifts in new commitment trends upon the outstanding levels of commitments is shown in Chart 8-8; outstanding commitments for securities advanced sharply in 1956 while an offsetting decline was registered in outstanding commitments for mortgages and real property.

A new phase of commitment trends began in late 1957 with the onset of a general business decline and a move in the direction of credit ease by the Federal Reserve authorities; by early 1958, net free reserves of the commercial banking system were increased to the $500 million level (Chart 8-1). As a result of the investor and borrower expectations created by this move to easier credit, plus the declining demands for short and long-term loans, interest rates on bank loans and corporate bonds fell sharply. Once again the familiar pattern emerged as life insurance companies shifted the emphasis of their forward commitments to the Government-insured mortgage market where interest rates remained fairly rigid and dammed-up demand for credit existed. Because the FHA maximum rate at this time was considerably higher than the maximum on VA loans, the build-up in commitments occurred largely in FHA loans as may be seen in Table 8-2 and Chart 8-5. The net effect of these market conditions and the change in monetary policy upon the level of outstanding commitments is shown in Chart 8-8 which traces the sharp decline in outstanding security commitments and the strong upsurge in the level of commitments for mortgage loans.

To recapitulate, a review of the period since 1952 indicates that as credit tightens, both as a result of market forces and Federal Reserve policy measures, life insurance companies shift their investment emphasis toward those outlets where the yields are flexible and rising, and away from those where the yields are rigid. The reverse is true when market forces and monetary policy move toward ease. Table 8-3 and Chart 8-6,

---

[9] This decline was to be expected for other reasons. After acquiring a large volume of VA and FHA mortgages in 1954-55, the life companies undoubtedly were moved to deemphasize these mortgages for diversification reasons.

TABLE 8-3
Net Uses of Funds in Selected Investments of Life Insurance Companies, 1947-1959

(In billions of dollars)

Year	Residential mortgages	Corporate bonds (U.S.)	U.S. Governments	State and local securities (U.S
1947	1.1	2.9	-1.6	*
1948	1.7	4.1	-3.3	0.3
1949	1.6	2.5	-1.5	0.2
1950	2.7	1.7	-1.8	0.1
1951	2.5	2.5	-2.4	*
1952	1.4	3.0	-0.8	*
1953	1.5	2.6	-0.4	0.1
1954	2.0	2.0	-0.8	0.5
1955	2.7	1.8	-0.5	0.2
1956	2.5	1.9	-1.0	0.2
1957	1.2	2.4	-0.5	0.1
1958	0.9	2.2	0.2	0.3
1959	1.3	2.0	-0.3	0.5

*Under $50 million.

presenting the net uses of funds in selected investments of life insurance companies since 1947, show the alternate peaks and valleys of life company net additions in holdings of corporate bonds and residential mortgages.

The purpose here is not to appraise the economic consequences of the impact of monetary policy on the direction of flow of life insurance company funds. It is simply to show the nature and extent of this impact. There has, of course, been much public discussion of the economic consequences. There is general recognition that the rigid interest rates on FHA and VA mortgages, along with flexible rates in other investment areas which are affected by Federal Reserve policy measures, produce alternate peaks and valleys in the availability of funds for government-insured and guaranteed mortgages. The instability in availability of VA and FHA financing has been severely criticized by many on the grounds that it is the reason for the instability of residential construction as a whole. Some observers have felt that this is a highly undesirable characteristic of residential construction. On the other hand, many observers argue that the ability of the Federal Reserve to function effectively to curtail the availability of VA-FHA credit when capital expansion is occurring elsewhere in the economy, and to stimulate residential construction through inducing greater availability of VA-FHA credit in a recession, is most advantageous from the viewpoint of general economic stability. Regardless of the merits of this question, there can be no question that monetary policy has a powerful impact on the direction of flow of life insurance company investments as between corporate bonds and residential mortgages, particularly VA-FHA mortgages.

Value of Assets. Monetary policy, by affecting the value of fixed-income assets, has exerted an important effect upon the ability of life insurance companies to raise investible funds through the sale of existing holdings. As interest rates rise in response to market pressures and restrictive credit policy, capital values of fixed-income obligations decline. To illustrate, the life companies held in early 1960 over $800 million of the U.S. Government 2½'s of March 1965-70 which were purchased at par in World War II. At the peak of interest rates in early 1960 these bonds were selling in the low 80's, so that life companies could only sell them at very substantial losses. The same situation applies to all of the fixed-income obligations in the portfolios of life companies—bonds and mortgages. Rising interest rates produced declining market values for these assets. This situation was equally applicable to all other investors. Of course, the life companies are able to carry practically all of these bonds in their statements at amortized cost. Losses arise only when the bonds are sold.

There are narrow limits to the ability of life insurance companies to absorb voluntary losses in order to raise funds for investment at higher yields. A number of state laws restrict the amount of surplus which a life company can have. New York State, for example, limits the surplus of mutual companies chartered in the state to no more than 10 percent of net policy reserves and policy liabilities. The purpose of the limitation is to prevent a company from accumulating unnecessarily large surplus funds at the expense of one generation of policyholders to the benefit of a later generation. In any event, the surpluses of many mutual life insurance companies are restricted in amount, so that sizable losses are readily apparent. Companies are reluctant to experience significant fluctuations in surplus, particularly reductions, because such a development is used competitively by rival companies as a sign of weakness in their financial position.

Consequently, as capital losses develop with respect to Government bonds and other fixed-income obligations, life insurance companies are discouraged from selling these obligations to raise investible funds. Thus, the rise of interest rates and the decline in capital values reduces the liquidity of life company assets. Since the spring of 1951, after the unpegging of the prices and yields of Government securities, we have experienced a pronounced upward trend of interest rates. During this period the declining prices of Government securities have at each stage in the decline acted to "lock" the companies into their holdings of Governments. This is not to say that life companies have not sold Governments and other securities at losses, but the losses have been a strong deterrent, as will be discussed presently.[10]

It will be helpful to look at the record with regard to life company holdings of U.S. Government securities. At the end of 1946 the life companies held $21.6 billion of Governments, amounting to nearly 45 percent of total assets of $48.2 billion. By the end of March 1951, life company holdings of Governments had been reduced to $12.6 billion, or 19 percent of total assets of $66.3 billion. In other words, during the period in which the prices of Government securities were pegged at par or better, the life insurance companies liquidated $9 billion of Government securities in order to invest in higher-yielding corporate bonds, mortgages, and other investments. After March 1951, the companies continued to reduce their holdings of Government securities, as shown in Table 8-4, but the pace has slackened noticeably as the market prices of Government bonds have declined and losses have deepened. At the end of 1959, holdings of Governments amounted to $6.8 billion, or 6 percent of assets. Admittedly, after the big volume of liquidation in the period from the end of 1946 through March 1951, life companies might have reduced the pace of their sale of Governments even if losses had not been involved. At the same time, however, there is no doubt that since March 1951 the deepening losses on Governments have been a powerful deterrent to sales. It is sometimes argued that life companies have reduced their holdings of Governments to about the minimum consistent with liquidity needs, and that in any event they will continue to hold about the present amount of long-term Governments in their portfolios. This overlooks the fact, however, that with the great cash flow provided to life companies from net cash income in excess of disbursements, mortgage amortization, sinking fund payments, and other sources of cash, the life companies today have little, if any, need for Government securities.[11]

When life insurance companies sell Government securities or other assets at losses, they do so, of course, to raise additional funds to acquire higher-yielding securities or mortgages. In selling securities at a loss, the life companies are required to weigh the amount of the loss against the higher return on the new securities acquired. If the higher return after taxes on the new securities makes up in a short time for the loss realized, the company is encouraged to dispose of securities at a loss. The important point is that losses will only be taken if the sufficiently higher

---

[10] During the past few years, the development of securities valuation reserves by life companies (Chapter 6), which are not included in the surplus account, has made it easier for some companies to dispose of a limited amount of securities at the prevailing losses.

[11] For a detailed discussion of cash flow, see Chapter 7.

TABLE 8-4
Holdings of U.S. Government Securities by
Life Insurance Companies
1946 - 1959

(In millions of dollars)

End of year	Amount	Percent of Total Assets
1946	21,629	44.9
1947	20,021	38.7
1948	16,746	30.2
1949	15,290	25.6
1950	13,459	21.0
1951	11,009	16.1
1952	10,252	14.0
1953	9,829	12.5
1954	9,070	10.7
1955	8,576	9.5
1956	7,555	7.9
1957	7,029	6.9
1958	7,183	6.7
1959	6,868	6.0

return is available. Thus, the willingness to absorb losses hinges upon the higher return.

In summary, the willingness and ability of life insurance companies to make new investments through the sale of existing assets is directly curtailed by moves of the monetary authorities toward a more restrictive policy. Although there is strong incentive for life companies to shift into higher-yielding securities, the necessity of taking a capital loss with an adverse effect upon surplus reduces the willingness to liquidate existing holdings of lower-yielding securities. Thus, monetary policy has a direct impact upon the total volume of new lending by life insurance companies.

Cash Flow. Another way in which monetary policy has an impact upon life insurance investment operations is through contributing to forces producing a decrease or increase in the cash flow of the companies. These forces are complex, but there is no doubt that, in addition to affecting the ability of companies to raise additional cash by selling assets, monetary policy does influence the cash flow of the companies in several ways. To take the case of policy loans, as interest rates move upward in response to market forces and a restrictive monetary policy, policyholders find it to their advantage to borrow on their life insurance policies with the life companies rather than the banks. This is because at a certain point the fixed policy loan rate stipulated in the policyholder's insurance contract becomes comparatively lower than the rate on policy loans charged by commercial banks. The policy loan rate for any company is a long-term contract rate (subject to statutory maximum) which stays static over the term of the contract unless amended by Board concession. The rise of policy loans of life companies in years of generally rising interest rates was shown in Chapter 2, Table 2-2. During the period 1955-59 in which the prime rate on bank loans had risen from 3 to 5 percent, policy loan extensions have increased steadily from $669 million in 1955 to $1,156 million in 1959. Likewise, when monetary policy is directed toward ease, there is a reverse tendency for policy loans to be placed with commercial banks at the then comparatively lower interest rates.

Of course, it may be argued that the cash flow of the companies really has not been affected, but that the life companies have merely been required to direct more of their cash to policy loans at the expense of other earning assets. Nevertheless, there can be little doubt that a rise in policy loans and the resultant decline of cash flow for investment in bonds and mortgages has a direct and immediate impact on the willingness of companies to enter into forward investment commitments. A company experiencing a rapid increase in policy loans is bound to pursue a more cautious forward commitment policy and to be more concerned about its liquidity position. Moreover, to the extent more life company funds must be available for policy loans, there are structural effects exerted on the capital markets which are important, e.g., there may be a greater degree of tightness in the availability of VA-FHA mortgage credit and more ready availability of business loans from commercial banks. Thus, the ramifications of the impact of monetary policy on the volume of policy loans are widespread. The effects on the capital markets are subtle but real.

Another way monetary policy affects the cash flow of life insurance companies is through the influence it exerts on mortgage repayments. As shown in Table 8-5, mortgage repayments constitute an important part of the gross cash flow of life companies. The regular amortization and partial prepayments on mortgages are not affected by monetary policy. However, an important effect is exerted on "other cash repayments." Much of these "other cash repayments" is the result of refinancing of the mortgages. In a period of monetary restriction and rising interest rates the conditions for refinancing become less and less favorable and thus unscheduled repayments decline. When credit is being eased, and in-

TABLE 8-5

Quarterly Cash Flow of Thirty-Nine Life Insurance Companies

(In millions of dollars)

	1957				1958				1959			
	I	II	III	IV	I	II	III	IV	I	II	III	IV
Gross inflow of investible funds												
Net increase in ledger assets	590	602	695	751	624	667	713	815	644	728	637	843
Net increase (-) or decrease in cash position	58	17	-65	97	-100	19	-110	66	-93	-12	139	90
Net increase (-) in policy loans	-54	-59	-61	-73	-68	-62	-44	-47	-56	-61	-74	-97
Mortgages (total)	380	385	403	416	399	406	504	490	500	493	486	461
Amortization and partial prepayments	270	269	271	299	293	274	321	304	324	307	302	324
Other cash repayments	109	110	128	111	105	131	180	184	174	178	184	135
Outright sales	1	5	4	5	1	1	4	1	3	7	1	1
Securities (total)	332	297	315	296	276	413	433	407	343	304	301	387
Bond maturities	81	98	108	116	114	125	115	151	121	135	146	161
Contingency sinking funds	15	17	17	18	11	14	16	16	11	13	16	13
Other security calls	40	27	23	42	23	42	56	48	30	41	29	42
Outright sales - Gov'ts	65	54	84	40	54	110	111	77	94	27	8	82
Outright sales - other securities	131	100	83	81	74	123	135	114	87	88	102	88
Sales of real estate	2	4	1	6	1	3	4	16	4	2	4	18
Other sales and repayments	5	12	11	16	10	11	11	12	11	11	11	11
All other sources of funds	14	6	1	-8	10	9	-4	3	4	1	3	1
Total investible funds	1,328	1,263	1,301	1,502	1,152	1,466	1,507	1,762	1,357	1,466	1,508	1,713

The thirty-nine companies hold approximately 57 percent of the assets of all United States life insurance companies.
Because of rounding, components may not add to totals shown.

215

terest rates are declining, refinancing and thus repayments rise. Here again, it may be argued that the over-all capital market impact is negligible because with fewer mortgage repayments, and thus a declining cash flow, there is also a corresponding and offsetting decline in the demand for credit for refinancing. Actually, however, there are important effects. The insurance company seeing its cash flow declining from lesser mortgage repayments (and possibly policy loans) must be more cautious about its forward commitments and its liquidity position. Moreover, declining mortgage repayments may have the effect of reducing the aggregate flow of funds into the residential mortgage market—that is, here also there may be important effects on the structure of the supply of loanable funds. This is because mortgage repayments are usually reinvested in mortgages.

Or to take another case, monetary policy has an important effect on the cash left with life insurance companies by policyholders or their beneficiaries under settlement options. Under various settlement options funds are left on deposit for investment by the companies at contractual interest rates. During a period of monetary restraint and rising interest rates, there is a tendency for cash left under option to be reduced as policyholders and their beneficiaries move their funds to take advantage of higher returns or capital gains available elsewhere. The rates of interest used by companies for these supplementary contracts (guaranteed plus excess rates) are closely related to the total portfolio rate of return of the company rather than the yields obtainable on new investments. On the other hand, when credit ease is being followed, and interest rates are declining, funds left on deposit with life companies tend to rise, thus expanding cash flow. Here also the important point is that, as cash flow rises or declines, life companies reflect the rise or decline in their commitment policy, and there are bound to be structural effects on the supply of funds.

Accordingly, monetary policy, to the extent it contributes to the variation in interest rates, has an important effect in a number of ways on the cash flow of life insurance companies. Rising interest rates tend to reduce cash flow available from life companies for new investments. To the extent that rising rates tend to attract funds elsewhere (as in the case of settlement options) or reduce demand at commercial banks (as in the case of some policy loans) there are nevertheless important structural effects on the market.

Forward Investment Commitments. Brief reference has already been made to the impact which monetary policy has upon the forward commitments of life insurance companies via the effect on cash flow. This impact needs to be considered in a broader context.

It is not unusual for the life companies of the United States as a whole to have substantial outstanding forward commitments, running as high as two-thirds of the annual gross cash flow of the companies.[12] At the present time, commitments of this magnitude would amount to 6 to 7 billion dollars out of a total annual cash flow of approximately $11 billion. These commitments would be to acquire residential mortgages, commercial and industrial mortgages, corporate bonds, state and municipal bonds, and other types of obligations. The life of these commitments would typically range all the way from a short period to a couple of years and in some cases even longer. It is clear that in determining the desirable volume of commitments at any given time, a company must have regard to its prospective cash flow. It must also have regard to trends in the demand for capital funds and in interest rates. Thus, expectations of life insurance companies about cash flow have an important bearing, as we have noted earlier, upon the commitment policies of these companies. Similarly, expectations about future developments in the capital markets, and about the trend of interest rates, exert an impact upon commitment policy. By their influence on these expectations, as well as through the more direct impact on interest rates noted above, the monetary authorities exert an important effect on life insurance company investing.

When demands for capital funds are running high and the Federal Reserve authorities are pursuing a policy of credit restraint, with interest rates moving upward, the expectation of life insurance companies (and other investors) is that interest rates are likely to go even higher. Under these conditions, there is naturally a somewhat reduced willingness of companies to expand their forward commitments, and there is a tendency for the average commitment period to be shortened. Likewise, in a period such as this there is a tendency for the companies to raise their commitment fees, i.e., charges made to the borrower against the undisbursed balance of a loan commitment. Thus, in a period of monetary restraint, the authorities encourage expectations by life insurance companies which lead the companies to alter their commitment policy in a way that reinforces monetary restraint. Similarly, when the Federal Reserve takes action to ease credit, and the effect of this easing plus declining demand for credit is to produce falling interest rates, the life insurance companies are then led to expect declining investment opportunities and lower interest rates. It is only natural at times like this for the life companies to seek to expand their forward commitments before rates decline further. They also are willing to commit their funds for a longer period, and on the basis of lower commitment fees. Thus, the expectations on the part of life insurance companies as created or encouraged by Federal Reserve policy actions lead life companies in a period of credit ease to take actions in accord with the objectives of the monetary authorities.

It is difficult to trace the effects described above in the aggregate

---

12 See Chapter 7, section on The Forward Commitment Process.

commitment figures of the life insurance companies. This is undoubtedly because the aggregate figures tend to mask individual company behavior. It is also because the effect of monetary policy upon commitments is marginal in nature, that is, companies tend to maintain a comparatively full commitment position at all times, with changes from this being determined by expectations. Nevertheless, the aggregate commitment figures do reveal the effects of expectations.

Table 8-6 and Charts 8-7 and 8-8 show the movement of outstanding commitments of the life insurance companies reporting commitment data to the Life Insurance Association of America since April 1951. The data are index numbers, with April 1951 equalling 100. The pronounced tendency for total commitments to rise in 1954, when the monetary authorities were pursuing a policy of active credit ease, suggests greater willingness to enter into forward commitments because of the expectation that rates would go lower. As noted earlier, the commitment buildup was largely in FHA-VA mortgages. The stability of total commitments in 1955 and early 1956, as the Federal Reserve moved toward credit restraint and interest rates began a gradual rise, may also be an evidence of reduced willingness to commit as rates were expected to rise. The rise of total commitments in the last three quarters of 1956 was the product of attractive offerings of industrial bonds at rising rates. It is significant that, as interest rates moved to record levels in 1957, total commitments tended to decline from the 1956 levels. In the first half of 1958, as interest rates fell sharply, forward commitments showed a noticeable rise. They continued to increase in the last third of 1958, when the expectation was for a further increase in rates, but they leveled out and tended to decline in 1959 as interest rates moved up to the highest levels since the early 1920's.

It would be a mistake to read too much into these figures because they are the product of many forces, not the least of which is the trend in cash flow and the expectations about cash flow. However, they do seem to bear out a common reaction of individual companies to changes in monetary policy.

In summary, it is clear that general credit controls, to the extent they cause interest rate changes and the expectation of interest rate changes, do exert prompt and important effects upon life insurance investments. (1) They influence the *direction* of flow of life company investments, encouraging an expanding flow of funds into VA-FHA mortgages during a period of credit ease, and an expanding flow of funds into corporate bonds and conventional mortgages (along with a contracting flow into VA-FHA mortgages) during a period of credit restraint. (2) They affect the *value of assets* held by life companies, and thus the ability of the companies to raise cash by sale of assets. (3) They influence the amount of *cash flow* of life companies through the effect interest rate changes have on policy loans, mortgage repayments, and funds left on deposit with

TABLE 8-6
**Index of Outstanding Commitments of Life Insurance Companies,
1951-1959**

(April 1951 = 100)

1951	Securities total	Mortgage loans and real property total	Total commitments outstanding
April	100	100	100
May	97	97	97
June	94	87	90
July	94	83	85
August	88	80	80
September	92	77	83
October	107	75	87
November	112	75	88
December	110	70	84
1952			
January	118	67	86
February	121	65	85
March	125	62	85
April	127	64	87
May	131	63	88
June	131	62	87
July	127	59	84
August	131	60	86
September	142	60	90
October	120	62	83
November	118	62	82
December	111	61	79
1953			
January	106	59	76
February	117	61	81
March	123	62	84
April	133	63	89
May	133	67	91
June	118	69	87
July	112	68	84
August	113	69	87
September	116	72	88
October	121	72	90
November	111	75	88
December	112	75	88
1954			
January	105	74	85
February	125	76	94
March	118	83	96
April	120	86	98
May	120	92	102
June	116	97	104

(Continued)

Table 8-6 (Continued)

1954	Securities total	Mortgage loans and real property total	Total commitments outstanding
July	107	101	103
August	120	109	114
September	128	115	120
October	128	118	122
November	129	123	125
December	105	123	116
1955			
January	101	123	115
February	103	124	117
March	100	124	115
April	97	123	113
May	100	125	116
June	108	123	119
July	101	122	114
August	110	124	119
September	111	124	119
October	115	122	120
November	125	125	125
December	117	121	119
1956			
January	115	118	117
February	116	120	118
March	114	122	119
April	127	128	128
May	132	132	132
June	136	132	134
July	136	130	133
August	140	130	134
September	156	128	138
October	164	124	139
November	180	115	139
December	164	110	133
1957			
January	178	102	133
February	177	100	131
March	175	97	129
April	177	97	130
May	176	96	129
June	173	96	128
July	169	96	126
August	166	95	124
September	155	97	122
October	158	97	122
November	159	100	125
December	139	95	114

(Continued)

Table 8-6 (Continued)

1958	Securities total	Mortgage loans and real property total	Total commitments outstanding
January	136	91	110
February	138	91	111
March	140	95	115
April	144	99	118
May	146	100	120
June	136	105	119
July	137	107	121
August	142	109	125
September	147	116	131
October	142	120	132
November	145	121	134
December	123	113	120
1959			
January	117	108	114
February	118	107	114
March	126	111	120
April	124	114	120
May	121	114	120
June	117	118	121
July	107	117	117
August	111	119	119
September	99	120	115
October	97	120	115
November	96	119	114
December	90	111	106

the companies under settlement options. (4) They affect the *forward commitment* policy of the companies through the influence exerted on investor expectations about the movement of interest rates.

Selective Credit Controls. There have been two types of selective credit controls which have affected the investments of life insurance companies, namely Regulation X and the Voluntary Credit Restraint Program. Both were an outgrowth of the emergency created in 1950 by the outbreak of the Korean War.

Regulation X was placed in effect in the autumn of 1950 under the terms of the Defense Production Act of 1950. It remained in effect until mid-1952. The regulation was designed to govern the expansion of residential mortgage credit, and thus home-building, by means of controlling the amount of down payment and the length of the amortization period. These terms on FHA mortgages were subject to regulation by the Housing and Home Finance Agency, on VA mortgages by the Veterans' Administration, and on conventional loans by the Federal Reserve Board. Naturally the life insurance companies were affected by the regulation, being one of the major home mortgage lenders in the country. The impact was, however, less than might have been expected because a large volume of commitments to provide financing on pre-Regulation X terms was built up by all types of mortgage lenders, and these commitments for the most part were ruled exempt from the regulation when it went into effect. Because of this backlog of commitments, along with the difficulty of drafting rules to cover the complicated functioning of the mortgage market, it is generally recognized that the restrictive effects on home-building of Regulation X were considerably delayed.

The Defense Production Act of 1950 also provided that the Federal Reserve Board organize a voluntary effort on the part of lending institutions to avoid inflationary uses of credit. With the outbreak of the Korean War there was much apprehension in the federal government that inflationary credit excesses would occur which the monetary authorities would be powerless to curb under circumstances in which they were still required to peg the prices of Government securities at par or better. There was apparently some thought that a system of rationing capital funds should be established, but it was decided that, aside from the enormous problems such a system would involve, it would be preferable to develop a voluntary effort on the part of lending institutions to control inflationary uses of funds. Accordingly in late 1950 and in early 1951, under the guidance and direction of the Federal Reserve Board, the Voluntary Credit Restraint Program (VCR) was organized.

The life insurance industry, through the Life Insurance Association of America and the American Life Convention, played an important role in the drafting and organizing of VCR, as did The American Bankers Association and the Investment Bankers Association of America. As the program got under way, other lending institutions such as the mutual savings banks and the savings and loan associations were brought into the effort. A national VCR Committee was established under the chairmanship of Oliver Powell, a member of the Federal Reserve Board. This committee had representation from all of the principal lending institutions, and it met regularly at the Federal Reserve Board in Washington to formulate VCR policy and to determine means to implement the program. Regional VCR committees were also formed; the life insurance business, for example, had one in New York, one in Chicago, one in Dallas, and one in San Francisco. The purposes of these committees were to disseminate information about VCR, issue interpretations of the program, and to review inquiries made by cooperating lending institutions regarding the inflationary or noninflationary nature of prospective loans. Through the national committee, data were obtained by the Federal Reserve Board to aid in judging the effectiveness of VCR. It was in this connection that the Life Insurance Association of America began the collection of data on forward investment commitments of life insurance companies.

The VCR Program was in effect until mid-1952, or for about a year and a half. The life insurance companies of the country were enthusiastic in joining the effort and were most conscientious in their desire to have the program be successful. This was, of course, also true of other types of financial institutions. It is exceedingly difficult to measure the accomplishments or lack of accomplishments of VCR. There is little doubt that it operated under serious handicaps, the most important of which was the great difficulty of defining what were and what were not inflationary uses of credit. It soon became obvious that in our complicated system of financing it was practically impossible to lay down any guidelines that would apply to all situations, even though general principles were developed and sent to cooperating lenders. Another important handicap was that investment commitments entered into prior to the start of VCR had to be honored, and here again there was a force which delayed the impact of the program, although it was not as serious as in the case of Regulation X.

In spite of these handicaps, VCR probably was much more effective than is commonly recognized. During the first several months in which it was in effect, the program served to focus attention of lending institutions on the importance of avoiding the extension of credit in uses which would lead to inflation. Thus, VCR helped to hold down the financing of transfers of real estate at inflated prices. It made lenders conscious of the need to restrict credit to uses in which there would be increased production of goods and services, and not mere transfers. In particular, VCR helped to restrict the flotation of capital issues by State and local government units where the proceeds were to be used for such purposes as veterans' bonuses. After March 1951, as general credit control powers were restored to the Federal Reserve authorities with the "accord," VCR became less essential. Moreover, the need for the program was reduced in 1952 after it became clear that the Korean War would be comparatively local in nature, and inflationary pressures subsided. This was recognized by lenders, which accounts for the relaxation of VCR by the lenders in the late stages of the program. VCR demonstrated, nonetheless, that in an emergency the lending institutions of the country can be enlisted in an effective voluntary effort to avoid obviously inflationary uses of credit. At the same time, however, it showed that there is no real substitute for impersonal general credit controls.

The Influence of Federal Debt Management Policies

Federal debt management policies also have a direct and important influence on life insurance company investments. By "debt management policies" is meant the policies with respect to the way in which the U.S. Treasury carries out its financing, either for cash or refunding purposes. Involved here are decisions with respect to maturities and rates, basis of allocating issues to subscribers, and similar matters.

In some respects, it might have been desirable to link debt management with monetary policy in discussing the impact on life company investments. The channels through which the impact is felt are similar. Just as Federal Reserve policy measures, by restricting or easing the availability of credit, affect the level of interest rates and investors' expectations, and hence life insurance company investments, so debt management actions can do the same. For example, by increasing the supply of long-term Government bonds, the Treasury exerts an influence toward higher long-term interest rates, or toward reducing the prospect for a decline in rates. Thus, the Treasury can play an important role in the movement of interest rates, and in investor expectations about the movement of interest rates. As we saw earlier in connection with general monetary controls, policies which have an impact on the level of interest rates and on investor expectations, as is the case with debt management, influence life insurance company investing in four main ways: (1) they cause shifts in the direction of flow of life company funds; (2) they affect the capital values of assets held by life companies, and thus the ability of companies to raise cash for investment; (3) they lead to changes in the cash flow of the companies; and (4) they affect the forward commitment policies of the companies.

Beyond these effects, the Treasury can have a powerful effect toward discouraging or encouraging inflation through its debt management policies. For example, if the Treasury persists in selling short-term securities exclusively, or even largely, whether these securities go into the commercial banks or not, the expectation of inflation is fostered. This expectation causes a rise of interest rates because it reduces the supply of funds available for the purchase of fixed-interest obligations such as bonds and mortgages, and it expands the demand for capital funds. The attractiveness of fixed-interest obligations is, of course, reduced when investors expect the value of the dollar to decline. In effect, a premium is required in the rate of interest to provide some compensation for a declining value of the dollar. In addition the expectation of inflation leads companies to "incentive financing" in which stock warrants are attached to the debt securities, and similar equity devices are employed. The reverse is true, of course, if debt management is conducted in a way which reduces the expectation of inflation. It should be pointed out that, in addition to debt management policy, monetary policy even more importantly affects life company investment policies through the impact it has upon expectations with respect to inflation. The same is true of other federal policy measures, notably, budgetary policy, and is also true of labor policy.

It will probably be helpful to cite a few specific instances of ways in which debt management affected life insurance company investing. These are merely some of the outstanding cases, but it should be recognized that debt management has a continuous impact upon interest rates, investor expectations, and hence upon investing operations. In early 1953, when there was much public discussion about the Treasury lengthening the debt, debt management undoubtedly contributed in some measure to rising long-term interest rates, and to the expectation of rising rates. So far as life insurance companies were concerned, the effects were more concentration of investment in corporate securities, a reduced flow of funds into VA-FHA mortgages, declining capital values, somewhat lower cash flow', and reduced willingness to commit funds. After the $3\frac{1}{4}$'s were brought out in only a limited amount, and the downturn of interest rates occurred in the second half of 1953 and 1954 as the result of market forces and monetary policy, the Treasury's failure to bring out any long-term bonds for an extended period undoubtedly contributed to lower rates and to the expectation of lower rates, with the consequences for life company investments which have already been traced in the discussion of monetary policy.

Another outstanding example occurred in 1958. It will be recalled that in the latter part of 1957 and through much of the first quarter of 1958 there was a sharp drop of interest rates caused mainly by somewhat reduced demands for capital funds, an easy money policy by the monetary authorities, and investor expectations that yields would continue to decline. A contributing factor to the sharp fall in Government bond yields was the belief that the Treasury would not undertake anything but short-term financing. These expectations had an impact on life insurance company investments along lines already outlined. In the early spring of 1958 the Treasury issued a long-term bond and thus aided to burst the expectation that interest rates would continue to fall. Here again an important effect was exerted upon life company investing.

Or to take another example, in the latter part of 1958 and 1959, as a larger proportion of Treasury financing was crowded into the shorter-term part of the market because of the interest ceiling, debt management unavoidably contributed to the expectation of inflation and thus to rising interest rates, with the effects on life insurance company investing described earlier.

Thus, federal debt management does have important influence on the investment activities of life insurance companies.

The Influence of Other Federal Policy Actions

Still other federal policy measures have an impact upon life insurance investments. One of the more important is government insurance and guaranty of residential mortgages. The availability of FHA insurance and the VA guaranty has made it possible for life companies and other investors to buy mortgages on a nationwide basis. It has broadened home ownership through making it possible for life companies and other investors to make low-down payment, long amortization-period loans. The availability of these loans in large amounts and at investment yields considerably in excess of those on Government bonds has induced life companies to replace a significant portion of their Government bond holdings with insured and guaranteed mortgages.

Another way in which life insurance companies have been affected by federal regulation is in the case of FHA mortgages, in which the housing authorities have had the power to regulate the down-payment and amortization period within the maximum permitted by law. This regulation has not, however, had much effect on life companies because they have usually as a matter of investment policy tightened the terms on FHA mortgages in a boom well in advance of any action by the authorities.

Another important type of federal regulation affecting life companies is that carried out by the SEC and the FPC under the Public Utility Holding Company Act of 1935. Under the terms of this act, the authorities have considered it their duty to control the redemption features in bond issues of utilities coming under their jurisdiction. Generally speaking, they have prescribed that bonds be callable at any time and that the call premium be limited to one interest coupon above the offering price. In a minority of cases they have permitted a five-year non-callable period. The justification stated by the authorities for requiring that bonds be callable is to assure the lowest possible financing costs, and thus the lowest cost of service to utilities customers.

During the past decade, and especially since 1953, the life insurance companies have attached great importance to obtaining fully adequate protection against the call of bonds which they hold. The sharp decline of interest rates in the second half of 1953 led to the calling of a number of issues of electric utilities bonds which had been offered to investors earlier in the year. This episode brought home the realization that under conditions of flexible monetary policy interest rates can rise sharply and then decline equally abruptly. Although recognizing the interests of electric utility power consumers, the life insurance companies are convinced that the best interests of their policyholders are served by buying bonds where there is adequate protection against call. Accordingly, the policy of the SEC and FPC has virtually removed the life insurance companies from the electric utility bond market. In 1953, for example, a survey showed that forty-seven companies purchased $332 million of electric utility bonds, whereas in 1956 the same companies acquired only $72 million. Generally speaking, the life companies limit their purchases of electric utility bonds to those that do provide call protection. In contrast, the life insurance companies have been heavy purchasers of industrial bonds in which they have been able to obtain satisfactory call protection.

Influence of Federal Income Tax on Investment Policy

Beginning with the 1942 Revenue Act and continuing until the passage of the Income Tax Act of 1959, the federal income tax imposed upon the life insurance companies was substantially a uniform percentage for all companies. The percentage could and did vary from year to year. The tax was based on income from interest, dividends, and rents; no account was taken of capital gains or losses. The apparently low rate was used in recognition of the peculiar structure of the life insurance business since most net investment income is required to support the reserves required by state laws, which in turn affects the cost of insurance.

The effect of such tax laws on investment policy was relatively simple. The "after tax" yield for all types of investment was in substantial proportion to the "before tax" yield. Capital gains could be taken with unbiased judgment. They were large for a few years because of special circumstances not likely to recur.

Under the 1959 Act conditions have become markedly different. No longer is the incremental yield a simple percentage of investment income. It is a complex function of many factors which differ widely both as between companies and at different times in the same company. Outstanding among these complexities is the implicit relationship between the principal deduction for reserve interest and the yield itself, whereby the deduction increases (but at less than a proportionate rate) with an increase in the investment yield. The tax is also imposed upon "underwriting income" and on the excess of net long-term capital gains over net short-term capital losses at a flat 25 percent rate. On part of the underwriting gain the tax is imposed at once and on part not until it is either accumulated beyond a specified limit or distributed to the stockholders.

The new tax is based on so many variables it is almost impossible to reach any generalized conclusions as to its effect on life insurance company investment policy. For the most part each company must analyze its own status and calculate its own results. It is possible, however, to predict cautiously a few general trends.

Since 1942, tax exempt bonds have been less attractive investments for life insurance companies than for other corporate investors and most individuals. The flat tax rate on investment income produced this result. Under the present law a somewhat greater interest in tax exempts will be the probable result. Beginning in 1955 life insurance companies had been denied the usual 85 percent intercorporate dividend credit. The 1959 Act, however, restores this credit. To the extent permitted by state investment statutes, therefore, stocks, both common and preferred, may be expected to be somewhat more attractive than they were under the immediately preceding laws.

Future investment policy will have to take account of possible capital gains. Some increased trading may be expected in order to offset capital losses against capital gains. On the other hand, there will be less incentive for life insurance companies than for other corporate taxpayers to prefer capital gains to ordinary income, inasmuch as the incremental tax rate for many companies will be close to 25 percent.

The popularity of purchase and lease-back arrangements may suffer somewhat. The newly imposed tax rules on valuation of property, depreciation, and amortization of principal along with the possibility of a capital gains tax and changing tax laws over time inject enough uncertainty into the investment picture to lessen the attractiveness of these investments for some companies.

With a few exceptions such as those noted, the new federal income tax law should not be expected to exercise a very great influence on life insurance company investments in general. For individual companies from time to time, however, the effect may be considerable.

Summary and Conclusions

In summary, it is sometimes asserted that the investment policies and activities of life insurance companies are largely unaffected by Federal policy measures, and particularly unaffected by monetary policy. This view is not substantiated by the facts.

General credit controls by the Federal Reserve authorities exert prompt and important effects upon life insurance investment operations. (1) They influence the direction of flow of life company investments, encouraging (because of the rigidity of FHA and VA rates) an expanding flow of funds into VA-FHA mortgages during a period of credit ease, and an expanding flow of funds into corporate bonds and conventional mortgages (along with a contracting flow into VA-FHA mortgages) during a period of credit restraint. (2) By having an impact upon interest rates, general credit controls affect the value of assets held by life companies, and thus the ability of the companies to raise cash for new investment by sale of assets. (3) They influence the total cash flow for investment of life companies through the effects interest rate changes have on policy loans, mortgage repayments, and funds left on deposit with the companies under settlement options. (4) They affect the forward commitment policy of the companies through the influence exerted on investor expectations about the movement of interest rates. That is, when general credit control policy contributes to the expectation of rising interest rates, life companies tend to be less willing to expand their forward commitments, with the reverse being true when policy leads to the expectation of falling rates.

During the Korean emergency in 1950-52 the life insurance companies were subjected to two types of selective credit control, namely Regulation X and the Voluntary Credit Restraint Program. Because of the buildup of forward commitments on pre-Regulation X terms, along with the difficulty of drafting rules to cover the complicated functioning of the home mortgage market, it is generally recognized that the restrictive effects on home-building of Regulation X were considerably delayed. The Voluntary Credit Restraint Program demonstrated that in an emergency the life insurance companies and other lending institutions can be enlisted in an effective voluntary effort to avoid obviously inflationary uses of credit, but at the same time it demonstrated that there is no real substitute for general credit controls.

Just as Federal Reserve policy measures, by restricting or easing the availability of credit, affect the level of interest rates and investors' expectations, and hence life insurance company investments, so federal debt management operations can influence life company investments in four main ways: (1) they cause shifts in the direction of flow of life company funds; (2) they affect the capital values of assets held by life companies, and thus the ability of companies to raise cash for investment; (3) they lead to changes in the total cash flow of the companies; and (4) they affect the forward commitment policies of the companies. Moreover, the Treasury can have a powerful effect toward encouraging or discouraging inflation through its debt management policies, with the expectation of continuing inflation or control of inflation having an important bearing on life company investments.

Other federal policy measures have an impact upon life insurance investments. One of these is government insurance and guaranty of residential mortgages. Another is the regulation by the FHA of downpayment and amortization terms on insured mortgages. Still another is the regulation by the SEC and FPC of redemption features in bond issues of utilities coming under their jurisdiction. The insistence by these authorities that bonds be immediately callable at low call prices has severely restricted life company purchases of utility bonds.

The new federal tax levied on life insurance companies is based on so many variables that it is virtually impossible to reach any generalized conclusions as to its effect on life company investment policy. Under the new law some companies will find tax-exempt bonds more attractive than formerly, common and preferred stocks will be somewhat more attractive because of the restoration of the intercorporate dividend credit, the popularity of purchase and lease-back investments may suffer somewhat, and investment policy will henceforth be required to take account of capital gains and losses.

Chapter 9

THE GURLEY-SHAW THESIS AND THE IMPACT OF MONETARY POLICY ON LIFE INSURANCE COMPANIES

The discussion in Chapter 8 has shown that the federal monetary and debt management authorities have a great deal of power to influence and control the investment operations of life insurance companies. This is, however, not in accord with the commonly accepted view, which is that the monetary authorities can exert a powerful control over the commercial banking system and the money supply but cannot exert any important control over the nonmonetary intermediaries. Arthur F. Burns has stated, for example, that:

Since the end of World War II the spectacular growth of the assets of financial institutions other than commercial banks reflects . . . the efficiency of financial markets in assembling "idle" funds and putting them to work in commerce and industry. This process not only can continue in the face of restrictions on the growth of commercial bank assets, but it is even likely for a time to be accelerated by a restrictive credit policy. A rise of interest rates increases the cost of holding demand deposits, on which commercial banks have been forbidden to pay interest since 1935. Hence, rising interest rates, especially if the movement is of considerable magnitude and duration, tend to stimulate both consumers and business firms to convert their cash balances into earning assets. This can often be done without any significant loss of liquidity. For example, when an individual draws on his checking account to buy a life insurance policy or to acquire savings and loan shares or to deposit funds in a mutual savings bank, he obtains against a financial institution a claim which can be readily converted into cash. The institution, in turn, having acquired ownership over a part of his demand deposit, now has additional money to lend to others who are likely to be active spenders. In these and other ways the loans of financial intermediaries can for a time grow quite rapidly even when the reserves of commercial banks are severely restricted by Federal Reserve actions.[1]

The basic ideas behind the view expressed by Burns have been de-

---

[1] Arthur F. Burns, *Prosperity Without Inflation*, pp. 50-51.

veloped by John G. Gurley and Edward S. Shaw.[2] Accordingly, it would be helpful to consider how their views compare with the ideas set forth in Chapter 8. Space will permit only a brief discussion of the Gurley-Shaw thesis, with the focus placed on its applicability to the life insurance companies.

Outline of the Gurley-Shaw Thesis

The general argument by Gurley and Shaw may be summarized as follows:

1) There is a spectrum of liquid assets which can be held by spending units in the economy. The most liquid, of course, is money itself, i.e., currency and demand deposits, but there are other liquid assets which are close substitutes for money, such as time deposits of commercial banks, mutual savings bank deposits, savings and loan shares, the cash values in life insurance, and so forth.

2) The monetary institutions of the country, i.e., the commercial banks, alone have the power to "create money" by buying "primary securities" (meaning such instruments as promissory notes, bonds, mortgages, etc.). However, nonmonetary intermediaries (such as mutual savings banks, savings and loan associations, and life insurance companies) issue their own "indirect securities" (for example, savings bank deposits, savings and loan association shares, and life insurance policies) for money, with this money in turn being used by the nonmonetary institutions to buy primary securities. These indirect securities are liquid assets in the hands of spending units, and these liquid assets are close substitutes for money. Thus, an increase in the liquid claims on nonmonetary institutions serves to reduce the demand by spending units for money itself, and accordingly such an increase in these liquid claims exerts an effect on the interest rate, the general price level, and the level of real national output.

3) The monetary authorities have direct control over the ability of the commercial banks to create money (demand deposits), and they have some control over the volume of time deposits of commercial banks by virtue of being able to control the interest rate paid on time deposits. However, they have no *direct* control over the ability of nonmonetary intermediaries to sell their liquid claims for money and thus add to the supply of close money substitutes in the hands of the public. Likewise, they have no control over the volume of loanable funds of these institutions.

---

[2] The discussion of the Gurley-Shaw views in this chapter is based on their book *Money in a Theory of Finance* (Washington, D.C.: The Brookings Institution, 1960), as well as Study Paper No. 14, "Liquidity and Financial Institutions in the Postwar Economy" by John G. Gurley, prepared in connection with the *Study of Employment, Growth and Price Levels* for consideration by the Joint Economic Committee of the Congress of the United States, January 25, 1960.

4) In a period in which the national economy has excess liquidity, and the general price level is tending to rise, the monetary authorities are handicapped in that they can control the amount of one type of liquid asset, namely money, but they cannot control the creation of liquid assets by nonmonetary intermediaries. In trying to offset the effect of the non-monetary source of liquidity, the monetary authorities are often required to be excessively restrictive with respect to the creation of money by the commercial banks. This raises serious questions about the profitability of commercial banks, their ability to raise capital, and thus their capacity to administer the payments mechanism of our national economy.

5) Indeed, the nonmonetary intermediaries sometimes function perversely from the viewpoint of the monetary authorities, as follows. When the monetary authorities restrict credit and the interest rate rises, the rate of return on primary securities (bonds, mortgages, etc.) goes higher, and thus the nonmonetary intermediaries are able to raise their "deposit rate" to attract funds. So, they are thus able to increase their sale of liquid claims for money, and their lending increases. Spending units, in turn, armed with more indirect securities (highly liquid in nature), are encouraged to reduce their demand for money. Thus, the interest rate is lower than it would have been in the absence of action by the non-monetary intermediaries, and the general price level is higher. So, the action by the nonmonetary intermediaries handicaps the effectiveness of restrictive monetary policy measures. Similarly, during a period in which the monetary authorities seek to ease commercial bank credit, the non-monetary intermediaries pursue a reverse course of action which also handicaps the authorities.

6) Accordingly, the question is raised as to whether direct controls should not be placed by government on the ability of nonmonetary intermediaries to sell their liquid claims for money.

Applying the Gurley-Shaw thesis to the period since the end of World War II, Gurley points out that at the close of the war the economy possessed a vast amount of money and close substitutes for money.[3] The market for these monetary and nonmonetary liquid assets was in equilibrium at abnormally low interest rates and at controlled price levels. The market for the current output of goods and services, on the other hand, at these low interest rates and price levels, was in a disequilibrium position, with excess demands prevailing almost everywhere. Thus equilibrium in the current output market was attainable only by increases in interest rates and commodity prices—the greater the increase in one the less the increase required in the other. The principal question facing the

---

[3] This application of the Gurley-Shaw thesis is taken from "Liquidity and Financial Institutions in the Postwar Period," *loc. cit.*, pp. 48-49. Most of the discussion here is a direct quotation from Gurley, with some abbreviation and simplification of technical terminology.

monetary authorities at this time was the extent to which commodity prices would have to rise to restore equilibrium in the market for current output.

Gurley goes on to state that given the amount of liquid assets, the level of real output, and the shape of the public's demand schedule for liquidity (which he assumed), the market for current output could have been brought into equilibrium only at substantially higher prices. This was because long-term interest rates were not sensitive to increases in commodity prices, and thus to reductions in real liquidity positions (after taking account of price changes), over long ranges of prices.[4] Consequently, the equilibrating mechanism for a good part of the postwar period had to rely principally on price increases and not on upward movements in interest rates to achieve equilibrium on all markets of the economy.

Further, Gurley points out that real output and nominal liquid assets (that is, uncorrected for price level changes), however, did not remain constant during the postwar period. The expansion in the supply of real output, which was accompanied by increases in financial-asset portfolios, by reducing excess demand in the current output market and by increasing the demand for liquid assets, diminished the extent to which price inflation was required to establish general equilibrium. Therefore, if nominal liquid assets had remained fairly constant in these years, the required price inflation would have been relatively modest, and the ultimate equilibrium level of interest rates would have been significantly higher. But nominal liquidity continued to grow rapidly, producing an excess demand for current output and an excess supply of liquid assets. Consequently, less upward pressure was placed on interest rates, while additional upward pressure was exerted on the price level. As it turned out, then, for at least a decade of the postwar period, the economy moved toward general equilibrium principally via price inflation rather than by upward movements in interest rates; the choice of this equilibrating channel was dictated by the expansion of nominal liquid assets.

Gurley goes on to note that this long-run adjustment process was accompanied by cyclical movements in economic activity. In the earlier stages of the postwar period, recessions reduced prices more than interest rates, and the subsequent expansions raised prices more than interest rates. In the later stages, recessions and expansions had much more impact upon interest rates than on prices. This was due to the fact that, in the earlier stages, the public was willing to lose and gain liquidity without much change in long-term interest rates. Therefore, the equilibrating process had to work primarily through changes in commodity prices. In

---

[4] There seems to be no recognition in Gurley's argument of the fact that Government bond yields, and hence interest rates generally, were pegged until March 1951.

the later stages, however, losses and gains in liquidity were accompanied by sharp changes in interest rates, since the public was highly sensitive to adjustments in its liquidity position, so that equilibrium could be attained without significant changes in commodity prices.

In the absence of direct controls over the nominal supply of liquid assets, states Gurley, the monetary authorities were greatly handicapped in their efforts to halt the growth of liquidity and so the rise in commodity prices. Despite fairly severe restraint on monetary growth, there was a large expansion of nonmonetary liquid assets during the postwar period, which mainly took the form of increases in liquid claims on financial institutions lying outside of the direct controls of the monetary authorities. This liquidity expansion forced the economy to attain general equilibrium by moving at first to substantially higher price levels and only later to higher interest rates.

Gurley notes that the growth of nominal liquid assets was based on purchases of primary securities (debts and equities of the nonfinancial sectors) by the monetary system and by nonmonetary intermediaries. He points out that almost $400 billion of primary securities were issued from 1947 through 1958, and financial institutions purchased $185 billion of them, creating approximately the same amount of liquid assets (demand deposits, savings deposits, savings and loan shares, cash values in life insurance, etc.). The largest gains were recorded in liquid claims on nonmonetary intermediaries, the supply of which was not directly controlled by the monetary authorities. In addition, the monetary authorities allowed sizable increases to occur in time deposits in the commercial banks. Thus, total liquid assets rose by $170 billion during this period, with $140 billion of them being in nonmonetary form. The increase in the money supply filled the small gap.

Gurley concludes that it is apparent that tight control of the money supply was not sufficient to prevent substantial gains in nominal liquidity generally, though the liquidity problem was aggravated by rapid growth in time deposits, which the monetary authorities could have prevented. With respect to financial factors, then, the postwar price inflation was due largely to the inheritance by the economy of an inflated volume of war-induced liquid assets and to the further expansion of these assets after 1946, which the monetary authorities were either unable or unwilling to control.

Some Questions About the Gurley-Shaw Thesis
Applicable to Life Insurance Companies

Against the background of the foregoing outline of the Gurley-Shaw thesis, it will be helpful to raise several questions about its applicability to life insurance companies. (1) Do life insurance policyholders as a general rule regard policy reserves as close substitutes for money? (2) Do life insurance companies have a "deposit rate" comparable to the deposit rate of mutual savings banks, savings and loan associations, and similar institutions? (3) Are life insurance companies free of direct control by the monetary authorities? (4) Assuming merit in the Gurley-Shaw argument, how should life companies be brought under control?

First, then, do life insurance policyholders as a general rule regard their policy reserves as close substitutes for money? Are these reserves regarded as liquid assets in the sense that, having policy reserves, life insurance policyholders are encouraged to reduce their demand for money itself? It is significant that Gurley himself seems to have some doubts on this question. He states:

> The term "liquid assets" is a shorthand expression for claims held by nonfinancial sectors of the economy that are considered by these sectors to be fixed in price and redeemable into money on demand. The money supply itself is the most liquid of these claims, but there are many other financial assets that serve as close substitutes for money for precautionary and diversification purposes, although these assets are not media of exchange. Close substitutes for money include time deposits in commercial banks, savings and loan shares, mutual savings deposits, shares and deposits in credit unions, deposits in the Postal Savings System, policy reserves in private life insurance companies, and U.S. Government savings bonds. There is, however, no hard and fast line between these financial assets and others.[5]

Gurley goes on to admit in a footnote to this passage, however, that "it may also be questioned whether the public looks upon policy reserves in life insurance companies as close substitutes for money," but he maintains that "the principal findings of this paper are not altered by these marginal changes." [6] Interestingly, in subsequent discussion he sometimes excludes policy reserves from his list of liquid assets, and sometimes includes them.[7]

What can be said about this question? It should be recognized at the outset that some policyholders are undoubtedly conscious of the cash values of their life insurance. In these cases policyholders do think of their cash values as liquid assets in the Gurley-Shaw sense. Even in these cases, however, policy reserves are probably far removed along the spectrum of liquid assets from such other liquid assets as time deposits, savings bank deposits, and the like. But, the point to be emphasized here is that the great majority of life insurance policyholders do not think of policy reserves as liquid assets. This has emerged clearly from the various surveys conducted by groups such as the Survey Research Center

---

[5] "Liquidity and Financial Institutions in the Postwar Period," pp. 3-4.

[6] *Ibid.*, p. 4.

[7] For example, on p. 23 he excludes policy reserves from a comprehensive list, and on p. 37 he includes them.

at the University of Michigan, in which most policyholders were completely unaware of reserves they were building through life insurance.[8] The fact seems to be that most people buy life insurance for *protection* and that the savings and investment element in permanent life insurance, although vital for the bulk of policyholders, would only be used in serious emergency. They may realize that they are building cash values, but it is an exaggeration to think that many policyholders regard these cash values as highly liquid assets.

Some light on this question may be shed by reviewing the record of the extent to which policyholders have drawn on liquid assets in the form of policy reserves. The two ways in which cash values may be drawn upon are through policy loans and cash surrenders. In Table 9-1 the total of

TABLE 9-1
Policy Reserves, Policy Loan Extensions, and Surrender Benefits
All U.S. Life Insurance Companies, 1952-1959
(In millions of dollars)

	(1)	(2)	(3)	(4)	(5)
	Total Policy Reserves	Total Policy Loan Extensions	Total Surrender Benefits	(2)+(3)	(4)÷(1)
1952	62,579	506	644	1,150	.018
1953	66,683	579	714	1,293	.019
1954	70,903	661	869	1,530	.022
1955	75,359	669	922	1,591	.021
1956	79,738	744	1,024	1,768	.022
1957	84,075	916	1,291	2,207	.026
1958	88,604	1,008	1,457	2,465	.028
1959	93,975	1,156	1,520	2,676	.028
1952-1959	621,916	6,239	8,441	14,680	.024

policy loans and cash surrender benefits for the life insurance business as a whole is related to total policy reserves during the period 1952-59. The figures for total policy reserves are not exactly equal to total cash values of life insurance, but they are quite close to the latter and are used

---

[8] For example, see *The Public Looks at Life Insurance, Report on a Pilot Survey,* conducted by the Life Insurance Agency Management Association, Research Report 1958-10, pp. 19 and 26-29; also, *Consumer Attitudes, Report on a Survey by Life Magazine,* Life Insurance Agency Management Association Research Report 1960-2, pp. 4-5; also *Life Insurance Ownership Among American Families,* 1957, Survey Research Center, Institute for Social Research, University of Michigan, pp. 47-53.

here because there are no industry-wide figures available on total cash values. As is apparent in the table, the use of policy reserves as a source of cash in this period (and the same would have been true in prior years) has been slight, averaging a little over 2 percent for the period as a whole. These figures do not include policy loans with commercial banks, for which we do not have countrywide totals, but in any event the inclusion of loans on policies by banks would not alter the percentage figures appreciably. Moreover, in recent years as policy loans with life insurance companies have increased noticeably, much of this increase has been a transfer of policy loans from the commercial banks as bank lending rates have risen and policyholders have found it more advantageous to borrow with the life companies at comparatively lower rates. In addition, it should be borne in mind that some portion of the increase in policy loans in recent years reflects the expanding sale of policies in which life company loans to policyholders are employed to pay the premiums. Certainly the actual use of policy reserves as a source of liquidity seems modest as compared with other forms of liquid assets listed by Gurley and Shaw. Withdrawals from mutual savings banks have averaged somewhat more than 25 percent of total deposits in these institutions, while the comparable withdrawal ratio for savings and loan associations has averaged close to 30 percent in recent years.

All of the evidence indicates, therefore, that policy reserves should not be classified as a "close substitute for money" or as a "highly liquid asset." They may be in the case of a small minority of more sophisticated policyholders, but for the overwhelming majority of policyholders their cash values in life insurance are far out at the end of the spectrum of liquid assets, if they are indeed recognized at all. In view of this, the Gurley-Shaw thesis has very limited applicability to the life insurance business for this reason alone, because the "close substitute for money" argument is crucial to the core of the Gurley-Shaw thinking.

There are, however, other questions of nearly equal importance which need to be considered. One of these is whether life insurance companies have a "deposit rate" comparable to the deposit rate of mutual savings banks, savings and loan associations, credit unions, and other types of nonmonetary intermediaries listed by Gurley and Shaw. Much of the Gurley-Shaw thesis is based on the framework of a "deposit rate." For example, they state:

> The willingness of nonmonetary intermediaries to supply claims on themselves, in real terms, depends on the rate of interest on primary securities that they buy, on the deposit rate on nonmonetary indirect debt that they sell, on their variable expenses in managing assets and liabilities, and on the types of primary securities available to them. An increase in the rate of interest on primary securities increases their willingness to supply nonmonetary indirect assets. They will also tend to supply less

claims on themselves when the composition of primary securities is unfavorable to their activities.[9]

This line of reasoning does not have much applicability so far as life insurance companies are concerned. It is argued here, and in many other places, by Gurley and Shaw that the net rate of return earned by nonmonetary intermediaries on primary securities, relative to the deposit rate they pay, determines their willingness to supply their own indirect securities to the public. In other words, in the case of a mutual savings bank, for example, the net rate of return earned by the bank on bonds and mortgages relative to the rate it must pay on deposits determines the willingness of the bank to expand its deposits, i.e., the indirect securities it supplies to the public. But, clearly, the rate of return earned on assets by life insurance companies relative to any "deposit rate" is not the determining factor in the willingness of life companies to sell their own indirect securities—life insurance policies. The willingness of life companies to expand their sale of permanent cash value insurance depends on whether the public is willing to pay the premiums necessary to cover the risks involved. It is true that in the calculation of life insurance premiums there is an assumption made about the rate of return which can be earned on policy reserves. This assumed rate might be thought of as a "deposit rate" for life companies. However, the premium is also based upon assumed life expectancy and assumed cost of administering the policy. Thus, the life insurance companies sell a product which is a combination of saving and protection, and to include them with institutions for which the deposit rate is of key importance does not make sense. The interest rate assumed in the calculation of dividends (or gross premiums for nonparticipating insurance) is closer to the "deposit rate" than the assumed rate for the determination of policy reserves, but even here the analogy of a deposit rate is not very realistic.

Again, Gurley and Shaw state:

> Private nonmonetary intermediaries are further aided if the monetary system's deposit rates are set at low levels and if monetary policy is generally restrictive. For then, assuming nonneutrality of money, rising interest rates on primary securities induce the private intermediaries to raise their own deposit rates for the purpose of attracting additional demand for their products. The growth of these intermediaries is also favored by governmental insurance of their indirect debts, by such insurance of at least some of the primary securities they purchase, and by the absence of competition from governmental lending institutions.
>
> Many of these factors are likely to be present during an upswing in private economic activity when aggregate demand for current output threatens to be excessive at prevailing price levels and when the Policy Bureau (the Federal Reserve authorities) attempts to protect these levels.[10]

---

9 *Money in a Theory of Finance*, pp. 204-205.
10 *Ibid.*, p. 229.

The above passage has little application to life companies.[11] Other passages could be cited to show the importance of the "deposit rate" in the Gurley-Shaw thesis. The important point in their thinking about the influence of the deposit rate is that, by altering the deposit rate, the intermediaries can take the initiative to increase or decrease liquid claims on themselves, and thus frustrate the efforts of the monetary authorities. The mechanism is the spread between the interest rate on primary securities and the deposit rate. So far as life insurance companies are concerned, it is certainly true that the rate of return on primary securities is of great importance. Whether the rate of return earned on invested assets is above or below the rate of interest assumed in policy contracts is vital to a company's successful operation. Certainly, a margin of the earned rate above the assumed rate aids a company to pay higher policyholder dividends, and thus to reduce the net cost of insurance. However, there is nothing in the life insurance field, from the viewpoint of selling liquid claims for money, in the nature of a "deposit rate." The only possible exception is the rate of return paid to beneficiaries in the case of funds left with the companies under settlement options. In this case,

---

[11] Actually, it has little applicability to any of the nonbank institutions for the following reason. Institutions such as mutual savings banks, life insurance companies, and savings and loan associations are long-term investors. As such, they hold in their investment portfolios securities and mortgages acquired over an extended period. For example, the life insurance companies hold Government bonds acquiring during World War II at a 2½ percent return, as well as mortgages acquired in 1959 to yield 6 percent. In a period such as the past fifteen years, as interest rates have risen, the yield on the *new* investments has shown a pronounced increase in many years, but the *average* on all investments has risen only slowly. In 1959, for example, new investments acquired by life companies probably averaged 5½-5¾ percent, whereas the average return on their assets as a whole was 3.96 percent. The accompanying table shows how slowly the average return on U.S. life company assets has changed since 1947. The slowness with which the average rate of return changes indicates how unrealistic the Gurley-Shaw argument is. The slow-moving average militates strongly against cyclical changes in the deposit rate, as argued by Gurley-Shaw. A similar situation would undoubtedly obtain with other types of financial intermediaries such as savings banks.

Year	Average Rate of Return on Life Insurance Invested Funds (before Federal taxes)
1947	2.88
1948	2.96
1949	3.06
1950	3.13
1951	3.18
1952	3.28
1953	3.36
1954	3.46
1955	3.51
1956	3.63
1957	3.75
1958	3.85
1959	3.96

however, it has not been customary for the companies to employ rate changes as a competitive device.[12]

Permanent cash value life insurance is a complicated bundle of utilities—protection, saving, investment, and so forth. The sale of life insurance has been primarily on the grounds of protection. The savings and investment aspect has not been prominent in most sales efforts. Consequently, the "deposit rate" type of reasoning has little application with life insurance companies. Actually, as the interest rate on primary securities has risen, the ability of the life companies to sell cash value insurance seems to have *declined*. The facts are that, as the average rate of return earned on assets by life companies has risen steadily since 1947, the companies have been selling a larger proportion of insurance involving no buildup of cash values. The underlying reason is in part that rising interest rates have been the product in large measure of price level inflation, which has provided a poor climate for the sale of permanent cash value policies. Actually, as discussed in Chapter 8, as interest rates on primary securities have risen, partly as the result of monetary policy, the cash flow of life companies for investment has tended to be restricted. In fact, as interest rates have risen throughout the economy, the growth of saving through life insurance seems to have been retarded (see Chapter 2), rather than favored as Gurley suggests.

We come now to the third question, namely are life insurance companies free of *direct* control by the monetary authorities. This can be considered briefly because of the detailed discussion in Chapter 8. As we saw in that discussion, Gurley and Shaw are correct in their view, of course, that life companies are not subject to *direct* control by the monetary authorities in the sense that the authorities can exert direct control over the money supply by controlling the volume of commercial bank reserves. However, the monetary authorities have powerful means to influence the loanable funds of life insurance companies, even though these means are indirect. By affecting interest rates the monetary authorities can have an important influence on (1) the direction in which life company investment funds flow, (2) the total amount of cash they have for investment, (3) their ability to sell assets and thus to raise additional funds for investment, and (4) their willingness to enter into forward investment commitments.

Actually, the flow of savings into investment through life insurance

---

12 It is a fact that in recent years companies have increased their discount on premiums paid in advance, as well as rates on deposit funds and group annuity guarantees. However, such alterations in rates are not made on a short-term cyclical basis which would act to frustrate countercyclical monetary policy, as the Gurley-Shaw thesis asserts. Rates are changed only very slowly in response to longer-run shifts in the demand for, and supply of, capital. Even if such rate increases do serve to attract savings to life companies (or to prevent losses of funds), it is difficult to see how this would have any adverse consequences from the general public's viewpoint.

companies provides an ideal framework for monetary policy to spread its influence, indirectly but powerfully, into the far-flung areas of the long term capital markets.

The final question to be asked is: assuming merit in the Gurley-Shaw thesis, how would life insurance companies be brought under direct control, and what would be the implications of such control? The heart of the difficulty, as seen by Gurley and Shaw, is the uncontrolled ability of life companies (and other intermediaries) to sell liquid claims upon themselves, i.e., to sell permanent cash value insurance and to retain policy proceeds through supplementary contracts on settlement options. This is, as we have seen, because increased liquid asset holdings by the public in the form of life insurance cash values enable the public to reduce its demand for cash and thus to affect interest rates, the general price level, the level of real output, and other economic variables. The increase of liquid assets held by the public in the form of life insurance cash values, maintain Gurley and Shaw, frustrates the effectiveness of monetary policy and requires greater restriction of the money supply than would otherwise be necessary, with possible damaging results to the commercial banking system. Accordingly, the mechanism of control implicit in the Gurley-Shaw argument is to affect the ability of life companies to increase their policy reserves by controlling their sale of cash value insurance.

Certainly Gurley and Shaw recognize that the enormous amount of saving through life insurance since 1900, and the use of this saving to finance real capital formation, has contributed greatly to the economic growth of our country. With our paramount domestic problem today being to stimulate even greater saving to finance an even greater rate of capital formation, and hence foster economic growth, it is doubtful that Gurley and Shaw really mean to advocate regulations which would restrain the accumulation of savings through life insurance during periods of monetary restraint. The current trend of life insurance saving, as discussed in Chapter 2, is already discouraging enough. Rather, the life insurance business should be given every encouragement by public policy to expand the sale of cash value insurance.

Conclusions About the Gurley-Shaw Thesis and Life Insurance Companies

Several conclusions emerge from this discussion, as follows:

1) The Gurley-Shaw thesis has little applicability to life insurance companies because (a) policy reserves are not regarded as liquid assets by the great majority of policyholders and are not a close substitute for money; (b) the life companies are not "deposit rate" institutions; and (c)

they have characteristics which differentiate them importantly from the deposit institutions.

2) Life insurance companies are powerfully affected by policies of the monetary authorities, even though not directly.

3) There is no convincing reason for instituting any direct control of life insurance companies by the monetary authorities. The indirect controls already available are powerful and fully adequate. The inevitable result of any direct control would be to injure the possibilities for further expanding the public's saving through life insurance, so greatly needed to facilitate a more rapid rate of national economic growth.

4) What is needed most, in connection with the Gurley-Shaw thesis, is a careful examination into the indirect ways in which monetary controls affect nonmonetary intermediaries. It is logical to expect that powerful indirect effects of monetary policy, similar to those felt by life companies, are also experienced by other nonmonetary intermediaries. Moreover, it is significant that Gurley and Shaw do not even mention two of the fastest-growing intermediaries, namely, the corporate uninsured pension funds and the state and local funds. Together, their annual growth in assets today is about as large as that of the life insurance business. The nature of these funds indicates that the Gurley-Shaw thesis would have as little applicability to them as it has to life insurance companies. Finally, the difficulties raised by Gurley and Shaw largely come down to changes in the velocity of money. One may well raise the question of whether the Gurley-Shaw thesis gives enough recognition to the fact that monetary policy is directed to regulating the *effective* supply of money, that is, the quantity multiplied by the rate of turnover. There is little doubt that a rise in the velocity of money has at times made the task of the authorities more difficult, but far from unmanageable.

Chapter 10

LIFE INSURANCE COMPANY INVESTMENTS AND NATIONAL ECONOMIC GROWTH

With the increasing focus of interest in the growth of the American economy, it is pertinent to consider the role which life insurance companies play in the process of economic growth. The economic growth of our national economy is the product of many factors: a growing and increasingly skilled labor force; a system of government which has nurtured individual free initiative, the spirit of inventiveness, and the willingness to assume investment risks; the great free trade area between the states which has made geographical specialization of production so effective; and many others. Important as these factors are, the heart of the economic growth process has, of course, been the willingness of the American people to save a significant proportion of their current income and to make these savings available for investment in the productive tools which have facilitated the expansion of our national output. Without the saving-investment process the American economy could not have developed such a great capacity to grow regardless of other favorable forces.

Life Insurance Companies in the Saving-Investment Process

As shown by Goldsmith's data, the principal channel of saving by the American people in the past sixty years has been life insurance.[1] During that period, over $106 billion of savings have been accumulated through life insurance. In 1900 the savings accumulated by the American people through life insurance amounted to the modest sum of $1.7 billion; by the end of 1959, accumulated life insurance savings had risen to $108 billion.

Chart 10-1 shows the record from 1910 through 1960 of the volume of

---

[1] Raymond W. Goldsmith, *A Study of Saving in the United States* (Princeton University Press, 1955); see especially Vol. I, pp. 448-460.

CHART 10-1

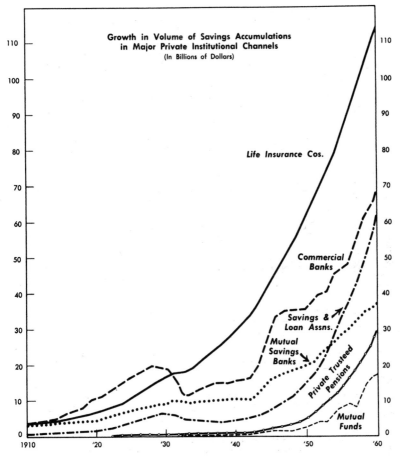

Growth in Volume of Savings Accumulations
in Major Private Institutional Channels
(In Billions of Dollars)

Life Insurance Cos.

Commercial Banks

Savings & Loan Assns.

Mutual Savings Banks

Private Trusteed Pensions

Mutual Funds

savings accumulations in major savings institutions. This chart is based on data from various private and government sources, brought together by the Business Research Bureau of the Metropolitan Life Insurance Company. Table 10-1 provides a detailed picture for 1948-60 of the highly important role life insurance companies play in the national capital markets, along with that of other types of financial institutions. This table presents sources and uses of capital funds in the national economy as a whole. The data measure the *net* new money supplied by various sources and the net uses of funds.

The tremendous growth of saving through life insurance is, of course, partly the product of a growing national economy. One would naturally expect life insurance sales to increase as the economy expands. More important, however, and easily overlooked, is the great contribution which the productive investment of life insurance funds has made to the growth

TABLE 10-1
Sources and Uses of Funds in the Capital Market, 1948-1960
(in billions of dollars)

Sources of funds	1948	1949	1950	1951	1952	1953	1954	1955	1956	1957	1958	1959	1960p
Life insurance companies	3.4	3.6	3.7	3.7	4.4	4.7	5.0	5.3	5.0	4.7	4.9	4.9	5.2
Savings and loan associations	1.2	1.3	2.1	2.0	3.1	3.7	4.2	5.7	4.9	4.9	6.3	8.4	7.0
Mutual savings banks	1.0	1.0	1.0	0.8	1.7	1.8	2.0	2.1	2.0	1.7	2.4	1.5	1.6
Corporate pension funds	0.7	0.7	0.9	1.3	1.5	1.7	1.9	1.9	2.2	2.6	2.7	3.2	3.3
Commercial banks	-1.7	6.1	6.6	6.0	9.1	4.1	10.2	4.8	4.4	5.1	15.2	4.2	9.3
Federal Reserve Banks	0.8	-4.4	1.9	3.0	0.9	1.2	-1.0	-0.1	0.1	-0.7	2.1	0.3	0.7
State and local funds	1.0	1.0	1.5	1.5	2.1	2.5	2.9	1.8	2.3	2.6	1.6	2.9	1.0
U.S. investment accounts	3.0	2.0	-0.1	3.1	3.6	2.4	1.3	2.1	2.3	1.2	-0.9	-0.7	1.4
Federal loan agencies	0.1	0.4	0.4	0.9	0.9	0.2	-0.1	0.6	0.9	1.6	0.6	2.5	1.7
Corporations	3.5	2.9	7.9	2.9	2.4	2.3	0.1	11.0	-1.1	2.1	0.7	8.3	1.5
Fire and casualty companies	1.0	1.1	0.8	0.7	1.2	1.3	1.2	0.9	0.5	0.8	0.9	1.5	1.4
Foreigners	-0.1	0.1	1.5	*	1.0	0.6	0.6	1.3	0.5	*	*	4.5	1.1
Individuals and others	4.4	3.2	2.0	1.8	5.0	5.2	1.8	8.7	8.1	6.8	4.0	14.6	3.0
Total sources	18.1	18.9	30.0	27.8	36.9	31.9	30.0	46.2	32.3	33.4	40.5	56.2	38.1
Uses of funds													
Corporate bonds	4.7	3.3	2.0	3.6	4.9	4.8	3.8	4.2	4.7	7.1	5.9	4.1	5.0
Corporate stocks	1.1	1.3	1.5	2.3	2.4	1.9	1.8	1.9	2.5	2.7	2.1	2.4	1.8
State & local government issues	2.2	2.3	3.1	2.4	3.1	3.5	4.2	3.5	3.3	4.9	5.9	5.4	4.0
U.S. Government issues	-4.1	4.3	-0.4	2.7	8.0	7.8	3.5	2.0	-4.1	-1.7	8.0	7.9	-0.6
Federal agency issues	0.3	-0.1	0.4	0.2	*	*	*	1.5	0.6	2.1	-0.5	2.2	*
Mortgages: 1-4 family	5.1	4.3	7.6	6.5	6.8	7.6	9.6	12.6	10.8	8.6	10.1	13.2	10.9
Other	2.2	2.1	2.6	2.9	2.3	2.3	2.8	3.6	3.8	3.5	5.2	6.0	4.5
Business credit	2.3	-2.5	8.1	5.2	2.9	-1.8	1.4	9.5	7.4	3.0	0.9	6.5	5.7
Consumer credit	2.8	2.9	4.1	1.2	4.8	3.9	1.1	6.4	3.6	2.8	0.3	6.4	3.9
All other credit	1.7	1.0	1.1	0.7	1.6	1.9	1.9	0.9	-0.4	0.5	2.7	2.1	2.7
Total uses	18.1	18.9	30.0	27.8	36.9	31.9	30.0	46.2	32.3	33.4	40.5	56.2	38.1

*Less than $50 million.   p - Preliminary.
Because of rounding, components may not add to totals shown.

246

of our economy. The following figures will illustrate how the life insurance business has contributed to economic growth.

During the period 1948-59, inclusive, one of pronounced economic growth, American business and industrial corporations borrowed *net new money* amounting to about $53 billion in order to aid in financing new plant and equipment and for working capital.[2] Of this total, nearly $29 billion was obtained from the life insurance companies of the country. In other words, about 54 percent of the net new money obtained in the capital markets by business and industrial corporations to finance their expansion, modernization, and working capital requirements in this period came from life insurance companies alone. About 66 percent of these funds went to business and industrial firms, with the remainder going to public utilities, and in small measure the railroads. It should be noted that the above figures refer to the *net new money* supplied by life companies to business and industry. Actually, due to repayment of existing loans by corporations, the life insurance companies made a much larger volume of loans to business and industrial corporations in this period. The Life Insurance Association of America compiles data which show that in order to increase their holdings of corporate bonds by $29 billion during 1948-59, the life insurance companies actually purchased approximately $58 billion of corporate bonds. These funds were invested imaginatively by the investment officers of life companies in a way that provided the financing for a wide variety of growth-producing ideas, as will be discussed presently.

But it would be a mistake to think that the investment of life insurance saving—and the contribution to economic growth—has been limited to the purchase of the bonds of business and industrial firms. During the same period, 1948-59, the life insurance companies added to their holdings of mortgages on business and industrial properties, and apartment buildings, in an amount equal to $8.5 billion. Since the total mortgage debt of this type increased by $32 billion in this period,[3] the life companies provided about 26 percent of the total of this financing. Thus, these are the funds which in the past twelve years have been employed to build office buildings, warehouses, department stores, shopping centers, and many other commercial and industrial facilities which have meant so much to the growth of the country. It is largely through this channel that life companies have provided millions of dollars of financing to small business concerns.

Perhaps most interesting is the enormous contribution which life insurance savings have made to better housing of our people, which certainly improves national productive capacity as well as our living standards.

---

[2] Estimates of Securities and Exchange Commission, cf. Federal Reserve Bulletin, January 1957 and 1961, p. 64.
[3] Economic Report of the President 1961, p. 181.

During these past twelve years the life insurance companies have expanded their holdings of mortgages on one- to four-family houses in an amount equal to $20 billion. In other words, about 20 percent of the total increase of $103 billion in home mortgage debt in the country as a whole during this period has gone to life insurance companies. But this again really underestimates the total impact of life insurance companies in home financing because it does not take account of amortization of mortgages and other mortgage repayments. Reliable information reported to the Life Insurance Association of America shows that since 1946 the life insurance companies of the country have actually made about $45.5 billion of home mortgage loans, of which $13.3 billion have been FHA-insured loans, $10.6 billion have been VA-guaranteed loans, and approximately $22 billion have been uninsured home loans. On the assumption that the average mortgage loan during this period was $10,000, the life insurance companies provided the financing making possible the purchase of homes by 4,550,000 American families.

These, then, are the principal ways in which the life insurance savings of our people have provided the financing of sound economic growth. They are not the only ways, however. There have been other types of life company investments of lesser magnitude such as the purchase of state and local government bonds which have provided the financing for toll highways and other public improvements. The same is true of direct investment in real estate and housing facilities, and many other investments.

Thus, the productive investment of life insurance savings has been a major source of the rapid growth of the American economy.

Specific Examples of Life Insurance Company Investments Which Have Contributed to Economic Growth

In order to be more specific about the ways in which life insurance company investments have contributed to national economic growth, several life companies were invited in early 1960 by the Life Insurance Association of America to provide examples of investments which they had made which facilitated economic growth. The examples which these companies provided are undoubtedly representative of the life insurance companies as a whole.

One major life insurance company reported that the Kaiser Steel Corporation, under an expansion program begun in 1952, increased its ingot capacity from 1,380,000 to 2,933,000 tons annually and finished products from 904,000 to 2,028,000 tons annually, at a total estimated capital cost of about $287,000,000. Of this amount, life insurance companies provided about $185,000,000 of the financing. McLouth Steel Corporation, under an expansion program also begun in 1952, increased ingot capacity from

550,000 to 1,865,000 tons annually and finished products from 493,000 to 1,378,000 tons annually, at a total estimated capital cost of $155,000,000. Of total outside financing of $125,000,000 obtained by McLouth, the life insurance companies provided $76,685,000. Or to take another example, Electric Energy Inc. obtained a total of $195,000,000 in financing from two major life insurance companies, beginning in 1951, to provide funds for the construction of a steam electric generating plant at Joppa, Illinois, primarily to supply power to the Atomic Energy Commission for its Paducah, Kentucky, project. Life insurance companies have had a substantial share in the jet re-equipment program of the airlines. During the past few years they have purchased, or committed to purchase, approximately $700,000,000 of airline debt, representing almost half of the estimated cost of 361 jet-powered aircraft acquired or on order by the airlines.

Another major life insurance company reported that it holds the entire debt outstanding of Perkin-Elmer Corporation, a company which manufactures scientific instruments primarily used for analysis of chemical compounds, and electronic-optical systems and components used for missile guidance and tracking, aerial photography, and bomb sights. In 1950 a loan of $400,000 was made to Perkin-Elmer to finance a new plant, and in 1956-57 an additional $1,480,000 was provided for plant expansion. In 1959 an additional loan of $1,000,000 was made to provide working capital. The same life insurance company reported that in 1959 it purchased $3,500,000 of the securities of Dixon Chemical Industries, Inc., to provide part of the funds this company needed to acquire a site and construct a sulfuric acid plant at Paulsboro, New Jersey. In 1959 the same life company made a commitment to provide additional financing of $2,750,000 for the construction of a hydrofluoric acid plant at Paulsboro. In another case, the same life insurance company in 1959 purchased $18,000,000 of the bonds of the Dundee Cement Company to provide part of the funds for the construction of a cement plant, with an annual capacity of 4,500,000 barrels, at Dundee, Michigan.

Another major life insurance company reported that during 1953-55 a group of life insurance companies loaned a total of $143,000,000 to Reserve Mining Corporation. These funds, together with capital provided by Reserve's owners (Armco Steel and Republic Steel), were used to build an iron ore beneficiation plant and related facilities at Babbitt and Beaver Bay, Minnesota. The plant, completed in 1956, processes taconite iron ore and has an annual capacity of 3,800,000 gross tons of iron ore pellets. The same life insurance company reported another case of financing it had provided to Texas Instruments, Inc. In 1953 Texas Instruments borrowed $2,500,000 for capital additions and working capital, and in 1956 a second loan of $10,000,000 was made to be employed in the construction of a semiconductor-components division plant.

Texas Instruments is engaged in the manufacture of various types of transistors, diodes, rectifiers, resistors, capacitors, and electromechanical systems. They are also engaged in the development and manufacture of specialized geophysical instruments and equipment for use in oil exploration, thermostatic and electrical controls, nuclear fuel element and cores, and other products. When the first loan was made to Texas Instruments in 1953, the company was small and limited in scope. Since then it has become a large factor in most of its fields, probably the major factor in transistors, and a highly important contributor to the "space age."

The same major life insurance company reported that since 1946 it has acquired $95,000,000 of the bonds of El Paso Natural Gas Company which has aided in the financing of two southern pipelines in Texas, New Mexico, and Arizona, with 80 percent of the gas being used in California. The financing has also aided in the development of El Paso's northern pipeline which delivers gas to Idaho, Oregon, and Washington. Similarly, the life company reported that in 1957 it joined with several life insurance companies in providing $107,000,000 of financing to the Houston Corporation, which owns all of the stock of the Coastal Transmission Corporation and Houston Texas Gas and Oil Corporation. These two latter companies constructed a mainline pipeline system for the transmission of natural gas from the Gulf Coast producing areas of Texas and Louisiana to markets in peninsular Florida, the last major population area in the United States which was without natural gas service. Still another example cited by the reporting life company was the financing of the Ohio Valley Electric Corporation. This company was incorporated in 1952 to supply the entire power requirements, under a twenty-five-year contract, of the Atomic Energy Commission's gaseous diffusion plant which was under construction in Pike County, Ohio. A total of $316,500,000 of bonds were sold to finance this project, the majority of which were bought by life insurance companies. Similarly, the Yankee Atomic Electric Company was incorporated in 1954 by eleven sponsoring New England electric companies for the purpose of constructing an atomic-powered steam electric generating plant in Rowe, Massachusetts. Of the total cost of the plant ($57,000,000), ten life insurance companies provided $20,000,000 of the financing. This is the first atomic electric plant to be built in New England, a high fuel cost area.

Several other interesting growth-producing investments were cited by another major life insurance company. For example, a $2,000,000 loan was made to Varian Associates to finance plant expansion for the production of Klystrom tubes used in the rapidly expanding fields of missiles, radar warning systems, and other communication systems. A $6,200,000 loan was made to Uranium Reduction Company to provide part of the financing for a new uranium processing mill. A $15,000,000 loan was made to Gulf States Paper Corporation to add new facilities and modernize and expand existing mill capacity in Alabama. This over-all program added substantially to paper industry capacity in the South.

Another major life company cited a number of growth-producing loans it had made to comparatively small business and industrial firms. For example, in 1956 it made a loan of $850,000 to Lincoln Service Corporation, an electric utility company serving a predominantly rural economy in Wyoming. The loan was to improve the company's transmission facilities to provide service for a number of small towns and for agricultural and ranching needs, in addition to some oil development. In 1947 a loan of $240,000 was made to Dairypak Incorporated (now Dairypak Butter, Inc.), a company which produces paper milk bottles. This company has prospered greatly and has come to the insurance company several times since 1947 to finance further growth, and in 1956, when the loan was last increased, it totaled $4,200,000. In another instance, the same life company in 1954 purchased $700,000 of notes of the Canal Barge Company, Inc., a contract carrier operating specialized oil and chemical tows on the Gulf Intracoastal Waterway and the Mississippi River and its tributaries. At the time of the original loan the company owned six towboats and ten tank barges with a net book value of $1,218,000. The insurance company has subsequently increased the loan twice, each time assisting Canal Barge Company in modernizing and upgrading the power and capacity of its fleet. In early 1960 negotiations were being completed to increase the loan to $2,000,000. The company now operates seven towboats and fifteen tank barges with a net book value of $3,604,000.

Another large life insurance company reported some typical examples of investments contributing to national economic growth. In 1952 several life insurance companies participated in total financing of $100,000,000 to the Iron Ore Company of Canada. Additional millions have been invested in the company by life insurance companies since that time. At the end of World War II, it was realized by the steel industry in this country that the iron ore deposits in the Mesabi Range of Minnesota would be inadequate to supply the iron ore requirements of an expanding steel capacity in the years ahead. The result was a world-wide search for ore deposits, and one of the largest discoveries was in nearby Labrador. However, hundreds of millions of dollars were required to finance the development of these resources, including the building of a railroad, a town-site, ore-docks, and open-pit mining facilities. A group of American steel companies and Canadian mining companies went ahead with the project, with financing obtained largely from U.S. life insurance companies, on the promise of the steel-company owners to purchase enough ore each year to provide enough funds to service the debt and thereby eventually to retire it.

The same life insurance company pointed out the great role life insurance companies have played in the postwar expansion of the aluminum industry. After the war the U.S. Government placed its emergency-built aluminum plants on sale. Both Reynolds Metals Company and Kaiser Aluminum & Chemical Company were extremely interested in purchasing these plants, but they did not have the financial resources or the credit rating at that time to finance the purchase of these plants. The result was an agreement worked out with the U.S. Government and the two aluminum companies whereby the government agreed to purchase any aluminum which could not be sold commercially from the output of these plants. On the basis of this agreement the life insurance companies were then able to finance the purchase of these plants by Reynolds Metal and Kaiser and in later years to finance several stages of aluminum expansion during and after the Korean War.

Another life company reported the following loans: a $10,000,000 loan in 1943 to Rohm & Haas which was used principally to expand the facilities for the manufacture of plexiglas; a $7,000,000 loan in 1952 to Copperweld Steel Company to modernize and expand their facilities for the production of copper-coated and aluminum-coated steel; a loan of $7,000,000 in 1956 to Air Products, Inc., for the expansion of oxygen production facilities; a loan of $1,900,000 in 1948 to Robinson Clay Products Co., Inc., to increase production of clay sewer pipe; a loan of $1,000,000 in 1959 to Neenah Foundry Company to construct a new plant making construction castings such as manhole covers, catch basin inlets, etc.; a loan of $500,000 in 1947 to Richard C. Remmey Son Company for plant expansion in connection with the production of fire brick used mainly by steel companies.

Another intermediate-sized life insurance company cited several interesting examples of growth-producing loans. One of these was a $2,000,000 loan in 1958 to the Jim Walter Corporation, a young firm which operates throughout the South constructing "shell" homes. The availability of this financing contributed greatly to the rapid growth of this company. In 1958 this life company made a $7,000,000 loan to the Okonite Company, a leading manufacturer of insulated wire and cable. This loan enabled the Okonite Company to close an outdated plant and move some of their operations to a modern facility with over 2½ times the floor space of the older plant. The loan permitted the company to abandon an old multi-story plant in a crowded city industrial district and to build a modern suburban plant that allowed increased productive efficiency and ample room for expansion. Still another example was a $1,000,000 loan in 1957 to the Hagan Chemicals & Controls, Inc., a producer of water treatment chemicals and automatic control devices.

Finally, one other medium-sized life insurance company listed several examples of growth-producing investments as follows: a $7,500,000 loan (part of total financing of $110,000,000 supplied by several life companies and other investors) in 1951-53 to the Chemstrand Corporation to provide funds for construction of plants to produce nylon and acrylic fibre; loans of $8,000,000 in 1956 and $2,500,000 in 1959-60 to Southern Nitrogen Company, Inc., to provide a portion of the funds needed to construct a plant for production of ammonia and its derivatives; a loan of $2,500,000 to Harry T. Campbell Sons' Corporation in 1958 to permit the company to increase its quarrying operations and manufacturing facilities to produce "Sacrete" for the fast-growing "do-it-yourself" market; a loan of $12,000,000 in 1952 to Kerr-McGee Oil Industries, Inc., to finance drilling and development and to finance drilling contracts and refining inventories; loans of $3,750,000 in 1953 and $875,000 in 1954 to Amoniaco Corporation to construct new plants and facilities for the manufacture of anhydrous ammonia; a loan of $7,500,000 in 1948 to Cit-Con Oil Corporation to provide part of the funds to finance one of the world's most modern plants for producing high quality motor oils and fully refined paraffin wax.

The above cases illustrate some of the countless ways in which life insurance company investments have aided the economic growth process in the United States. The investments have been in small firms, large firms, comparatively new firms, old firms, and firms in almost every community in the country.

Loans to Small Business and Industrial Concerns

Although it is generally recognized that life insurance investments have contributed to the economic growth of the United States, it is often assumed that life company loans are almost entirely in large amounts and to the large firms of the country. Some of the examples presented earlier show that life company loans are often small in amount and to relatively unknown business and industrial concerns. But it will be helpful here to provide additional information on the extent to which life insurance companies make smaller business loans, for much of the vigor of our national economy comes from the dynamic growth of small business firms.

As the result of a request from Representative Wright Patman, Chairman of the Select Committee on Small Business of the House of Representatives, the Life Insurance Association of America in 1957 conducted a survey of life insurance company lending to business and industry during the period 1953-56, inclusive. The survey covered sixty-seven reporting life insurance companies whose combined assets totaled almost $74 billion at the end of 1956, thus accounting for 77 percent of the assets held by all life insurance companies. The basic data in the survey included the number of loans and dollar amounts authorized each year for investment in business and industrial bonds, public utility bonds, and mortgage loans to business and industry. The data were classified in terms of the total size of borrowing involved, the asset-size of the borrower, the principal business of the borrower, and the rate of interest on the loan.

The results of this survey illustrate how life insurance companies lend to borrowers of all size groups. The combined totals of life insurance loans through investments in business and industrial bonds, public utility bonds, and business and industrial mortgages are shown in Table 10-2

TABLE 10-2
Life Insurance Loans to Business and Industry
By Type of Investment and Amount Authorized

	1953	1954	1955	1956
	(In thousands of dollars)			
Corporate bonds and notes:				
Business and industrial	2,776,486	2,624,475	2,678,717	3,390,966
Public utilities	1,146,448	802,839	482,844	428,937
Business & industrial mortgages	749,548	1,067,697	1,191,151	1,268,761
Total	4,672,482	4,495,011	4,352,712	5,088,644

for the years 1953 through 1956. These data represent the dollar amounts *authorized* during each year for investment in the forms indicated, reflecting the year in which the loan decision became final rather than the time at which funds were actually disbursed.[4]

From a total of $4.7 billion in 1953 the amounts authorized declined to $4.5 billion in 1954 and to $4.4 billion in 1955, followed by a rise to almost $5.1 billion authorized in 1956.[5] Investment in public utility bonds declined steadily over this period, while loans authorized for business and industrial bonds remained fairly constant until a substantial rise took place in 1956. Amounts authorized for mortgage loans to business and industry have risen steadily in each year, increasing from $750 million in 1953 to $1,269 million in 1956.

A further breakdown of these annual totals, classified according to the total size of loan involved, appears in Table 10-3. As in all similar tables to follow, the heading "Total Size of Loan" refers to the *total amount borrowed* by the business concern whether through a security offered publicly to thousands of investors, a direct placement with several financial institutions, or a mortgage loan from a single life insurance

---

[4] The time lag between loan authorization and final disbursement varies from several days to several months. The data in this survey thus more accurately reflect market conditions prevailing in a given year than would statistics on disbursements of loan funds.

[5] In analyzing these figures, it should be kept in mind that in 1954 and 1955 an increase in residential mortgage authorizations (not included in this survey) offset the decline in authorizations to finance business and industry.

TABLE 10-3
Life Insurance Loans to Business and Industry[1]
By Size of Loan, Amount Authorized and Number of Borrowing Operations[2]

Total size of loan	1953 Number[2]	1953 Amount	1954 Number[2]	1954 Amount	1955 Number[2]	1955 Amount	1956 Number[2]	1956 Amount
				(Amounts in thousands of dollars)				
Under $50,000	2,007	48,804	2,072	50,446	2,064	50,725	1,953	50,121
$50,000 - $100,000	815	56,419	934	63,672	981	67,108	1,075	73,834
$100,000 - $250,000	858	127,033	1,072	160,684	1,170	179,754	1,214	184,456
$250,000 - $1,000,000	595	269,327	809	378,212	863	396,591	823	393,175
$1,000,000 - $5,000,000	362	713,117	468	856,837	448	855,629	498	1,007,836
$5,000,000 - $10,000,000	83	402,003	75	371,916	104	496,329	99	504,984
$10,000,000 and over	146	3,055,779	175	2,613,244	158	2,306,576	188	2,874,258
Total	4,866	4,672,482	5,605	4,495,011	5,788	4,352,712	5,850	5,088,664
				(As percent of total number and total amount)				
Under $50,000	41.3	1.0	37.0	1.1	35.7	1.2	33.4	1.0
$50,000 - $100,000	16.8	1.2	16.7	1.4	17.0	1.5	18.4	1.5
$100,000 - $250,000	17.6	2.7	19.1	3.6	20.2	4.1	20.7	3.6
$250,000 - $1,000,000	12.2	5.8	14.4	8.4	14.9	9.1	14.1	7.7
$1,000,000 - $5,000,000	7.4	15.3	8.4	19.1	7.7	19.7	8.5	19.8
$5,000,000 - $10,000,000	1.7	8.6	1.3	8.3	1.8	11.4	1.7	9.9
$10,000,000 and over	3.0	65.4	3.1	58.1	2.7	53.0	3.2	56.5
Total	100.0	100.0	100.0	100.0	100.0	100.0	100.0	100.0

[1]Includes investments in business and industrial bonds, public utility bonds and mortgage loans to business and industry. The survey does not include investment in residential mortgages. The importance of residential mortgages is indicated by the fact that during 1953-1956 the life insurance business as a whole made $16.7 billion of residential mortgage loans, of which $5.3 billion were VA guaranteed and $3.4 billion were FHA insured. Although exact figures are not available, it is well known that many of these residential mortgage loans are in fact small business loans. Likewise the survey does not include farm mortgage loans, which are really business loans. During 1953-1956 the life insurance business made 120,913 farm mortgage loans, for a total of $1,779,759,000 or an average loan of $14,719.

[2]These data are based on the supplement to the survey report, which corrects the *gross* number of authorizations for duplicate reporting by two or more life insurance companies purchasing part of the same bond issue. Consequently, the statistics represent the number of borrowing operations in which business and industrial firms obtained loans from life insurance lenders, either through bonds or through mortgages.

company. The dollar amounts shown in the body of the table represent the aggregate loan authorizations by the reporting life insurance companies. For example, authorization to invest in a public utility bond issue totaling $50 million has been recorded in the survey opposite the line "$10,000,000 and over," even though a single company may have authorized the purchase of only $100,000 of the issue or all reporting life companies may have authorized the purchase of $900,000 of the issue.

Life insurance participation in loans totaling $10 million and more accounted for a high proportion of all business and industrial loan authorizations shown in Table 10-3, but the importance of this size of loan in the total was less in 1956 than in 1953 or 1954. On the other hand, the dollar amounts authorized in the loan categories below $250,000 rose in each year since 1953, while the relative importance of such authorizations increased from 4.9 percent of the total amount in 1953 to 6.1 percent in 1954 and 6.8 percent in 1955; in 1956 the percentage of loans under $250,000 returned to the 1954 level.

Table 10-3 also shows the number of borrowing operations in which business and industrial firms obtained loans from the reporting life insurance companies, either through bonds or mortgages. Of the total number of borrowing operations reported for this period, almost three-quarters were for loans involving less than $250,000. Borrowing operations for less than $250,000 in which life insurance companies provided loan funds rose steadily in number from 3,680 in 1953 to 4,242 in 1956. Data on the number of borrowing operations have been obtained by means of a supplementary survey which was designed to eliminate the duplication in reporting by two or more companies on separate bond issues in which more than one life company participated.[6] In the case of mortgage loans to business and industry, participation by more than one company in a single loan occurs rarely if at all, and the number of authorizations originally reported in the survey reflect the number of borrowing operations that took place in each loan category.

The average dollar amounts authorized by each company for investment in each loan category are shown in Table 10-4. These average amounts have been computed by dividing the total amounts authorized as shown in Table 10-3 by the gross number of authorizations reported by the companies, before adjustment for duplicate reporting. In the smallest category, loans under $50,000, the average authorization

---

[6] Life insurance companies responding to the survey were originally requested to report the number of authorizations and dollar amount authorized in each category of "Total Size of Loan." Combining the sixty-seven company reports inevitably produced duplication in cases where several companies participated in a direct placement by a single borrower, or purchased part of a bond issue offered publicly to life insurance companies and other investors.

TABLE 10-4
Life Insurance Loans to Business and Industry
By Size of Loan, Average Amount Authorized, and Average Interest Rate

(Amounts in thousands of dollars)

Total size of loan	1953 Average amount	1953 Average rate	1954 Average amount	1954 Average rate	1955 Average amount	1955 Average rate	1956 Average amount	1956 Average rate
Under $50,000	24	4.97	24	4.96	25	4.95	26	5.15
$50,000 - $100,000	69	4.80	68	4.79	68	4.75	69	5.00
$100,000 - $250,000	147	4.74	150	4.64	154	4.66	153	4.92
$250,000 - $1,000,000	428	4.66	449	4.54	436	4.61	446	4.90
$1,000,000 - $5,000,000	1,308	4.48	1,391	4.29	1,403	4.38	1,448	4.80
$5,000,000 - $10,000,000	1,331	4.28	1,603	4.04	2,287	4.28	2,225	4.60
$10,000,000 and over	2,702	3.90	2,465	3.74	2,657	3.98	2,860	4.36
Grand average	742	4.11	658	4.00	638	4.20	723	4.55

amounted to about $25,000 throughout the period. For loans involving $10 million and over, the average authorization by individual companies was around $2.5 million, reflecting the participation in loans involving more than one investor.

Table 10-4 also presents a summary of survey results of average interest rates [7] on life insurance investments, classified by total size of loan. The grand total average of interest rates shows a decline from 4.11 percent in 1953 to 4.00 percent the next year, followed by an increase to an average 4.20 percent in 1955 and a further rise in 1956 to 4.55 percent. These trends parallel the movement of interest rates in the long-term capital markets during this period. After rising in the first six months of 1953, market yields declined steadily during the last half of 1953 and during 1954, while the years 1955 and 1956 were characterized by a generally rising trend of interest rates as demands for long-term funds outstripped the supply of savings.

The inverse relationship of interest rate levels to the total size of loan is shown clearly in Table 10-4, with larger loans commanding lower rates than smaller loans. For example, in 1954 life insurance investments in loans of less than $50,000 were authorized at rates averaging 1.22 percent higher than the rates for loans involving over $10 million of borrowing. This is to be expected because the smaller loans are more expensive to make and to administer, and the risk usually much greater. As capital market conditions changed between 1954 and 1956, the entire schedule of interest rates rose. The larger loans experienced the sharpest increase in rates and the smaller loans the least increase, as is shown by the persistent upward progression from an increase in nineteen basis points in the case of the smallest loans to sixty-two basis points for the largest class. Thus, borrowers in the smallest loan category paid an average interest rate of 5.15 percent in 1956 or only seventy-nine basis points above the rate on loans in the largest category.

These developments are set forth in greater detail in the summary of survey results in Table 10-5 which shows the absolute and percentage changes in average rates on each category of loan size. Between 1954 and 1955 the rates on larger loans rose by twenty-four basis points, while the rates for smaller loans declined somewhat from the average of 1954. Rates on all categories increased in 1956 over the 1955 average but the rise was substantially greater for large borrowings than for the smaller loans. Expressing the same trends as a percentage increase in borrowing costs, the contrast between large and small loans is even more striking.

---

[7] The average rates reported by participating companies are the gross contract rates on each transaction, weighted by the dollar amount authorized for that transaction. The interest rates shown in the survey tables roughly represent the cost of borrowing rather than net yield to the investor since they take no account of administrative expenses and other fees.

TABLE 10-5
Absolute and Percentage Changes in Average Interest Rates
on Life Insurance Loans to Business and Industry
by Year and by Total Size of Loan

Total size of loan	Absolute increase (+) or decrease (-)			
	1953-1954	1954-1955	1955-1956	1954-1956
	(Rates in percent per annum)			
Under $50,000	- .01	- .01	+ .20	+ .19
$50,000 - $100,000	- .01	- .04	+ .25	+ .21
$100,000 - $250,000	- .10	+ .02	+ .26	+ .28
$250,000 - $1,000,000	- .12	+ .07	+ .29	+ .36
$1,000,000 - $5,000,000	- .19	+ .09	+ .42	+ .51
$5,000,000 - $10,000,000	- .24	+ .24	+ .32	+ .56
$10,000,000 and over	- .16	+ .24	+ .38	+ .62
Grand average	- .11	+ .20	+ .35	+ .55

Total size of loan	Percent increase (+) or decrease (-)			
	1953-1954	1954-1955	1955-1956	1954-1956
Under $50,000	- .20	- .20	+4.04	+ 3.83
$50,000 - $100,000	- .21	- .84	+5.26	+ 4.38
$100,000 - $250,000	-2.11	+ .43	+5.58	+ 6.03
$250,000 - $1,000,000	-2.58	+1.54	+6.29	+ 7.93
$1,000,000 - $5,000,000	-4.24	+2.10	+9.59	+11.89
$5,000,000 - $10,000,000	-5.61	+5.94	+7.48	+13.86
$10,000,000 and over	-4.10	+6.42	+9.55	+16.58
Grand average	-2.68	+5.00	+8.33	+13.75

As may be seen in Table 10-4, average borrowing costs on loans under $50,000 rose by nineteen basis points between 1954 and 1956, for a percentage increase of 3.83 percent; the rise of average rates on loans of $10 million and over was sixty-two basis points or a rise of 16.58 percent in the cost of such borrowing.

These figures show, therefore, that life insurance lending to smaller business concerns in 1953-56 was very active. The experience in subsequent years has undoubtedly paralleled that of 1953-56.

Summary

The basic factor underlying the economic growth of the United States has been the willingness of the American people to save a substantial proportion of their income and thus to make funds available for the expansion of the country's stock of capital goods. During the past sixty years the life insurance companies of the country have provided the largest channel of personal savings into productive investment. Life insurance savings have contributed heavily to the expansion of industrial plant and equipment, to the growth of our public utilities and railroads, and to the development of commercial facilities. In addition, the life companies have played a large role in home mortgage financing and have thus contributed to making Americans the best-housed people in the world. Capital expenditures by state and local government units have also been financed in large measure by the life insurance companies. In response to competitive forces in the capital markets, life insurance savings have flowed into investments in the areas of greatest need, and they have been available to comparatively small as well as large business and industrial firms.

Chapter 11

LIFE INSURANCE COMPANIES
AND ALLOCATION OF CAPITAL

Allocation of Funds to Competing Uses

In judging the effectiveness of life insurance companies as financial intermediaries engaged in the channeling of savings into various investment outlets, the question arises as to how well they have performed their function as allocators of capital. Have the funds accumulated through life companies been directed into those investment areas where they have been most productive in an over-all economic sense? Has the investment of these funds contributed in the most desirable way to the social, as well as the economic, make-up of the country? A scientific answer to these important questions would require an alternative experience by which to compare, i.e., what would have happened in the absence of life insurance companies? Lacking such a scientific basis for comparison, it is possible to re-examine what actually occurred from the standpoint of the allocation of capital and resources.

Accordingly, this chapter appraises the performance of life insurance companies in our financial system in terms of (1) economic priorities and (2) social priorities. This discussion necessarily draws upon points that have been made in earlier chapters of this monograph.

Economic Priorities in a Market System. The United States economy is, of course, primarily a market economy, one in which the free play of market forces brings about the allocation of resources and the financial command over these resources. In such an economy, demand and supply influences, through their impact upon relative price relationships, lead to the shifts in the factors of production which are necessary to a flexible and dynamic economy. An increase in demand makes itself felt initially through an upward pressure on the price, followed by a greater willingness to provide the demanded service or commodity at the higher price. The increase in supply serves to satisfy the increased demand, but draws resources away from those areas in which demand has declined relatively. The ability of a market economy to respond quickly to meeting increased demands depends upon its ability to adapt by shifting resources and keeping its productive factors mobile and flexible.

The financial side of a free market economy is likewise dependent upon the mobility and flexibility of capital and credit—the ability to shift toward those areas where demand is strongest and the economic need for funds is greatest. In the financial markets, it is the price of money or the rate of return on investments which indicates the relative scarcity or abundance in any particular sector of the capital and credit market. Thus, a rise in the demand for long-term capital by business and industry will be indicated by rising yields on corporate bonds; this rise will tend to divert funds into the corporate bond market and away from other areas where demand is less pressing.

Life insurance companies qualify as efficient allocators of financial resources in a market economy for the following reasons. First, their investments are made in almost every sector of the capital market and they are constantly considering a wide array of potential investment outlets. The scope of these outlets has been documented in Chapter 3 which reviewed the investment trends of life insurance companies over past decades. Second, as seen in Chapter 4, the investment decisions of life insurance companies are based on a philosophy of maximizing their rate of return, within the bounds of state investment laws and the principle of safeguarding the security of the principal invested. The incentive for life companies to maximize their rate of return on investments arises from the effect of this return upon policyholders' dividends and on the net cost of insurance, thus becoming an important factor in the competition among the companies in their sales of life insurance to the public. Under these conditions of a wide variety of investment outlets and a yield-maximizing philosophy of investments, life insurance companies allocate their funds to those investments where the rate is highest, i.e., where the economic priorities fixed by the market are the greatest. It may be concluded, therefore, that life insurance companies perform most efficiently in a market system to allocate available savings among the wide range of competing demands from various sectors of the economy.

The Influence of Social Priorities. In addition to economic priorities, there are a number of social priorities which have affected the allocation of life insurance funds. It might be noted that social priorities are not necessarily noneconomic, and they may in fact make themselves felt through economic or financial channels. Among such social priorities in recent years has been the enormous need by the federal government during World War II for the financial means to implement the military requirements of a global war; life insurance companies met this need by increasing their holdings of Government securities to over 45 percent of their total assets. Immediately following the war, the social priorities accorded to housing facilities in urban areas were recognized by the life companies through the erection or financing of large-scale housing projects to meet existing shortages. The more general social priorities accorded to home ownership have been given national recognition through the insurance and guaranty programs of the Federal Housing Administration and the Veterans Administration, and life companies have been one of the largest suppliers of residential mortgage funds under these programs. These and other illustrations of the recognition of social priorities by life companies have been described more fully in Chapter 4.

Responsiveness to Shifting Demands and Needs

Timing of Response in the Short-Run. It has already been shown that life insurance companies perform efficiently as allocators of capital to competing uses because of their policy of yield maximization and the wide range of investment markets in which they function. The question remains as to how rapid is the responsiveness of life company investment officers to changing market conditions. Is the response to shifting demands swift or sluggish? Do life companies move quickly in taking advantage of more attractive yields in particular markets or is there a considerable passage of time before the direction of investment emphasis is changed?

The discussion in Chapter 8 of the forward commitment trends of life insurance companies since 1953 clearly demonstrates the sensitivity of life company investment policy to changing interest rates and shifts in market demands. When market conditions and monetary policy took a new direction and produced a changing pattern of investment yields, forward investment commitments also shifted from bonds to mortgages or vice versa. These shifts in commitments reflected not only the new conditions of underlying demand and supply factors, but also stemmed from expectations concerning the future direction of monetary policy and interest rates.

It is of considerable importance that the responsiveness of life companies to short-run changes shows itself in forward commitments, since this stage of the financial process has the most immediate impact upon production and employment. Forward commitments are intimately linked with advance planning of investment decisions by business and industry and by the home construction field. Availability of funds through forward commitments has the power to set into motion forces in the real world of production, whether it be starts of residential construction, or the placement of orders for factory equipment for expanded production, or the letting of contracts for office building construction. Thus, shifts in demand for financial resources, acting to change yield differentials and bringing a shift in forward commitments of life companies, have a rapid impact upon actual business activity even in advance of the actual disbursement of the committed funds.

Long-Run Adjustments to Change. Perhaps the best answer to the question of whether life companies respond to changing economic needs over time is to examine information obtained by the Life Insurance Association of America about the experience of forty-nine U. S. legal reserve life insurance companies which have provided data allocating their various investments to regions over a period of thirty-five years. The regional distribution of the investments of these companies on a combined basis has shifted noticeably over the years.

As seen in Table 11-1 the increase in total assets of the forty-nine com-

TABLE 11-1
Assets—By Regions—Forty-Nine U.S. Legal Reserve Life Insurance Companies
(In millions of dollars)

	1924		1959		Increase 1959 over 1924	
	Amount	%	Amount	%	Amount	%
New England	$ 365	3.8	$ 3,424	3.6	$ 3,059	838.1
Middle Atlantic	2,086	21.6	15,916	16.6	13,830	663.0
East North Central	1,720	17.8	17,046	17.8	15,326	891.0
West North Central	1,909	19.8	6,737	7.0	4,828	252.9
South Atlantic	878	9.1	10,690	11.2	9,812	1117.5
East South Central	524	5.4	4,528	4.7	4,004	764.1
West South Central	575	5.9	9,963	10.4	9,388	1632.7
Mountain	318	3.3	3,862	4.0	3,544	1114.5
Pacific	508	5.3	11,182	11.7	10,674	2101.2
Foreign & not allocated	779	8.0	12,495	13.0	11,716	1504.0
Total	9,662	100.0	95,843	100.0	86,181	892.0

panies, from $9,662 million to $95,843 million, was 892 percent in the thirty-five-year period. Some of the regions had increases that were considerably higher, notably the Pacific (2,101 percent) and the West South Central regions (1,632 percent). Some were markedly lower, e.g., the West North Central (252 percent) and the Middle Atlantic states (663 percent). It is also interesting to note that the largest investment dollarwise shifted from the Middle Atlantic to the East North Central region, while the investment in the New England states dropped lower than in the Mountain states in the same period.

The table also shows the proportion of life insurance investments in the regions in the two years, 1924 and 1959. The Pacific states have increased their share of total invested assets very considerably and the West South Central states have likewise a bigger share of the total assets in 1959. However, the share of assets invested in the West North Central states decreased from nearly 20 percent in 1924 to 7 percent in 1959. The share of the Middle Atlantic states also declined to 16.6 percent from nearly 21.6 percent. These figures reflect, of course, the changing geographical structure of our national economy as the country has developed.

The adaptability of life insurance investments to economic changes is also apparent in the case of types of investment outlets. As noted in Chapter 3, farm mortgages were almost as important as mortgages on city property in the early 1920's. The forty-nine company study shows that in 1924, over 60 percent of the farm mortgages were on property located in the West North Central region (Appendix Table 11A-3). This region in 1959 had less than a third of the farm mortgages. Dollarwise, less was invested in farm mortgages in this region in 1959 than was invested there in 1924. Every other region has increased its total dollar investment in farm mortgages in the thirty-five years, although the relative importance of farm mortgages has decreased from 18.7 percent of the total assets of the forty-nine companies in 1924 to 2.7 percent of total assets in 1959.

In 1924 mortgages on other than farm property ($2.0 billion) constituted 20.9 percent of total assets (Table 11-2). In 1959 the investment

TABLE 11-2
Assets—By Types of Investment—
Forty-Nine U.S. Legal Reserve Life Insurance Companies

(In millions of dollars)

	1924		1959		Increase 1959 over 1924	
	Amount	%	Amount	%	Amount	%
U.S. Government bonds	$ 688	7.1	$ 5,434	5.7	$ 4,746	689.8
State, county, municipal bonds	611	6.3	2,976	3.1	2,365	387.1
Railroad bonds & stocks	2,110	21.9	3,545	3.7	1,435	68.0
Public utility bonds & stocks	448	4.6	15,347	16.0	14,899	3325.7
Other bonds & stocks	140	1.5	25,157	26.2	25,017	17869.3
Total bonds & stocks	3,997	41.4	52,458	54.7	48,461	1212.4
Farm mortgages	1,802	18.7	2,612	2.7	810	45.0
Other mortgages	2,019	20.9	29,647	31.0	27,628	1368.4
Total mortgages	3,821	39.6	32,259	33.7	28,438	744.3
Real estate	176	1.8	3,019	3.2	2,843	1615.3
Policy loans	1,188	12.3	3,740	3.9	2,552	214.8
Cash	101	1.0	897	.9	796	788.1
Other	380	3.9	3,469	3.6	3,089	812.9
Total	9,662	100.0	95,843	100.0	86,181	892.0

had grown to $29.6 billion, or 31.0 percent of total assets. Whereas in 1924, 43.6 percent of the $2.0 billion was invested in the Middle Atlantic states (Appendix Table 11A-3), by 1959 it was down to less than 15 percent of the $29.6 billion. By 1959, the greatest investment in "other mortgages" was in the East North Central states, $5.4 billion; the next largest in Pacific states, $5.2 billion; in the South Atlantic states, $4.5 billion; in the Middle Atlantic states, $4.4 billion; and in the West South Central states, $3.8 billion (Appendix Table 11A-1). Only in the New England states was the investment in non-farm mortgages exceeded by any other type of investment.

Railroad securities were the most popular type of investment in the early 1920's. In 1924, they were $2.1 billion or 21.9 percent of the total assets. By 1959 the total investment in railroad securities was $3.5 billion, an increase of 68 percent from 1924, but this constituted only 3.7 percent of the total investments held that year.

Investment in public utility bonds and stocks has increased 3,326 percent in the thirty-five-year period from $0.4 billion in 1924, representing 4.6 percent of total assets, to $15.3 billion in 1959, or 16 percent of total assets. In 1924, 40 percent of the public utility investment was in the Middle Atlantic states; in 1959, 17.9 percent of the total public utility investment was there. In 1924, the public utility investment in the East North Central states, $100 million, was second in amount or 21.9 percent. In 1959, the public utility investment in the East North Central states of $2.9 billion (18.8 percent) was the largest regional investment in public utilities. The relative importance of the public utility investments in the West South Central states (2.8 percent in 1924, 12.8 percent in 1959), in the South Atlantic states (5.4 percent in 1924, 10.4 percent in 1959), in the Mountain states (2.1 percent in 1924, 7.0 percent in 1959), and in the East South Central states (2.2 percent in 1924, 5.3 percent in 1959) points up the shift of investments from one region to another.

In many ways one of the most interesting developments in the thirty-five-year picture is the increasing investment by the forty-nine life companies in securities of business and industrial corporations other than railroads or public utilities. This category is labeled "other bonds and stocks" in Table 11-2. The investment in these securities constituted a modest $140 million or 1.5 percent of total assets in 1924—but in 1959 the $25,157 million constituted 26.2 percent of total assets. Perhaps the shift in the regional pattern is not significant, but 47.5 percent of the $140 million in 1924 was invested in New England and the Middle Atlantic states, while 19.8 percent of the $25,157 million in 1959 was so invested. By 1959 investments in these bonds and stocks represented one-fifth of the total investment in every region except the Mountain and Pacific states. In 1959, the investment in securities of business and industrial corporations was larger than the investment in securities of railroads or public utilities except in the Mountain states where the investment in public utilities was greater.

As has been noted, life insurance companies have been permitted in recent years to acquire real estate for investment purposes. Approximately 80 percent of the $3.0 billion invested in real estate at the end of 1959 was in real estate acquired for investment purposes—apartment houses, housing developments, hotels, warehouses, factories, shopping centers, etc. Dollarwise, the Pacific states have increased their investment from $9 million in 1924 to $551 million in 1959. The Middle Atlantic states went from $87 million in 1924 (4.2 percent of the regional investment) to $1,209 million in 1959 (7.6 percent of the regional investment). The investment in the Middle Atlantic states is 40 percent of the $3.0 billion invested in real estate. This is less proportionately than the $87 million in the Middle Atlantic states in 1924, which was 49 percent of all real estate held.

It is evident, therefore, that life insurance companies have been most responsive to the changing capital requirements of the American economy. This is true not only of the way in which they have shifted their investment emphasis from one type of outlet to another as the result of changing market demands; it is also true of the way in which the geographical distribution of their investments has changed over time in response to the development of new industrial areas. The life companies have contributed greatly to the development of a competitive national capital market.

Ability to Innovate. A remaining question relates to the ability of life companies to innovate in response to new demands in the economy. Are the companies staid and conservative in their investment policy, clinging to the established methods and the traditional outlets, or are they able and willing to work out new investment techniques and to consider unconventional forms of investment to finance the changing needs of the economy?

An impressive list of innovations may be cited to demonstrate the ability of life companies to meet the need for new forms of investment or new techniques of financing during the past several years. In some instances it has been necessary to amend state investment laws to allow such innovations to be introduced, but the passage in many states of "leeway" or "basket" clauses now provides flexibility, within prescribed limits, to depart from conventional practice in investment policy.

A few examples from recent years will illustrate the willingness of life companies to invest their funds in new ways or through new outlets. As previously mentioned, the erection and management of large-scale housing projects brought life companies into new fields during and immediately after World War II. These pioneering efforts in the use of their funds were designed to alleviate the critical shortage of urban housing. Another frontier of investing was crossed when life companies worked out the purchase-lease-back technique in which an office building, a warehouse, or other real property of a business corporation is purchased by a life company and then leased to the selling corporation for its use. This technique allows a business concern to raise new money without adding to its long-term indebtedness. Oil and gas production loans, based on the expected revenue from proven oil reserves still underground, are another innovating form of investment. The financing of pipeline construction in the postwar period has been facilitated by life company loans based on delivery contracts and certificates of necessity issued by the Federal Power Commission.

Mortgage loans are traditionally based on real property, i.e., land and buildings. The concept of a security based on physical assets has been extended more recently to "floating property" in the form of barges operating in inland waterways and ocean-going super-tankers carrying petroleum. Ship mortgages and variations on this approach have become fairly common investments by life companies during the postwar period.

These and other techniques of investing have been developed in recent years and have proved to be sound and successful investments from the standpoint of the life insurance companies, while meeting the financial needs of business for raising capital in new ways or for special purposes. By exhibiting their willingness to explore and develop new forms of financing, life insurance companies have demonstrated that they are able to keep pace with the changing requirements of a modern industrial economy.

Summary

Life insurance companies eminently qualify as efficient allocators of financial resources in a market economy for the following reasons. First, they invest in almost every sector of the capital market and they are constantly considering a wide array of potential investment outlets. Second, the investment decisions of life insurance companies are based on a philosophy of maximizing their rate of return, within the bounds of state investment laws and the principle of safeguarding the security of the funds invested. Life insurance companies thus allocate their funds in a wide variety of ways to those investments where the rate is highest, i.e., where economic priorities fixed by the market are the greatest. Life insurance companies therefore perform most efficiently in a market system to allocate available savings among the wide range of competing demands from various sectors of the economy.

In addition to economic priorities, a number of social priorities have affected the allocation of life insurance funds. Immediately following the war, for example, the social priorities accorded to housing facilities in urban areas were recognized by the life companies through the erection or financing of large-scale housing projects to meet existing shortages. The more general social priorities accorded to home ownership have been given national recognition through the insurance and guaranty programs of the Federal Housing Administration and the Veterans Administration. Life companies have been one of the largest suppliers of residential mortgage funds under these programs.

Life insurance company investments have been highly responsive to the changing geographical structure of the American economy. During the past thirty-five years there has been a significant shift in investment emphasis from the older areas of the country to the rapidly developing areas such as the Pacific Coast and the West South Central states. Similarly, there have been important changes in the past thirty-five years in the types of investments life companies have made. Farm mortgages have declined in importance and city mortgages have increased sharply. Railroad securities, once the largest investment holding, have dwindled in importance, whereas there has been a sharp increase in holdings of public utility and industrial bonds.

Moreover, an impressive list of innovations may be cited to demonstrate the ability of life companies to meet the need for new forms of investment or new techniques of financing. In some instances it has been necessary to amend state investment laws to allow such innovations to be introduced, but the passage in many states of leeway or basket clauses now provides flexibility, within prescribed limits, to depart from conventional practice in investment policy.

A few examples from recent years will illustrate the willingness of life companies to invest their funds in new ways or through new outlets. The erection and management of large-scale housing projects brought life companies into new fields during and immediately after World War II. Another frontier of investing was crossed when life companies worked out the purchase-lease-back technique in which the real property of a business corporation is purchased by a life company and then leased to the selling corporation for its use. Oil and gas production loans, based on the expected revenue from proven oil reserves still underground, are another innovating form of investment. The financing of pipeline construction in the postwar period has been facilitated by life company loans based on delivery contracts and certificates of necessity issued by the Federal Power Commission. Many other investment innovations may be cited.

The record shows, therefore, that life insurance companies have proved to be a highly efficient means for channeling capital funds into those areas of the national economy, and into those uses, in which market demands have been strongest. They have responded quickly and imaginatively to the changing capital requirements of the American economy.

Appendix to Chapter 11

Allocations to regions are made in the following ways:

Mortgages, real estate, and cash on the basis of physical location of property covered.

Bonds and stocks:

U.S. Government—on the basis of the regional distribution of civilian population of U.S.

State, county, and municipal—on the basis of location of issuing authority.

Mortgage—on the basis of location of property, plant, or equipment covered.

Debenture bonds and stocks—on the basis of location of tangible property (for railroads, on the basis of miles of track).

Regions (as used by U.S. Bureau of Census):

New England: Maine, New Hampshire, Vermont, Massachusetts, Rhode Island, Connecticut

Middle Atlantic: New York, New Jersey, Pennsylvania.

East North Central: Ohio, Indiana, Illinois, Michigan, Wisconsin.

West North Central: Minnesota, Iowa, Missouri, North Dakota, South Dakota, Nebraska, Kansas.

South Atlantic: Delaware, Maryland, District of Columbia, Virginia, West Virginia, North Carolina, South Carolina, Georgia, Florida.

East South Central: Kentucky, Tennessee, Alabama, Mississippi.

West South Central: Arkansas, Louisiana, Oklahoma, Texas.

Mountain: Montana, Idaho, Wyoming, Colorado, New Mexico, Arizona, Utah, Nevada.

Pacific: Washington, Oregon, California.

TABLE 11A-1

Investments—By Regions—By Types of Investment, 1924, 1959
Forty-Nine U.S. Legal Reserve Life Insurance Companies
(millions of dollars)

	Total Investment	New England	Middle Atlantic	East North Central	West North Central	South Atlantic	East South Central	West South Central	Mountain	Pacific
1924										
U.S. Government Bonds	$ 688	$ 48	$ 145	$ 141	$ 80	$ 91	$ 56	$ 67	$ 23	$ 38
State, County, Municipal Bonds	611	18	43	55	40	69	33	33	17	35
Railroad Bonds and Stocks	2,110	48	336	532	289	262	175	138	174	126
Public Utility Bonds and Stocks	448	29	180	98	34	24	10	12	9	43
Other Bonds and Stocks	140	26	40	20	4	5	4	1	2	12
Total Bonds and Stocks	3,997	169	745	846	446	450	278	251	225	254
Farm Mortgages	1,802			289	1,099	66	92	192	26	38
Other Mortgages	2,019	52	881	349	219	209	76	59	27	119
Total Mortgages	3,821	52	882	637	1,318	275	167	251	53	156
Real Estate	176	31	87	12	12	10	3	2	4	9
Policy Loans	1,188	90	329	209	127	140	74	68	35	81
Cash	101	23	42	12	6	3	2	1		3
Other	380		2	3				2		5
Total	9,662	365	2,086	1,720	1,909	878	524	575	318	508
1959										
U.S. Government Bonds	5,434	308	1,030	1,115	467	775	364	504	199	577
State, County, Municipal Bonds	2,976	116	350	504	81	251	108	199	55	207
Railroad Bonds and Stocks	3,545	61	589	894	471	456	235	309	234	198
Public Utility Bonds and Stocks	15,347	768	2,747	2,883	1,044	1,596	811	1,971	1,080	1,542
Other Bonds and Stocks	25,157	868	4,103	4,487	1,356	2,209	1,002	2,433	520	2,091
Total Bonds and Stocks	52,458	2,120	8,820	9,883	3,419	5,287	2,519	5,417	2,087	4,615
Farm Mortgages	2,612	5	37	451	853	174	154	416	269	243
Other Mortgages	29,647	642	4,416	5,362	2,000	4,499	1,662	3,845	1,326	5,194
Total Mortgages	32,259	647	4,453	5,813	2,853	4,672	1,817	4,261	1,595	5,437
Real Estate	3,019	273	1,209	451	125	244	37	54	39	551
Policy Loans	3,740	267	989	720	290	412	133	198	127	492
Cash	897	112	415	135	47	41	17	26	8	56
Other	3,469	5	29	44	3	34	5	7	6	31
Total	95,843	3,424	15,916	17,046	6,737	10,690	4,528	9,963	3,862	11,182

Relative Investments—By Regions—By Types of Investment, 1924, 1959
Forty-Nine U.S. Legal Reserve Life Insurance Companies

	Total Investment	New England	Middle Atlantic	East North Central	West North Central	South Atlantic	East South Central	West South Central	Mountain	Pacific
1924										
U.S. Government Bonds	7.1%	13.2%	7.0%	8.2%	4.2%	10.4%	10.7%	11.7%	7.2%	7.5%
State, County, Municipal Bonds	6.3	4.9	2.1	3.2	2.1	7.9	6.3	5.7	5.3	6.9
Railroad Bonds and Stocks	21.9	13.2	16.1	30.9	15.1	29.8	33.4	24.0	54.7	24.8
Public Utility Bonds and Stocks	4.6	7.9	8.6	5.7	1.8	2.7	1.9	2.1	2.8	8.5
Other Bonds and Stocks	1.5	7.1	1.9	1.2	.2	.6	.8	.2	.6	2.4
Total Bonds and Stocks	41.4	46.3	35.7	49.2	23.4	51.3	53.1	43.7	70.8	50.0
Farm Mortgages	18.7			16.8	57.6	7.5	17.6	33.4	8.2	7.5
Other Mortgages	20.9	14.2	42.2	20.3	11.5	23.8	14.5	10.3	8.5	23.4
Total Mortgages	39.6	14.2	42.3	37.0	69.0	31.3	31.9	43.7	16.7	30.7
Real Estate	1.8	8.5	4.2	.7	.6	1.1	.6	.3	1.3	1.8
Policy Loans	12.3	24.7	15.8	12.2	6.7	15.9	14.1	11.8	11.0	15.9
Cash	1.0	6.3	2.0	.7	.3	.3	.4	.2		.6
Other	3.9		.1	.2				.3		1.0
Total	100.0	100.0	100.1	100.0	100.0	99.9	100.1	100.0	99.8	100.0
1959										
U.S. Government Bonds	5.7	9.0	6.5	6.5	6.9	7.2	8.0	8.1	5.1	5.2
State, County, Municipal Bonds	3.1	3.4	2.2	3.0	1.2	2.3	2.4	2.0	1.4	1.9
Railroad Bonds and Stocks	3.7	1.8	3.7	5.2	7.0	4.3	5.2	3.1	6.1	1.8
Public Utility Bonds and Stocks	16.0	22.4	17.3	16.9	15.5	14.9	17.9	19.8	28.0	13.8
Other Bonds and Stocks	26.2	25.4	25.8	26.3	20.1	20.7	22.1	24.4	13.5	18.7
Total Bonds and Stocks	54.7	61.9	55.4	58.0	50.8	49.5	55.6	54.4	54.0	41.3
Farm Mortgages	2.7	.1	.2	2.6	12.7	1.6	3.4	4.2	7.0	2.2
Other Mortgages	31.0	18.8	27.7	31.5	29.7	42.1	36.7	38.6	34.3	46.5
Total Mortgages	33.7	18.9	28.0	34.1	42.3	43.7	40.1	42.8	41.3	48.6
Real Estate	3.2	8.0	7.6	2.6	1.9	2.3	.8	.5	1.0	4.9
Policy Loans	3.9	7.8	6.2	4.2	4.3	3.9	2.9	2.0	3.3	4.4
Cash	.9	3.3	2.6	.8	.7	.4	.4	.3	.2	.5
Other	3.6	.1	.2	.3	.0	.3	.1	.1	.2	.3
Total	100.0	100.0	100.0	100.0	100.0	100.1	99.9	100.1	100.0	100.0

TABLE 11A-3

Relative Investments—By Types of Security—By Regions, 1924, 1959

Forty-Nine U.S. Legal Reserve Life Insurance Companies

		New England	Middle Atlantic	East North Central	West North Central	South Atlantic	East South Central	West South Central	Mountain	Pacific
U.S. Government Bonds	1924	7.0%	21.1%	20.5%	11.6%	13.2%	8.1%	9.7%	3.3%	5.5%
	1959	5.7	19.0	20.5	8.6	14.3	6.7	9.3	3.7	10.6
State, County, Municipal Bonds	1924	2.9	7.0	9.1	6.6	11.2	5.5	5.3	2.8	5.7
	1959	3.9	11.8	16.9	2.7	8.4	3.6	6.7	1.8	7.0
Railroad Bonds and Stocks	1924	2.3	15.9	25.2	13.7	12.4	8.3	6.5	8.2	6.0
	1959	1.7	16.6	25.2	13.3	12.9	6.6	8.7	6.6	5.6
Public Utility Bonds and Stocks	1924	6.5	40.3	21.9	7.6	5.4	2.2	2.8	2.1	9.6
	1959	5.0	17.9	18.8	6.8	10.4	5.3	12.8	7.0	10.0
Other Bonds and Stocks	1924	18.7	28.8	13.9	2.5	3.4	2.9	.7	1.5	8.5
	1959	3.5	16.3	17.8	5.4	8.8	4.0	9.7	2.1	8.3
Total Bonds and Stocks	1924	4.2	18.6	21.2	11.2	11.3	7.0	6.3	5.6	6.3
	1959	4.0	16.8	18.8	6.5	10.1	4.8	10.3	4.0	8.8
Farm Mortgages	1924	.0	.0	16.0	61.0	3.7	5.1	10.7	1.5	2.1
	1959	.2	1.4	17.3	32.7	6.6	5.9	15.9	10.3	9.3
Other Than Farm Mortgages	1924	2.6	43.6	17.3	10.9	10.4	3.7	2.9	1.3	5.9
	1959	2.2	14.9	18.1	6.7	15.2	5.6	13.0	4.5	17.5
Total Mortgages	1924	1.4	23.1	16.7	34.5	7.2	4.4	6.6	1.4	4.1
	1959	2.0	13.8	18.0	8.8	14.5	5.6	13.2	4.9	16.9
Real Estate	1924	17.5	49.3	7.0	6.9	5.5	1.7	1.4	2.0	4.9
	1959	9.0	40.1	14.9	4.1	8.1	1.2	1.8	1.3	18.2
Policy Loans	1924	7.6	27.7	17.6	10.7	11.8	6.2	5.8	2.9	6.8
	1959	7.1	26.4	19.2	7.8	11.0	3.6	5.3	3.4	13.2
Cash	1924	22.5	41.9	12.4	5.5	3.2	1.7	1.4	.4	3.0
	1959	12.5	46.3	15.1	5.2	4.5	1.8	2.9	.9	6.3
Total Assets	1924	3.8	21.6	17.8	19.8	9.1	5.4	5.9	3.3	5.3
	1959	3.6	16.6	17.8	7.0	11.2	4.7	10.4	4.0	11.7

274

COMMISSION ON MONEY AND CREDIT

Members

Frazar B. Wilde, CHAIRMAN
Chairman, Connecticut General Life Insurance Company

H. Christian Sonne, VICE CHAIRMAN
New York, New York

Adolf A. Berle, Jr.
New York, New York
(Withdrew to serve as Chairman of the U.S. State Department Latin American Task Force.)

James B. Black
Chairman of the Board, Pacific Gas & Electric Company

Joseph M. Dodge
Chairman of the Board, The Detroit Bank and Trust Company
(Resigned October 7, 1960.)

Marriner S. Eccles
Chairman of the Board, First Security Corporation

Lamar Fleming, Jr.
Chairman of the Board, Anderson, Clayton & Co.

Henry H. Fowler
Fowler, Leva, Hawes & Symington
(Resigned February 3, 1961, on his appointment as Under Secretary of the Treasury.)

Gaylord A. Freeman, Jr.
Vice Chairman, The First National Bank of Chicago
(Appointed April 29, 1960.)

Fred T. Greene
President, Federal Home Loan Bank of Indianapolis
(Died March 17, 1961.)

Philip M. Klutznick
Park Forest, Illinois
(Resigned February 8, 1961, on his appointment as United States Representative to the Economic and Social Council of the United Nations.)

Fred Lazarus, Jr.
Chairman of the Board, Federated Department Stores, Inc.

Isador Lubin
Arthur T. Vanderbilt Professor of Public Affairs, Rutgers University

J. Irwin Miller
Chairman of the Board, Cummins Engine Company

Robert R. Nathan
President, Robert R. Nathan Associates, Inc.

Emil Rieve
President Emeritus, Textile Workers of America, AFL-CIO
(Appointed May 19, 1960.)

David Rockefeller
President, The Chase Manhattan Bank

Beardsley Ruml
New York, New York
(Died April 18, 1960.)

Stanley H. Ruttenberg
Director, Department of Research, AFL-CIO

Charles Sawyer
Taft, Stettinius & Hollister

William F. Schnitzler
Secretary-Treasurer, AFL-CIO
(Resigned April 28, 1960.)

276

Earl B. Schwulst
President and Chairman of the Board, The Bowery Savings Bank

J. Cameron Thomson
Retired Chairman of the Board, Northwest Bancorporation

Charles B. Shuman
President, American Farm Bureau Federation

Willard L. Thorp
Director, Merrill Center for Economics, Amherst College

Jesse W. Tapp
Chairman of the Board, Bank of America, N.T. and S.A.

Theodore O. Yntema
Chairman, Finance Committee, Ford Motor Company

Advisory Board

Lester V. Chandler
Professor of Economics, Princeton University

Richard E. Neustadt
Professor of Public Law and Government, Columbia University

Gerhard Colm
Chief Economist, National Planning Association

Paul A. Samuelson
Professor of Economics, Massachusetts Institute of Technology

Gaylord A. Freeman, Jr.
Vice Chairman, The First National Bank of Chicago
(Resigned April 29, 1960, on his appointment to the Commission.)

Sumner H. Slichter
Lamont University Professor, Harvard University
(Died September 27, 1959.)

Leo Grebler
Professor of Business Administration, University of California (Los Angeles)

Edward S. Shaw
Professor of Economics, Stanford University

Raymond W. Goldsmith
Professor of Economics, Yale University

Neil H. Jacoby
Dean, School of Business Administration, University of California (Los Angeles)

Alan H. Temple
New York, New York

Richard A. Musgrave
Woodrow Wilson School of Public and International Affairs, Princeton University

Jacob Viner
Professor of Economics, Emeritus, Princeton University

Staff

Bertrand Fox
Research Director

Eli Shapiro
Deputy Research Director

Date Due